D0221007

THE FLEXIBLE FIRM

The Flexible Firm

Capability Management in Network Organizations

Edited by
JULIAN BIRKINSHAW AND PETER HAGSTRÖM

OXFORD
UNIVERSITY PRESS

OXFORD

UNIVERSITY PRESS

Great Clarendon Street, Oxford OX2 6DP

Oxford University Press is a department of the University of Oxford.
It furthers the University's objective of excellence in research, scholarship,
and education by publishing worldwide in

Oxford New York

Athens Auckland Bangkok Bogotá Buenos Aires Cape Town
Chennai Dar es Salaam Delhi Florence Hong Kong Istanbul Karachi
Kolkata Kuala Lumpur Madrid Melbourne Mexico City Mumbai Nairobi
Paris São Paulo Shanghai Singapore Taipei Tokyo Toronto Warsaw

and associated companies in Berlin Ibadan

Oxford is a registered trade mark of Oxford University Press
in the UK and in certain other countries

Published in the United States
by Oxford University Press Inc., New York

© The several contributors 2000

The moral rights of the author have been asserted

Database right Oxford University Press (maker)

Reprinted 2001

All rights reserved. No part of this publication may be reproduced,
stored in a retrieval system, or transmitted, in any form or by any means,
without the prior permission in writing of Oxford University Press,
or as expressly permitted by law, or under terms agreed with the appropriate
reprographics rights organization. Enquiries concerning reproduction
outside the scope of the above should be sent to the Rights Department,
Oxford University Press, at the address above

You must not circulate this book in any other binding or cover
and you must impose this same condition on any acquirer

ISBN 0-19-829651-7

Printed in Great Britain
on acid-free paper by
Bookcraft (Bath) Short Run Books
Midsomer Norton

To Ross and Duncan
To Oliver and Andrea

Acknowledgements

We are heavily indebted to a number of different companies for their help in getting this research programme off the ground, and for seeing it through to completion. The names of all the 300-odd individuals who helped us in the course of the research would run into several pages, so instead we highlight below our key contacts in each company, as representatives of their respective organizations.

At the Institute of International Business (IIB), special thanks go to Kjell Nordström, our colleague who was instrumental in getting the programme started and in giving it the high level of visibility it required in Swedish business circles. Thanks to Örjan Sölvell, the director of IIB. Örjan was a tireless supporter of the CaMiNO programme, and he provided institutional support to ensure that we got the level of resources we needed to make it work. Lotte Brandt also deserves special mention for her help in pulling the chapters together in the latter stages of the programme.

Mats Dellham, co-founder of Askus and now a director of Askus K-W, was the linchpin of the programme. He put forward the initial ideas for a research programme on capability management and network organizations, and he was responsible for building up enthusiasm for the programme in the five partner companies. We are also indebted to many other individuals at Askus K-W for their help, most notably Gunnar Backlund, Björn Stattin, and Ann-Louise Palm. Askus K-W provided valuable insights into the changes going on in the partner companies. They also organized the partner meetings and provided financial support.

In Ericsson our key sponsor was Britt Reigo, executive vice-president for human resources, and our lead contact was Pär-Anders Pehrson, director of competence and leadership. Other individuals who provided ongoing support to specific projects were Gösta Lemne, Lars Åkeson, Björn Törnstrand, Stig-Rune Johanson, and Christina Callmer.

Pharmacia & Upjohn went through a lot of changes in the course of the programme, including a move of their headquarters from London to New Jersey. Jan Ekberg, former chairman, was the initial sponsor for our research. Other important contacts during the programme were Håkan Åström, Les Hudson, Mark Moore-Gillon, Lennart Olving, and Jacques Vernet.

SEB (formerly Skandinaviska Enskilda Banken) provided strong support through Jacob Wallenberg, chairman, Suzanne Grufman, senior vice-president for human resources, and Beatrice Engström-Bondy. Other individuals to whom we are particularly indebted are Magnus Cavalli-Björkman, Anders Lindqvist, and Eva Dämbeck.

In Skandia Ola Ramstedt, executive vice-president for human resources, was our lead contact and sponsor. Other individuals who provided invaluable assistance included Björn Wolrath, Hans-Erik Anderson, Leif Edvinsson, Kenneth Sandén, and Anders Högstrom.

Volvo, another company that went through great changes during the years of our research, also provided excellent support. Our key sponsor was Claes Malmros, group executive responsible for corporate strategy, and our lead contact was Jan Blennius, vice-president for corporate strategy. Many other Volvo executives also provided active support to the research, including Leif Johanson (who became chief executive during the programme), Charles Hunter-Pease, Gerd Peter, Kurt G. Larsson, and Anita Beijer.

To these executives, and many others not named, we give our heartfelt thanks. Grounded research of the type undertaken during this programme requires a lot of face-to-face meetings, and over the course of the last three years these individuals have been very generous with their time, and with their thoughts on the important issues facing their organizations. Doing this sort of research is rather like doing a jigsaw puzzle, with each interview or questionnaire representing another piece of the puzzle that has to be fitted in with all the others. Unlike a jigsaw, however, there is no one right answer. So for the readers of this book, and in particular anyone from the above companies who is reading it, our hope is that you find the picture we have put together to be both attractive and novel.

J.B. and P.H.

Contents

Notes on the Contributors

David Arnold is an Assistant Professor at the Graduate School of Business Administration, Harvard University.

Niklas Arvidsson is a doctoral candidate at the Institute of International Business, Stockholm School of Economics.

Julian Birkinshaw is an Assistant Professor at London Business School.

Henrik Bresman is a doctoral candidate at the Massachusetts Institute of Technology, Boston.

Carl Fey is an Assistant Professor at the Stockholm School of Economics.

Peter Hagström is an Assistant Professor at the Institute of International Business, Stockholm School of Economics.

Stefan Jonsson is a doctoral candidate at the Institute of International Business, Stockholm School of Economics.

Patrick Regnér is a doctoral candidate at the Institute of International Business, Stockholm School of Economics.

Maurizio Sobrero is an Assistant Professor at the University of Bologna.

Robin Teigland is a doctoral candidate at the Institute of International Business, Stockholm School of Economics.

Omar Toulan is an Assistant Professor in the Faculty of Management, McGill University.

Figures

Tables

Introduction

This volume is the result of a novel type of partnership between researchers and corporations. The fundamental idea of this partnership was for academics to present preliminary research ideas for a 'relevance test' by the firms. Having vetted their early thoughts in this fashion, the participating firms then provided resources and sites for the ensuing research. The resultant collection of research papers addresses a wide variety of different research topics, and utilizes very different methodologies, but the papers share a number of common themes that have sprung directly from the research programme known as *Capability Management in Network Organizations* (CaMiNO). While it may seem a little self-indulgent, we will nevertheless use this space to provide some background on the CaMiNO programme.

The programme was hatched in 1996, at a meeting between researchers at the Institute of International Business (IIB) and Askus K-W, a Stockholm-based consulting company. As close observers of contemporary changes in the world of business, we decided the time was right for a large-scale investigation into the ways in which firms were responding to their evolving business environment. Like all other observers, we had an intuitive sense of what changes appeared to be most important. In particular, three such tendencies stood out:

1. a pressing need to identify and build core capabilities,
2. a greater ability to work effectively with partner firms in an 'extended enterprise' model, and
3. the rapid development of an effective IT infrastructure to hold the firm and its partners together.

These three issues became the cornerstones of the research programme, and they also naturally provided us with the name for the programme, Capability Management in Network Organizations.

The research programme took place over the period 1997–9. In addition to the involvement of IIB and Askus K-W, there were five partner firms: Ericsson, Pharmacia & Upjohn, SEB, Skandia, and Volvo. These partner firms provided some funding and open-door access as research sites in return for direct feedback to them on the results of the programme. While we were free to undertake our research in whichever firms we chose, these five firms provided the raw data for most of the work reported in this book.

While academia–industry collaborations are quite common, it is worth while to identify a couple of the features of the CaMiNO programme that we believe made it an unusually rich experience for the participants. First, the single location of the research team provided for an unusually high level of interaction between researchers. While we would not all claim to subscribe to the same school of thought, there are still certain ideas, references, research methods, and epistemological norms that find their way into all of our writings. Readers are, of course, free to judge for themselves, but our expectation is that you will find quite a coherent picture emerging from the eleven chapters in this volume.

Secondly, we decided to encourage, rather than resist, the input of the companies into the early design of our research agenda. A number of partner meetings were held in the first half of the programme, at which we both presented our ideas and listened to the ideas of the partner companies about what issues should be researched and how it could be done. Needless to say, we reserved the right to ignore their suggestions in order to avoid going down the slippery slope into contract research, but more often than not they provided the spark for a new project, or for a new angle on an old project.

Which brings us to the theme of the book. While the name 'Capability Management in Network Organizations' was with us from the start, we initially saw it as an umbrella theme, broad enough to cover most issues that are germane to the study of contemporary organizations. However, as the research progressed, it became apparent that there were more commonalities between the various research projects than we had at first hoped for. In particular, while some of us were studying the network of external relationships a firm had with its suppliers and customers, others were looking inside the firm at the networks of interactions between individuals and between different organizational units. These two research domains are very different at one level, at least when one thinks in terms of the formal, legal boundaries of the firm. Indeed as one reviewer of this book commented, it was not obvious a priori that the two domains really fitted together into a single volume.

But armed with the findings from our research projects, several of which spanned the external and internal networks of the firm, we were able to draw out the logic presented in Chapter 1, that capability development is a multi-level phenomenon. Some capabilities are developed in the external network, some are developed at the level of the firm, and others are developed at the sub-firm level in the networks between operating units and individuals. This analysis also led us to the title of the book—'The Flexible Firm'. The logic here is that network organizations are inherently more flexible than traditional hierarchical firms, which is an important characteristic in a fast-changing business environment. Flexibility can therefore be seen as a meta-capability that network organizations need to develop.

The research programme, in other words, enjoyed a symbiotic relationship with its constituent projects. It provided the initial impetus for a number of specific research projects, and a broadly defined domain within which they were defined. But over time the individual projects provided some specific and important insights that ended up being incorporated back into our higher-level thinking about capability management and network organizations. While this two-way process of interaction was intended at the start, it is gratifying to see that we were also able to create a programme that was greater than the sum of the parts. This volume represents the formal reporting of the research for an academic audience and thoughtful managers. It is hoped that one or more books will follow in the next couple of years with a view to disseminating the key ideas more broadly.

While this Introduction is mostly about what is in the book, it is also worth mentioning a couple of the projects that are not reported here. Niclas Lilja, a former colleague at IIB, undertook a detailed historical analysis, supervised by Peter Hagström, of the evolution of the organization structures of the five partner companies. Nils Andersson, with supervision from Julian Birkinshaw, looked at the business development initiatives in SEB and Skandia. Heike Zätterström, again with assistance from Julian Birkinshaw, studied the outsourcing of manufacturing activities in P&U, Volvo, and Ericsson. The findings from these research projects were written up separately, and distributed to the relevant people in the companies, but for reasons of coherence and timeliness they did not find their way into this volume.

1

Network Relationships Inside and Outside the Firm, and the Development of Capabilities

JULIAN BIRKINSHAW

1. Introduction

Over the last decade the literature on strategic management has come to be dominated by the resource-based view of the firm, a theoretical perspective which is concerned with understanding how the firm's resources and capabilities can lead to competitive advantage. While considerable progress has clearly been made, most theoretical work in this area builds on the simplifying assumption that the firm is—or at least can be usefully modelled as —a monolithic entity. For example, Amit and Schoemaker (1993) talk about resources as factors that are owned or controlled by the firm and capabilities as the firm's capacity to deploy resources. However, as the firm becomes increasingly heterogeneous internally (Ghoshal and Bartlett 1990; Hedlund 1986) and more interconnected with suppliers, customers, and competitors outside (Nohria and Eccles 1992; Snow *et al.* 1992), it is important to challenge the assumptions on which the RBV is built, and consider whether the 'firm' is actually the relevant level of analysis. It is now recognized, for example, that some resources and capabilities are built in the relationship with important suppliers or customers (Dyer and Singh 1998). And other capabilities seem to emerge at the subsidiary or divisional level and are then transferred or disseminated to other sub-units (Birkinshaw and Hood 1998; Szulanski 1996). These examples suggest that if we are to understand fully the internal drivers of competitive advantage, we need to work with a more disaggregated conceptualization of the firm—one that recognizes the importance of both sub-firm and supra-firm entities as sources of rent-generating resources and capabilities.

The starting-point in this book is to view the firm not as a monolithic entity but as an organizational network. More specifically, the firm is viewed as a network of relationships between sub-units, groups, and individuals, which is in turn embedded in a wider network of relationships with customers, suppliers, competitors, and other entities. This network perspective has been used in the field of organization studies for decades, and in recent years it has become increasingly popular as a way of analysing the internal and external workings of the firm (see Nohria and Eccles 1992, for an overview). However, it has not so far been used explicitly in conjunction with the resource-based view of the firm. There are good reasons for this, not least because the two schools of thought have very different objective functions (the RBV is concerned with firm-level competitive advantage; the network literature is far more descriptive and seeks to understand how network position affects action). Our belief, none the less, is that a network perspective can usefully inform the resource-based view of the firm, and it is the purpose of this book to show that this is the case. The overarching thesis of the book is that valuable capabilities are built at multiple levels inside the firm and in the firm's external network of relationships. It thus follows that competitive advantage can be gained by those firms that are best able to identify, build, and appropriate the value from those capabilities.

While the argument so far has been made in terms of the academic literature, there is an important managerial angle that should also be mentioned. If we think in terms of the emergence of the 'virtual' firm that undertakes a few core activities but manages all others through partnerships and outsourcing contracts, what is the basis for its competitive advantage? Obviously the core activities are part of the answer, but in addition it seems logical to argue that the ability to manage external relationships and build value through them is also important. Certainly, managers will argue that this is the case, but they will also typically acknowledge that they see this increasingly 'networked' world as a threat, because it is not obvious exactly what capabilities they need to build to be successful. One of the intended contributions of this book, then, is to begin to make sense of the threats and opportunities of this new business environment, and to figure out what sorts of capabilities firms need to build to be successful in it.

1.1. Key Findings from the Research

What, then, are the capabilities that firms need to build in order to be successful as network organizations? At a meta-level, we see the core capability as *flexibility*—hence the title of the book. Flexibility means an ability to adapt aspects of the organization rapidly in the face of new opportunities or threats in the environment. Network organizations are inherently more flexible than hierarchical organizations, but they still need to be configured in such a way that adaptation and rapid responsiveness can be achieved.

At a more specific level, the research studies presented in this volume suggest a number of important capabilities that network organizations need to develop:

1. Relationships with customers and suppliers may appear dyadic, but they typically involve multiple individuals on either side of the relationship, each with an imperfect knowledge of the entire relationship. Thus, an important capability in managing customer or supplier relationships is internal co-ordination—the ability to manage the internal flow of information about the partner firm, the specification of a lead individual, the development of systems to support them, etc. This finding is discussed in detail in Chapter 2 (Sobrero and Toulan), Chapter 3 (Birkinshaw, Toulan, and Arnold), and Chapter 4 (Bresman).

2. Outsourcing of activities has important benefits, but managing the interface with the outsourcing partner is a far from easy task. Chapter 6 (Jonsson) shows that it is necessary to build vicarious capabilities at the interface, not just absorptive capacity, if that relationship is important to the innovatory capacity of the firm.

3. Central to the idea of a network organization is the ability to tap into external sources of knowledge in the business environment. The significant role of peripheral organizational units in external knowledge co-ordination is illustrated in Chapter 5 (Regnér), which stresses the crucial role of alternative strategy creation paths. Chapter 4 (Bresman) shows that a great deal of internal co-ordination and group diversity is needed for knowledge to be effectively internalized. And Chapter 7 (Teigland) shows that tapping into external sources of knowledge can be positive or negative, depending on the task being performed.

4. It is widely recognized that transferring best practices internally is far from trivial (e.g. Szulanski 1996). However, it is not enough just to get the transfer process right. Equally importantly, the firm has to learn to identify where those best practices lie in the first place. As shown in Chapter 9 (Arvidsson), many firms do not know what they know, and as a result their so-called best-practice transfers end up being mediocre-practice transfers.

These points represent important highlights from the ten chapters that follow this one, but they do not do justice to the detailed and systematic research that lies behind them, nor do they pick up on all the issues that are addressed. We therefore urge you to read the book in its entirety. While each chapter was written separately, there is a strong common thread between them, both in terms of the empirical material and with regard to the theoretical ideas that are introduced in this chapter.

This chapter serves three functions. First, it provides some background on the concept of the network organization, and explains why it is important to study contemporary firms in this way. Secondly, it puts forward the argument—hinted at above—that the development of resources and capabilities occurs at multiple levels inside and outside the firm. This argument represents the core theoretical contribution of the book, and it also provides a consistent theme that is subsequently developed in various ways in the nine empirical chapters. Finally, we provide an overview of the nine empirical chapters in the book. The final chapter (Chapter 11) provides a summary of the book, picks up on a number of the common themes that emerge, and offers some perspectives on future research directions.

2. Network Organizations

2.1. What is a Network Organization?

This is not the place to undertake a detailed analysis of the definition of a network organization or a review of the network literature. Briefly, a network can be defined most simply as a set of nodes linked by a set of social relationships of a specified type, but of course this definition is so broad as to encompass just about anything. For the purposes of this book, then, it is important to be clear that we see networks as something more specific, namely, an emerging alternative to the traditional hierarchical model of organization that grew up in the early years of this century. Baker (1992: 399) puts forward a useful distinction in this regard:

The network organisation is a specific organisational type, but the mere presence of a network of ties is not its distinguishing feature. All organisations are networks—patterns of roles and relationships—whether or not they fit the network organisation image. Organisational type depends on the particular pattern and characteristics of the network. For example, a network characterised by rigid hierarchical subdivision of tasks and roles, vertical relationships, and an administrative apparatus separated from production is commonly called a bureaucracy. In contrast, a network characterised by flexibility, decentralised planning and control, and lateral as opposed to vertical ties is closer to the network organisation type.

This book subscribes to Baker's definition of a network organization type, i.e. in terms of flexibility, decentralization, and lateral ties. It is also an attractive definition for two other reasons. First, it says nothing about firm boundaries, in that these characteristics can just as easily be observed outside as inside the firm. Secondly, the distinction between bureaucracy and network organizations highlights a shift in emphasis from the former to the latter that has been under way for some twenty years (more on this later).

In terms of the extant literature on network organizations, let it suffice to acknowledge that it is extensive and multi-disciplinary, and that it exists at several levels of analysis—notably the individual level, the sub-firm level, the firm level, and the industry–regional level. For reviews, see, among others, Flapp *et al.* (1998), Koza and Lewin (1998), Nohria and Eccles (1992), and Powell (1990).

2.2. Network Organizations as New or Emerging Forms

An important issue to consider in terms of the literature on network organizations is the recurring argument that they are a new or emerging form of organization. Many authors have observed the increasing use of alliances and network relationships, and argued that they are a response to the hypercompetitive or turbulent business environment of the current time (e.g. Doz and Hamel 1997; Gomez-Casseres 1994; Nohria and Eccles 1992). Others go further, suggesting that we are witnessing a fundamental change in the nature of wealth creation and the organization of work. In a vastly simplified form, the argument is that network organizations will come to dominate the information age through their inherent flexibility and responsiveness in the way that large hierarchical firms dominated the industrial age on account of their ability to achieve economies of scale and scope (e.g. Best 1990; D'Aveni 1994; Kelly 1998; Illinitch *et al.* 1996).

It is difficult to know how to treat this argument. On the one hand, there are clearly changes going on in the global economy that are driving, and being driven by, changes in the way firms are organizing. On the other hand, it is important not to lose one's sense of historical perspective. While it is convenient to caricature the organizations of the post-war years as bureaucratic and rigid, the reality is that many of the 'new' approaches to organizing have been around in some shape or form for centuries.

Our approach in this book is essentially to sidestep this discussion of paradigm shifts and new organizational forms. In large part the work described here is phenomenon-driven, in that we are studying issues or practices that firms are currently experimenting with or changing. This approach requires an explicit comparison with what went before, but it does not require us to frame the change in terms of a wholesale shift in the environment or the logic of business. While there may indeed be paradigm-shifting changes under way, we prefer to position the current research more conservatively in terms of an ongoing process of co-evolution between firms and the business environment.

2.3. Networks, Hierarchies, and Markets

An alternative perspective on the network terminology will also be mentioned. Transaction cost economics argues that the 'hierarchy' and the 'market' can be seen as alternative ways of mediating transactions (Coase 1937; Williamson 1975). However, it is commonly argued that the pure forms of hierarchy and market are rarely seen. Instead, most transactions actually lie in the 'swollen middle' (Hennart 1993), as hybrids that have elements of both hierarchy and market.

The network organization, as described here, can be seen as a hybrid that is neither pure market nor pure hierarchy (Jarillo 1988; Powell 1990; Thorelli 1987). This conceptualization also allows us to distinguish between two different species of network organization (see Figure 1.1). One is the relationship that the core firm has with a set of legally independent partner firms. These firms interact with one another through the market system, but in relationships that are built on behaviours one would normally associate

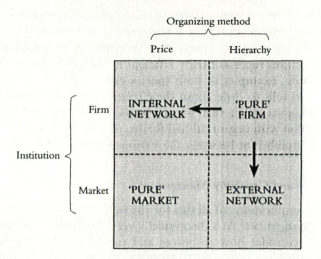

FIG. 1.1. Two forms of network organization

with common ownership: norms of reciprocity and trust, sharing of knowledge, and investments in relationship-specific assets. A variety of popular terms are used to characterize these sorts of relationships, including the virtual organization, the extended enterprise model, and the business network. Here we simply use the term 'external network' to refer to relationships beyond the legal boundaries of the core firm.

The second species we refer to as the internal network. This is the set of relationships between subsidiaries or divisions of the same legal firm that interact with each other on a quasi-market basis. Under this arrangement each division has sufficient degrees of freedom to make most of its own resource allocation decisions, while still working in close co-operation with its affiliated divisions. Thus, for example, one sees many large firms giving their divisions a choice of whether (and at what price) to buy from an internal supplier, or whether to source from an outside party. This choice promotes flexibility in the buying division, and enhances competitiveness in the supplier division. At the same time, because the two units are commonly owned, it is in their interests to come up with a mutually acceptable solution. Again, there are many variants of this approach, some of the better known being the inter-organizational network, the heterarchy, the self-organizing system, and the internal market.

It should be noted that these two species, while quite distinct, typically represent complementary rather than competing approaches to organizing. For example, companies like Skandia AFS and ABB make extensive use of external network partnerships and internal network structures. The reason for this is that both network forms can be seen as a shift away from the traditional hierarchical form of organization, and as such offer many of the benefits of market transacting but without many of the costs (Hennart 1993).

Interestingly, it is by no means clear whether, or to what extent, these network structures represent truly efficient modes of organization. As this book will show, examples of both species can be seen in most large firms today, but this tells us little about their relative efficiency or effectiveness. Rather, it suggests either that we are in the middle of a period of active experimentation with organizational forms, or that there is something close to a neutral equilibrium between the various forms (Simon 1991).

2.4. Networks and Capability Management

What are the implications of all this for the other half of the research theme, capability management? At a theoretical level the network conceptualization allows us to consider how resources and capabilities develop at different levels of analysis—in the internal network, in the external network, or at some other level. This proves to be quite an insightful line of thinking, as the following section will show.

At an applied level the network approach also has some important implications. If we accept the basic premiss that there are ongoing changes in the way firms are organizing themselves, it follows that firms will need to develop a new set of capabilities to be able to manage effectively—such things as working with external partners, transferring capabilities between subsidiary units, or building an information technology infrastructure that meets the needs of both internal and external parties. The identification of these sorts of capability is one of the common themes of the book. Thus, while it is written in an academic style for an academic audience, there are also valuable conclusions for practising managers in most chapters.

It is also interesting to speculate that there may be some form of 'meta-capability' in network management that some firms are able to develop that allows them to integrate a number of different capabilities, or provides them with the foresight to stay one step ahead of their competitors. The argument is similar to that made by Percy Barnevik, ex-CEO of ABB, when he claimed that the capability to manage a multinational firm effectively was hard to copy and thus a source of competitive advantage. It may be that some firms have, or are developing, network management capabilities that will provide them with a long-term source of advantage in an increasingly networked world. Unfortunately, this is a question that we do not currently have a good answer to, but it is addressed in a number of places in the book.

3. A Multi-Level Perspective on Capability Development

The resource-based view of the firm (RBV) is currently established as the dominant paradigm in strategic management. Rather than see firm success as a question of clever positioning *vis-à-vis* other actors in the industrial environment (Porter 1980), the RBV argues that competitive advantage originates in the unique bundle of resources and capabilities owned by the firm. To the extent that these resources and capabilities are valuable in the market-place, rare, hard to substitute, and hard to imitate, they will result in competitive advantage (Barney 1991). There has been an enormous body of literature published in the last ten years that qualifies, adapts, and extends this argument (e.g. Amit and Schoemaker 1993; Conner 1991; Peteraf 1993), but the basic logic remains the same.

There is a related but distinct body of literature referred to as the dynamic capabilities perspective, which is concerned with the 'mechanisms by which firms accumulate and dissipate new skills and capabilities' (Teece *et al.* 1997: 19; see also Dierickx and Cool 1989; Kogut and Zander 1992; Nelson and Winter 1982). This perspective builds on the same principles of resource heterogeneity, but it is more focused on the dynamics of capability development than the stocks of resources and capabilities at any given point in time.

Both the resource-based view and the dynamic capabilities perspective typically work with the simplifying assumption that resources and capabilities can be modelled at the firm level. As noted earlier, resources are seen as stocks of available factors that are owned or controlled by the firm, while capabilities are the firm's capacity to deploy resources, usually in combination, using organizational processes to effect a desired end (Amit and Schoemaker 1993). This may be the relevant level of analysis in most cases, but there is considerable empirical evidence, as well as good theoretical reason, to suggest that other levels of analysis are equally valid.

Consider first the supra-firm level of analysis. Many firms today are formally linked to other independent firms through joint venture arrangements, licensing agreements, or suchlike. Others have more informal but equally important relationships in the form of strategic alliances, outsourcing arrangements, value-adding partnerships, and so on. All of these relationships involve some level of 'deeper' interaction than would be expected in a traditional arm's-length relationship, and as such they become an important opportunity for mutual adaptation, learning, and idea generation (Dyer and Singh 1998; Hamel 1991; Håkansson and Johanson 1992; Kogut 1988). Even more importantly, many of these relationships involve investments in relationship-specific activities and the bringing-together of complementary resources and capabilities. In the words of Dyer and Singh (1998: 660), the argument is that 'a firm's critical resources may span firm boundaries and may be embedded in interfirm resources and routines'.

The sub-firm level of analysis also offers potential for enriching our thinking about the sources of critical resources and capabilities. By modelling the firm as an inter-organizational network, it becomes apparent that individual units often have considerable discretion over resource allocation and over the choice of activities that they partake in. These individual units, in other words, have their own distinct set of resources and capabilities that emerge as a function of the particular characteristics of the local environment (Birkinshaw and Hood 1998; Frost 1998; Ghoshal and Nohria 1989), the existing activities of the unit (Galunic and Eisenhardt 1996), and the initiative of unit management (Birkinshaw 1995), to name a few of the important determinants. Moreover, it is also apparent that these resources and capabilities cannot always be seamlessly transferred or disseminated between units. Research has shown that there is often a considerable variation in capability level between units in the same firm (Liebenstein 1966) and that transfers of practices between units are often fraught with problems (Arvidsson 1999; Szulanski 1996; Zander 1991). And in terms of physical or human resources, the costs of moving them between locations often exceed the benefits. The point, in other words, is that for whole classes of resources and capabilities, the appropriate level of analysis for understanding them is the sub-firm unit. For many others—such as patents, IT systems, or the organization culture—the firm is still the more appropriate level of analysis.

Finally, it should also be realized that the network relationships between sub-units can be a source of critical capabilities in the same way that the relationships between firm and supplier can. For example, Hansen (1996) and Tsai and Ghoshal (1998) model unit-level outcomes such as innovation and time to market as a function of the network of relationships that the unit has with other internal units. Another way of making this point is to hypothesize the case of a firm internalizing its relationship with a strategically important supplier as discussed by Dyer and Singh (1998). In such a case, it is obvious that while the governance systems surrounding that relationship have changed, much of the rent-generating capacity of the relationship remains the same.

In sum, the implication of this discussion is that the development of valuable resources and capabilities occurs at multiple levels of analysis. By using a network perspective, we can more effectively conceptualize what the appropriate levels are, and thus we can build a more comprehensive framework for understanding how and where competitive advantage is achieved.

There is one link missing in the above logic, namely the issue of rent appropriation. It is a central tenet of the resource-based view that firms will only realize above-average profits if they can capture or 'appropriate' the rents that accrue from these valuable resources and capabilities (Amit and Schoemaker 1993; Peteraf 1993; Teece 1987). In terms of the current discussion then, it is important to identify the sources of capabilities inside and outside the firm, but it is equally critical that we understand how different stakeholders appropriate the value emanating from those capabilities. For example, when capabilities are developed at the supra-firm level, we can expect the division of profits from those 'relational rents' to be a function of the relative bargaining power of the two parties, all else being equal (Dyer and Singh 1998: 657). And even when capabilities are developed within the firm, it is possible for other stakeholders to extract value from them, as well as for the rents to be dissipated in the process of using them (Ghemawat 1991). In short, the step from valuable capabilities to competitive advantage —regardless of the level of analysis—is far from guaranteed.

A more detailed investigation of these ideas will not be attempted here. Theory-building is still at a relatively rudimentary level, so it is probably more valuable to build a body of strong empirical evidence of the sources of capability development at this stage, and then revisit the theoretical issues subsequently. The following nine chapters represent a first attempt in this direction.

4. Overview of the Book

Figure 1.2 provides a graphical illustration of the themes of the nine empirical chapters. The horizontal axis represents the level of analysis. Six chapters are concerned with the relationship of the firm to its external network, though to varying degrees they also examine the internal network. Three chapters are focused primarily around internal network issues. The vertical axis represents the distinction between exploration and exploitation (March 1991), where exploration is about identifying new opportunities and exploitation is about making use of existing ones. The ability to balance exploration and exploitation is central to firm success, in that a deficiency in either will result in failure (short-term failure if exploitation is entirely neglected; long-term failure if exploration is entirely neglected). As Figure 1.2 indicates, the nine

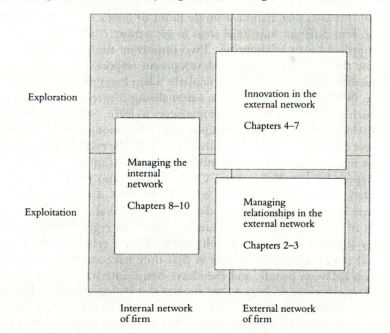

FIG. 1.2. Overview of chapters

chapters are split fairly evenly on this dimension, and several are explicitly concerned with how organizations achieve a balance between exploration and exploitation. By mapping the chapters in this way, it is possible to identify three broad groupings that we use to structure the book. Below we consider each of these groups in turn.

4.1. Managing Relationships in the External Network

Part I consists of two chapters. Chapter 2 (Sobrero and Toulan) is concerned with how firms structure their relationships with supplier firms. Chapter 3 (Birkinshaw, Toulan, and Arnold) focuses on the relationship with global customers.

A consistent finding comes out in these two chapters: that the effective management of long-term relationships with suppliers and customers requires as much focus on internal co-ordination issues (between functions and divisions) as on the relationship itself. This is because such relationships are often so complex and multifaceted that they cannot be managed by a single individual or by multiple unco-ordinated individuals. In terms of the theme of the book, then, it suggests that firms operating in a network organization have to develop an internal co-ordination capability to create strong relationships with suppliers and customers.

In Chapter 2 Maurizio Sobrero and Omar Toulan describe a detailed study of Volvo and its strategic relationships with forty-seven suppliers. Unlike most studies in this area that assume a single point of contact, they survey individuals in four different functional areas to get a more comprehensive picture of the supplier–buyer relationship. Two important findings emerge. First, they show that giving the supplier development responsibilities can enhance the performance of a given task, particularly when that task is complex. Outsourcing, in other words, may mean externalizing control as well as production, which is a hard lesson for most managers to learn. Secondly, they show that knowledge about the relationship is dispersed among several individuals in different functions. This suggests that to manage the relationship effectively there is a need for more effective internal co-ordination across functions.

In Chapter 3 Julian Birkinshaw, Omar Toulan, and David Arnold look at the relationship of the focal firm with its customer, and more specifically with those key customers that are designated as global accounts. Based on a survey of fifty-eight global account managers in eight European firms, the study attempts to understand why some of these relationships are more successful than others. The answer is that they have stronger internal co-ordination between people, and they have better internal support mechanisms. Obviously these findings do not suggest that building a good relationship with the customer is unimportant. Rather, the authors argue, most account managers probably do a good job of that, so the internal factors end up deciding between the high and low performers.

4.2. Innovation in the External Network

Part II consists of four chapters. Chapter 4 (Bresman) and Chapter 5 (Regnér) both focus on the role of links into the broader external network as a means of getting access to new and valuable ideas. Chapter 6 (Jonsson) examines how it is possible to innovate effectively in a 'virtual' firm where most value-adding activities are not actually controlled by the firm. Chapter 7 (Teigland) moves the level of analysis down to the individual level, in a study that compares the external and internal sources of knowledge used by individuals when they solve difficult problems.

Unlike the chapters in Part I, these four are concerned with the use of the external network for exploration—for tapping into new ideas, and for combining knowledge in different places. A common theme is the need to balance the short-term exploitational needs of the firm with the longer-term demands for exploration. While the four chapters address different aspects of this problem, they all end up identifying approaches that firms can use to achieve a better balance between these conflicting demands.

Chapter 4, by Henrik Bresman, is a detailed study of the process of in-licensing of pharmaceutical compounds by Pharma Inc. (a pseudonym). Bresman uses the term 'external integrative capability' to refer to the process of identifying, evaluating, and internalizing knowledge about in-licensing compounds. The study reveals one important finding: that the level of variation in team structure over the life of a project is strongly associated with both current and future project performance. Individual projects benefit from multiple perspectives. But more importantly, there is evidence of a learning curve, as the external integrative capability is built up within the firm.

In Chapter 5 Patrick Regnér undertakes a detailed analysis of four 'strategy creation' cases: Ericsson's mobile telephony business, Pharmacia & Upjohn's consumer healthcare business, Autoliv's automotive safety business, and AGA's entry into Eastern Europe. His analysis suggests that in all four cases the strategy creation process occurred in the periphery of the firm, and through linkages with independent external actors. Regnér argues that the ability to assimilate external knowledge, often from entirely different industries or spheres of activity, is pivotal to the development of new strategies. He also describes the internal processes that transpired in the four cases as these new strategies built legitimacy within the firm.

Stefan Jonsson starts with an interesting dilemma in Chapter 6. A firm that outsources most of its value-adding activities to partner firms will typically gain in flexibility and efficiency in the short term, but runs the risk of reducing the quality of interaction between activities, and thus impoverishing its capacity for innovation. This dilemma is addressed through a detailed case-study of Skandia AFS, a firm that has moved a long way down the 'virtual' road but that is still very innovative. He argues that Skandia has resolved the dilemma by beefing up the interface with partner firms—through key account management, wholesaling support, and investment manager management. These interfaces provide an increase in absorptive capacity and provide the two-way interaction necessary for effective innovation.

In Chapter 7 Robin Teigland describes a study of the knowledge acquisition strategies of the 200 employees of Icon Medialab, a web design company based in Stockholm. Building on the idea that most learning in organizations occurs through almost invisible communities of practice, she asked individuals what sources of internal and external knowledge they used when solving difficult problems and what means of communication they used. The central finding was that the choice of network depended a lot on the individual's objective. On-time performance was best facilitated through use of codified internal sources of knowledge. Creativity was enhanced through external codified sources of knowledge and social contacts outside work. Thus, both internal and external personal networks are important, but they affect performance in different ways.

4.3. Managing the Internal Network

Part III looks primarily at how subsidiaries and divisions within the firm relate to one another. Chapter 8 (Birkinshaw and Fey) uses the metaphor of the internal market to understand how resources are allocated within R. & D. organizations. Chapter 9 (Arvidsson) looks at the identification of best practices in marketing and sales subsidiaries, and how these practices are transferred between units. Finally, Chapter 10 (Hagström) considers the role of information technology systems as an enabler of strategy in a network organization.

A couple of interesting themes emerge from these three chapters. First, internal networks are characterized by a blend of co-operation and competition: individual units work together, but they are also expected to compete with one another for resources. This approach captures some of the benefits of a market system while not sacrificing any of the advantages of ownership. Secondly, it is apparent that most of the internal knowledge flow and co-ordination problems within the firm arise not through structural inadequacies but on account of cognitive and behavioural limitations.

In Chapter 8 Julian Birkinshaw and Carl Fey describe a study of R. & D. organizations in five firms (ABB, Ericsson, HP, Pharmacia & Upjohn, Omega), using the internal market metaphor. Essentially they argue that one can usefully model the relationship between a corporate research centre and a business unit as a quasi-market one, in which both supplier and buyer potentially have a choice about who to sell to or buy from. The analysis reveals that only ABB, and to some degree Ericsson, operate in a manner that approximates the internal market. The authors also note that the internal market approach appears to enhance efficiency quite nicely, but with some negative implications for long-term effectiveness.

Chapter 9, by Niklas Arvidsson, is a detailed analysis of 171 sales and marketing subsidiary units in seven different multinational firms. He argues that all the research on transfers of best practice is built on the important but untested assumption that there is some agreement on what the best practice is, and where it is held. The research reported in the chapter then goes on to challenge this assumption. More specifically, by asking both subsidiary unit and corporate headquarters to rate the marketing capabilities of each unit, Arvidsson is able to show that there is frequently a lack of agreement about where the best practices lie. Furthermore, by looking at the patterns of transfers of practices between units, he shows that transfers frequently do not flow from high performers to low performers. The implication of this research is that much greater awareness of the whereabouts of valuable capabilities is needed for firms to manage their internal knowledge in an effective way.

In Chapter 10 Peter Hagström offers a detailed analysis of the role played by information technology (IT) in network organizations. Based on his experiences in a large number of Swedish multinational firms, Hagström argues that IT can play a rather sophisticated role in facilitating, and some-times even driving, the emergence of network organizations. For example, IT enhances the firm's control over its world-wide operations, but it also makes it possible to identify and cash in on local initiatives when they occur. In terms of the internal market logic presented in Chapter 8, IT fosters greater communication and transparency, and ultimately a more market-like set of relationships within the firm. IT can also foster more effective relationships with external firms, but the gulf between potential and reality here is much larger than it is with internal systems.

Finally, Chapter 11, by Peter Hagström, provides a summary of the major themes of the book and highlights a number of important issues that arise in the empirical chapters. Some reflections on the research process, and suggestions for future research directions, are also mentioned.

PART I

Managing Relationships in the
External Network

2

Task Partitioning, Communication Activities, and the Performance of Supplier Relations in Product Development

MAURIZIO SOBRERO AND OMAR TOULAN

1. Introduction

The relationships a firm has with its suppliers can be a valuable source of competitive advantage. The benefit from these relationships can accrue in many ways. Previous work on supplier–manufacturer relationships (Clark 1989; Lipparini and Sobrero 1994; Liker *et al*. 1995; Dyer 1996), as well as alliances (Roberts and Berry 1985) and joint ventures (Harrigan 1986; Cohen and Levinthal 1990), have grouped these potential benefits into two categories: increased efficiency, and the tapping of competencies or resources unavailable inside the firm. Given the difference in goals, however, one would also expect there to be a difference in the way these two types of relationships should be managed. With this in mind, the objective of this chapter is to address three related research questions: Along what lines do these supplier–manufacturer relationships differ from each other? Is there a fit between relationship type, management of the relationship, and performance? What does this mean in terms of the individual actors which make up the relationship?

In addressing the first question, we take as a starting-point the distinction made above between efficiency- and competence-seeking relationships. We elaborate upon this classification by focusing on the characteristics of the task being performed (Alexander 1964; Thompson 1967; Clark 1985; von Hippel 1990; Sobrero 1996), as well as the distribution of expertise between the supplier and the manufacturer. Through a cluster analysis we then identify different management models in the design and development process which focus on the actual distribution of roles and responsibilities between the two parties. We then correlate these two factors, task characteristics and management model, to see whether a fit between the two leads to higher performance of the relationship. This differs from previous studies, which, rather than focusing on the fit between task characteristics and management model to explain supplier performance, have focused on contextual aspects of the relationship, such as trust (Ring and Van de Ven 1992; Ring 1996), commitment (Anderson and Weitz 1989; Heide and George 1990; Heide and Miner 1992), or power asymmetries (Pfeffer and Nowak 1976; Van de Ven and Walker 1984; Joskow 1987).

In the final part of the chapter, after having identified differences in supplier management at the level of the overall relationship based on asymmetric distributions of expertise and task characteristics, we change levels of analysis and focus on the individuals actually responsible for the day-to-day management of the supplier relationship. In this case, however, we focus not on the distribution of knowledge about the parts being supplied but rather on knowledge about the supplier itself and its relationship with the manufacturer. Differences in supplier knowledge across functional areas within the firm are then explained in part using data on communication patterns.

Together, the various parts of the chapter point to the complexity of supplier relationships. Not only do they vary one from the other in terms of what is being performed, but they must also be managed in different ways so as to achieve the highest performance. The difficulty of managing these relationships in a differential manner, however, is increased by the fact that interaction with and knowledge of the supplier are dispersed among various actors in the firm. In the pages which follow, these questions are addressed using the results from a survey on supplier relations conducted at one of the divisions of Volvo in 1998. In total, forty-seven supplier–manufacturer relationships are analysed.

2. Empirical Setting

In selecting a site in which to address the research questions identified above, it was important to choose one in which suppliers played a major role in the success of the firm in question, particularly in the area of design. In addition, the firm needed to have enough supplier relationships so as to be able to identify variance both in the task being performed and in the way in which the relationship is managed. The Volvo Corporation meets both of these criteria. Given its relative size, Volvo is in a position in which it cannot afford to retain all the necessary skills to produce its cars in-house. For many parts, it does not have the necessary scale on which to spread the fixed costs of development. This fact is aggravated by the changing nature of the industries in which it operates, where one is witnessing a growing increase in the number of parts requiring electrical and/or computer engineering skills, traditionally outside the domain of the company. As such, Volvo's success is in many ways dependent upon the success of its supplier relationships, through which it can tap external sources of expertise. In addition to being critical, these relationships are also numerous in the case of Volvo, so much so that it was decided to focus on one project within one of the company's divisions.

There are forty-seven parts suppliers for the project in question. The suppliers themselves range in size from small local players to large multinationals. In addition, they produce products which vary in task complexity and for which the requisite expertise is dispersed between Volvo and the supplier. In fact, in nearly two-thirds of the cases Volvo personnel identified the supplier as having more of the expertise needed to design and develop the part.

3. Methodology

With the empirical setting chosen, it was decided that the best way to collect the required data would be to survey those individuals responsible for the forty-seven project suppliers in each of four functional areas within Volvo: design, purchasing, pre-series quality assurance, and series quality assurance. After a number of interviews at Volvo these four groups were identified as being the ones responsible for the majority of the interaction between Volvo and its suppliers. A total of 188 surveys were administered to the forty-five individuals responsible for the forty-seven suppliers: twelve from design, ten from purchasing, thirteen from pre-series quality assurance; and ten from series quality assurance. In each case individuals were asked to complete one survey per project supplier for which they were responsible.

The survey itself was designed over the course of two months, following roughly twenty-five interviews with Volvo personnel in each of the areas identified above. It was then pre-tested on five Volvo managers. The survey was designed to cover issues relating to the supplier itself as well as its relationship with Volvo. In addition, respondents were asked to evaluate the supplier relationship on a number of criteria. The survey consisted of three main parts. The first covered basic information about the supplier and its relationship with Volvo. This was followed by a section covering various areas of competence, for which the respondent was asked to evaluate the supplier. Finally, the third section focused on the specific role the supplier played in the project in question, focusing on design and problem-solving activities.[1]

Remission rates were quite high, compared to traditional surveys. We received responses from twenty-nine of the forty-five individuals (individual remission rate of 64 per cent), for a total of 101 surveys (survey remission rate of 54 per cent). Responses covered the whole set of forty-seven suppliers. Breakdowns by functional area can be found in Table 2.1. On average individuals filled out three to four surveys each, though this varied from

---

[1] A copy of the questionnaire is available upon request from the authors.

TABLE 2.1. *Response rates by functional area*

Functional area	Sent (no.)	Received (no.)	Response rate (%)
Design			
Individuals	12	6	50
Surveys	47	16	34
Purchasing			
Individuals	10	8	80
Surveys	47	34	72
Pre-series quality assurance			
Individuals	13	5	38
Surveys	47	11	23
Series quality assurance			
Individuals	10	10	100
Surveys	47	40	85

one to eleven as a result of both intra- and inter-functional differences. Certain functions such as design, because of the nature of the work, have a smaller number of suppliers assigned to each individual. In addition, within the same function different numbers of individuals were responsible for different numbers of suppliers, depending on the complexity of the relationships and the parts being provided.

4. The Role of Suppliers in the Development Process

Empirical analyses in different industries and countries offer convergent evidence on the role of suppliers in promoting shorter and more efficient innovation cycles, suggesting that vertical relationships in new product development can be activated with two objectives in mind: (*a*) to increase the overall efficiency of the process, or (*b*) to tap into external resources otherwise inaccessible. In either case it is key to look at the extent to which suppliers actively participate in the development process as well as the criticality of their engineering efforts.

Imai and colleagues' work on supplier–manufacturer relationships in new product development (Imai *et al.* 1985) presents evidence from five in-depth case-studies of Japanese firms in the electronics, photographic equipment, and automotive industries. Together with stressing the organizational issues involved in the process and their distinctiveness with respect to US approaches, frequent, repetitive, and long-lasting relations with suppliers are pointed out as contributing to faster and more flexible new product development processes. The early involvement of suppliers in the development process and high levels of communication flows across firms

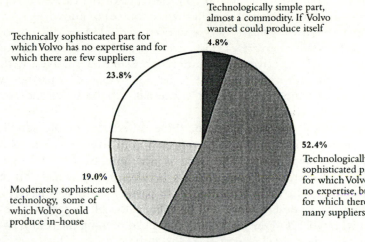

Technologically simple part, almost a commodity. If Volvo wanted could produce itself
4.8%

Technically sophisticated part for which Volvo has no expertise and for which there are few suppliers
23.8%

52.4%
Technologically sophisticated part for which Volvo has no expertise, but for which there are many suppliers

19.0%
Moderately sophisticated technology, some of which Volvo could produce in-house

FIG. 2.1. Parts characteristics and suppliers' involvement

are focused on as driving forces for faster releases of new devices and prompt responses to competitors' moves.

Similar arguments, although at an industry level, are made by Håkansson (1987, 1989), who provides evidence through different case-studies of how the strengths of certain Swedish industries are based on this nexus of contacts between suppliers and manufacturers. Research in the world automobile industry (Clark 1989; Liker *et al.* 1995; Dyer 1996, 1997) supports these arguments with empirical evidence at the project level. *Ceteris paribus*, greater supplier involvement is shown to account for roughly one-third of the Japanese advantage in engineering hours and four to five months of their lead-time advantage.

More recent work in electronics (Nishiguchi 1995), packaging machinery (Fruin 1992), and home appliances (Sobrero 1996) supports these conclusions, but also highlights the co-ordination and monitoring problems arising from a multi-partner structure. Sobrero and Roberts (1998) used fifty dyadic supplier–manufacturer relationships drawn from three new product development projects to show that the type of knowledge being partitioned and its level of interdependence with the rest of the project are important predictors of relationship performance. Further, the analyses demonstrate a clear trade-off between short-term efficiency-increasing and longer-term learning-enhancing relationship types.

A first look at our data confirms that suppliers were involved in the project in question for different reasons (Figure 2.1). Only one-fourth (23.8 per cent) of the total set of forty-seven relationships is related to parts which Volvo could produce in-house if wanted. On the contrary, 76.2 per cent of the relationships are initiated because the supplier has a distinctive expertise, which Volvo could not replicate. In 23.8 per cent of the cases Volvo had few opportunities to choose among alternative sources of knowledge, as the supplier market on those parts was either concentrated or did not offer technologically valid alternatives. However, in 52.4 per cent of the cases the supplier could be selected among different possible alternatives. In these cases it is therefore important not only to be able to identify a partner who has a knowledge which is not available internally, but also to understand which partner one should choose.

As suggested by previous research, these differences in the supplier's expected contribution should also be reflected in different relation-specific organizational arrangements. The issue is not only to acknowledge an asymmetric distribution of competencies between the partners, but also to structure the relationship accordingly. In particular, choices have to be made as to how the design work will be split, who will be responsible for what, and who will act as the integrating figure, combining the results of the interaction with the overall project. To look at these issues, which represent specific areas of managerial attention for the organization of the supplier–manufacturer interaction in new product development, we can rely on the application of the theory of design to innovation activities. A first distinction can be made between concept definition and design activities. Concept definition activities are targeted to the understanding of alternative design concepts for approaching a specific problem, and to the selection of one of these concepts (Marple 1961). Subsequently, problem-solvers must shift their attention to define clearly the functional parameters of the selected design concept (Alexander 1964). Design activities represent this next step, during which the selected detailed solutions are technically carried through to the rest of the project. Clearly the two sets of activities are interdependent and are often characterized by intense iterative cycles. Theoretically, however, they can be used to represent two distinct sets of activities within a development project.

To explore the extent to which Volvo structured the forty-seven relationships in question in different ways with respect to the distribution of responsibilities of concept definition and design activities we focused on the part of our questionnaire specifically dedicated to how problem-solving and design activities had been organized. Our goal was to obtain a measure of the differences–similarities among the relationships observed with respect to the organizational arrangements chosen. To do so, we first used multidimensional scaling on the seven questions addressing different aspects of how the development work was partitioned between Volvo and the supplier. The procedure proved to be numerically stable (Kruskal stress level $= 0.127$, RSQ $= 0.954$) and we therefore decided to use the resulting values as our starting values for the subsequent step of the analysis, where we used hierarchical cluster analysis to partition the relationships observed into homogeneous groups. Since the starting values are an aggregate measure

TABLE 2.2. *Differences in the organization of design and problem-solving activities*

	Group 1 mean value	Group 2 mean value	Between-group difference significant at
Who takes the lead in the project?	2.21	4.22	$p < 0.001$
Where is the design work performed?	1.93	4.56	$p < 0.001$
Who identifies the general boundaries of the problem?	4.07	5.41	$p < 0.001$
Who identifies the specific technical solution?	3.21	4.96	$p < 0.001$
Who chooses the final solution?	4.50	6.73	$p < 0.001$
Who is responsible for integrating the design work with the overall project?	6.07	6.83	$p < 0.001$

Note: Responses are based on a seven-point Likert scale where 1 = supplier, 4 = split equally, 7 = Volvo.

of the differences in the way design and problem-solving activities were partitioned between Volvo and the supplier in all the forty-seven relationships observed, relationships organized in a similar way should cluster together. In our calculations we applied the average linkage between group method to define the difference between two clusters as the average of the distances between all pairs defined by the members of the cluster. This solution is particularly helpful to emphasize between group differences, which is what we are interested in. Three significant groups emerged from our analysis. One group, composed of ten of the forty-seven observations, is characterized by the relevant presence of missing values in many of the questions we were interested in. We therefore decided to focus on the remaining two groups, which include all other thirty-seven observations, representing about 80 per cent of our sample, and showing very interesting differences along all the selected organizational dimensions. The first group is characterized by relationships in which the supplier plays a dominant role, while the second group includes all cases where Volvo is the lead partner within the relationship. Table 2.2 reports the mean values for each group on the responses for the questionnaire related to the organization of design and problem-solving activities.

Volvo always retains project integration responsibility, although for some parts belonging to the first group the supplier is called to give a contribution also in this specific area. Within group 1 the supplier takes the lead in the relationship, and participates actively in the definition of the general boundaries of the problem as well as the subsequent technical solutions, where its expertise is critical in selecting the final choices. In these cases almost all of the design work is done by the supplier. Within group 2, although the leadership within the relationship seems to be shared between the partners, Volvo is more actively working on the knowledge scope dimension, both at the level of the general problem definition, and at the level of functional parameter specification. Accordingly, it is Volvo who chooses the final solution, although the supplier has still to perform some relevant design work in order to implement it.

These differences in how problem-solving responsibilities are allocated between the partners suggest giving greater consideration to the characteristics of the work being performed. Organizational scholars have long been studying how alternative ways of integrating and co-ordinating the work of multiple units can result in better outcomes, depending on the characteristics of the task being performed. Traditionally, the unit of analysis in these fit models is the organization, and the unit of observation is the transaction among different entities within it. A similar approach, however, can easily be extended to the analysis of inter-organizational relationships. In our case, in fact, we observe how different organizational co-ordination choices are made to structure different types of supplier contributions to the development process.

Several models of fit have been used to determine the most effective co-ordination choices (Scott 1990). Selection models limit their analysis to univariate context structure relations, failing to account for the multidimensional nature of the context and of the structure and not explicitly considering performance implications (Van de Ven and Drazin 1985). Interaction models focus on explaining variation in performance from the interaction of organizational structure and context. Their main limitation, however, is that they determine each structural dimension independently of the others without investigating possible substitution and trade-off effects.

Systemic models, on the contrary, advocate that 'the understanding of context-structure performance relationships can only advance by addressing simultaneously the many contingencies, structural alternatives and performance criteria that must be considered holistically to understand organization design' (Van de Ven and Drazin 1985: 519). Systemic models adopt a deviation approach, where ideal profiles summarizing different combinations along a set of organization-structuring variables are compared with alternative solutions along a set of performance measures.

To analyse the impact of different structuring decisions on how the design process was managed and how problem-solving activities were divided between the partners in our set of relationships we decided to adopt a systemic approach. As we have seen so far, in fact, there are many different aspects within these two specific areas where alternative organizational design choices can be applied. Similarly, there are different ways in which a relationship's performance can be evaluated (Sobrero and Roberts 1998).

Respondents were asked to evaluate each of their suppliers on twelve different dimensions. These dimensions were derived from an initial set developed during the preliminary phase using previous research and adding some dimensions which were considered critical in the particular Volvo setting. Some of these dimensions are concerned with an operational evaluation of the collaboration (i.e. the respect of deadlines, the ability to produce prototypes, the quality level of the supplier). Others refer to the presence, or absence, of specific capabilities within the supplier organization (i.e. unique technological expertise, ability to identify the root of the problems, the speed of responsiveness). Others referred more generally to the ease of working with the supplier (i.e. willingness to visit Volvo, willingness to open one's own facilities, willingness to listen to Volvo concerns). Judgements on each dimension were expressed on a seven-point Likert scale (1 = poor performance, 7 = excellent performance).

To analyse the role of fit between relationship-specific organizational arrangements and the different measures of performance we constructed six deviation measures to be correlated with our twelve performance indicators. For example, we would expect that for parts where the supplier has a significant knowledge and expertise, Volvo should outsource most of the design work to speed up the development process and make the most of the relationship. All deviation indicators are calculated as the absolute difference between two sets of items. One set is composed of indicators of relationship-specific task characteristics expressed as criticality (i.e. degree of importance of the component developed for the whole project), complexity (i.e. how difficult was the design and development work associated to that specific component), and expertise distribution (i.e. the degree of competence asymmetries between Volvo and the supplier about that specific component). The second set of items is composed of the organizational choices along the design and problem-solving activities dimensions. A description of how the fit indices are calculated is included in Appendix 2.1.

We therefore developed three deviation measures capturing the fit between the distribution of design responsibilities and criticality of the task, technical complexity of the part, and relative expertise of the partners. Each one of these three measures is composed of two deviation indicators, with reliability coefficients equal to 0.76, 0.85, and 0.79, respectively. We then developed three other deviation measures for the fit between the distribution of problem-solving responsibilities and criticality of the task, technical complexity of the part, and relative expertise of the partners. Each one of these three measures is composed of four deviation indicators, with reliability coefficients equal to 0.72, 0.82, and 0.81 respectively. From the way our questions were formulated we expect the difference to be large when there is coherence (fit) between the inter-organizational choice and the nature of the task.

TABLE 2.3. *Compositional fit for relationship characteristics, supplier's involvement in design and problem-solving activities, and relationship performance*

Performance indicators	Criticality fit		Complexity fit		Expertise fit	
	Design	Problem-solving	Design	Problem-solving	Design	Problem-solving
Respect for initial budget	0.45[a]	—	0.41[a]	—	—	—
Speed of responsiveness to Volvo's concerns	0.34[b]	—	—	—	—	—
Respect for deadlines in development	—	—	0.32[a]	—	—	—
Technological expertise or uniqueness	0.41[b]	0.34[b]	—	—	—	—
Willingness to open up facilities to Volvo	—	0.34[b]	—	0.54[c]	—	—
Willingness to visit Volvo	—	—	—	0.31[a]	—	—
Ability to identify roots of problems	0.36[b]	0.48[c]	—	—	0.49[c]	0.30[a]
Producing prototypes	0.31[a]	—	—	—	0.41[b]	0.32[a]
Listening to Volvo's problems	0.28[a]	—	—	—	—	—
Defect rates in production	0.32[a]	—	—	—	0.35[b]	—
Delivery time and respect for deadlines in production	—	—	—	—	—	—
Overall ease to work with	—	0.40[b]	—	—	—	—

[a] $p < 0.10$.
[b] $p < 0.05$.
[c] $p < 0.01$.

Table 2.3 reports the results of our correlation analysis, and shows that managing supplier–manufacturer relationships differentially based on task characteristics and expertise distribution does in fact lead to higher performance. For complex and critical parts where the supplier is responsible for design activities there is a higher respect for the initial budget. In the case of complex parts, there is a greater respect for development deadlines. In the case of critical parts there is also a greater speed in responding to Volvo's concerns, a greater ability to identify the roots of problems, to produce prototypes, to decrease defect rates in production, and to demonstrate a higher technological expertise.

Higher supplier involvement in problem-solving activities for critical and complex parts shows a similar tendency. When we focus on the fit between the partners' expertise distribution and design responsibilities, we notice that, when the supplier is more competent and also more involved both in the design and in the problem-solving activities, it shows a greater ability to identify the roots of the problems, to produce prototypes, and to decrease defect rates in production.

What these results imply is that to leverage external relationships effectively in knowledge-intensive transactions such as product development projects, there must be a strategic allocation of resources and responsibilities between the partners reflecting competence asymmetries (Figure 2.2). Whenever the component is not critical for the rest of the project and is not technically complex, design and problem-solving activities can more easily be incorporated by the original equipment manufacturer (OEM) even for parts where the overall expertise is low. Especially when facing a pool of internal technical resources already established and working, the relationship-specific co-ordination costs offset the savings from not investing internally.

On the other hand, whenever external partners do have a distinct set of competencies in areas unfamiliar to the OEM which are also technically complex and critical for the performance of the whole project, it pays to subcontract design and development efforts. Rather than denying the economic importance of these transactions, our results suggest that a short-term strategy of internal control over a critical resource generates inefficiencies due to the lack of knowledge and expertise. The effects are twofold. On the one hand, by internalizing control over activities not mastered by the existing company's resources, problem-solving cycles evolve through inefficient trial and error processes, triggered by ineffective design concept identification and functional parameter definition. On the other hand, by centring the whole process on an internal perspective, the opportunities to learn from the relationship and absorb new ideas and solutions decrease, as the partner's knowledge and experience is under-utilized and often directed towards more familiar domains.

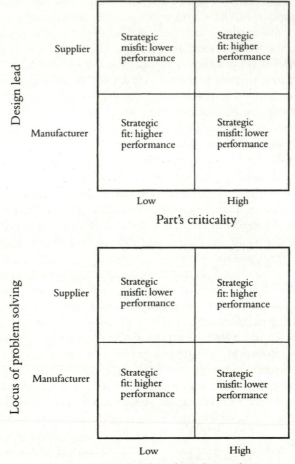

FIG. 2.2. Inter-organizational fit and performance in supplier–manufacturer relationships for new product development

5. From Companies to Individuals: Knowledge Distribution and Communication Patterns

Given that there is an impact on performance as a result of managing supplier relationships in a differential manner, the issue becomes even more complicated by the fact that this tailoring of management approaches involves not just one person on each side of the relationship but rather several. As was mentioned in Section 3, four groups in particular form the bulk of the interaction with the supplier: design, purchasing, pre-series quality assurance, and series quality assurance. As will become apparent in the tables which follow, however, the breadth of knowledge not only about the supplier but also about its relationship with Volvo can vary dramatically from one group to another.

In evaluating the effectiveness of inter-firm relationships such as these, and in particular ones involving product development, much attention has been given in the literature to the importance of absorptive capacity (Cohen and Levinthal 1990) in producing high performance outcomes. In other words, prior common experiences, or human co-specialization (Dyer 1996) between the two parties to the relationship, allow for more effective learning. In most cases, absorptive capacity is viewed from the point of view of possessing a common knowledge about the technology or product being developed so as to allow the recipient firm to absorb the innovations of the supplier. However, we view this as but one aspect of absorptive capacity. An equally important and sequentially prior aspect relates to possessing knowledge of the supplier's abilities and its relationship with the OEM. Without detailed knowledge of the supplier's strengths and weaknesses, the recipient firm is at a disadvantage in terms of exploiting the supplier's abilities; nor will it know where to invest in terms of technical absorptive capacity. Likewise, knowledge not only about the supplier's abilities but also about aspects of its relationship with the OEM provides the context needed to make informed strategic decisions.

With this in mind, we attempt to map the distribution of knowledge on these two matters, supplier abilities and relationship characteristics, across the four functional groups mentioned above. Each respondent was asked to express his/her knowledge about twenty-three aspects of each supplier's competencies. The questions were expressed in multiple-choice format with the last option in each case being 'I don't know'. These twenty-three questions were classified under the headings listed in Table 2.4, which cover both general qualifications and specific functional abilities. The scores presented in Table 2.4 express the percentage of respondents in each of the four functional groups in Volvo who claim to have knowledge of the supplier's ability regarding that issue.

Focusing on the results across the four Volvo functional groups, what becomes evident is that there is an uneven distribution of knowledge across the four groups. On the one hand, the designers and series quality assurance personnel tend to have more specialized knowledge about the supplier. In the case of the former, the knowledge tends to be focused around upstream activities, while for the latter it is more centred around downstream activities, which matches the functional specialization of each group. If the designers and series quality assurance groups can be classified as specialists, the opposite is true of the purchasers and pre-series quality engineers. They are called upon to be generalists, possessing basic knowledge about the various capabilities of the supplier, which supports their role as relationship integrator and link between the various functions on both

TABLE 2.4. *Knowledge of supplier abilities by functional area* (% claiming to have knowledge)

Supplier aspects	Functional area			
	Designers	Purchasers	Pre-series quality assurance	Series quality assurance
Overview	97	100	64	32
Competence	94	100	100	55
Product development	100	100	93	25
Productivity	54	97	67	16
Received quality	53	92	91	48
Logistics	35	100	97	32
Environment	25	84	77	13

Note: The value reported for each aspect is the average value of between two and five specific questions on each topic.

sides of the relationship. Another way to view them would be as gatekeepers, to use Allen's (1977) terminology, where they serve as nodes in the relationship structure of the organization.

A somewhat different picture emerges when one moves from knowledge about the supplier's competencies to knowledge about its relationship with Volvo (Table 2.5). While one would expect knowledge of functional abilities of the supplier to be more localized in different groups within Volvo, one would expect basic knowledge of the company's relationship with Volvo to be more widely dispersed. However, the commonality of knowledge amongst the four groups is limited to the age of the relationship and whether or not Volvo has an alternative supplier for the same parts. In most cases, knowledge of the relationship with Volvo is concentrated in the purchaser function. Basic relationship characteristics such as the volume purchased and evolution of prices reside essentially only with the purchaser. Furthermore, while most respondents across the three groups have an idea about the dependency of Volvo on the supplier, the same is not true of the dependency of the supplier on Volvo. When it comes to issues surrounding product development, however, the purchasers take second place to the designers. While the former claim to be knowledgeable about the contractual and legal issues surrounding development, the same is not true of the dedication of resources from both parties to the development process itself. The dispersion of knowledge of various aspects of the supplier relationship, particularly between purchasing and design, serves to reinforce the diffuse nature of these relationships and the difficulty of centrally managing them.

TABLE 2.5. *Knowledge of supplier relationship by functional area* (% claiming to have knowledge)

Supplier aspects	Functional area			
	Designers	Purchasers	Pre-series quality assurance	Series quality assurance
Basic characteristics				
Age of relationship	75	97	91	65
Cost of parts purchased by Volvo	88	97	9	3
Volume purchased by Volvo	6	94	0	0
Evolution of prices	0	74	36	5
Dependence				
Volvo on supplier (alternate supplier)	100	100	73	83
Supplier on Volvo (Volvo as % of total sales)	13	90	100	15
Product development				
Resources devoted by Volvo	84	19	18	0
Resources devoted by supplier	81	16	18	0
Contracting for development	88	80	57	1
Patenting results	75	58	36	0

One way of explaining the results from Tables 2.4 and 2.5 is to look more closely at the communication patterns of each of the four functional areas. This is particularly important for relationships involving joint product development, in which the inherent uncertainty of the activity demands extensive and elaborate information exchanges both to support individual efforts and to align the multiple activities performed within the project. Research on communication shows that frequent contacts between the subjects involved in problem-solving activities lead to faster and more effective solutions (Allen 1986; Bastien 1987; Carter and Miller 1989). Studies on project teams document how better-performing groups are engaged in more frequent and extensive communication both within and outside the group (Ancona and Caldwell 1992).

In addition, numerous findings stress the role of different information-transferring media in enhancing the process. Direct verbal contacts and personal interactions (Dyer 1996), either through meetings or phone calls, allow faster recognition than written communication of potential conflicts among interdependent tasks. Information technology based tools, such as a shared computer aided design platform or groupware technologies, have recently attempted to combine the richness of information deriving from oral communication and its more rigorous formalization through written codification such as drawings, specifications, and the like, contributing to improving project development performance (Orlikowsky 1993).

Extracting from the Clark and Fujimoto (1991) conceptual framework to organize information transfer processes, and more recent empirical work (Hartley *et al.* 1997), we identified two dimensions to structure the exchange of information with suppliers: (1) the frequency of communication; and (2) the type of media used to exchange information. Also, given the multi-functional approach of our study, we added a third dimension, (3) the point of contact within the supplier with whom the information is exchanged.

The survey respondents were asked a number of questions relating to each of these three issues. The first focused on how each person divided their time amongst the various personnel within the supplier. Respondents were given five options: sales manager; design engineers; logistics personnel; top management; and other. Table 2.6 presents the average allocations for each of the four Volvo functional groups. As is evident from the table, the point of contact for each group tends to be relatively specialized. As might be expected, there is a relatively high correlation between one's own functional specialization and that of the personnel one communicates with at the supplier. Purchasers maintain 'thick' or dense ties (Dyer and Nobeoka 1998) with the supplier's sales manager, and relatively weak ties with all other functional areas at the supplier. The series quality assurance personnel are even more specialized in their communication patterns, devoting 87 per cent of their time to other quality personnel. Only in the case of designers and pre-series quality assurance is there more than one thick tie.

TABLE 2.6. *Distribution of Volvo communication with suppliers* (% of contact with supplier)

Supplier personnel	Volvo personnel			
	Designers	Purchasers	Pre-series quality assurance	Series quality assurance
Sales manager	49.3	69.2	34.9	6.1
Design engineers	46.1	14.1	10.8	1.4
Logistics personnel	2.2	4.1	2.3	5.2
Top management	2.2	8.7	7.6	0.4
Other (quality)	3.1	1.6	44.5	87.0

In order to obtain a complete picture of the communication patterns, however, one must combine the results of Table 2.6 with those of Table 2.7, which describes the average frequency with which each group interacts with the supplier's personnel. Respondents were asked to score the frequency with which they communicated with each group in the supplier, using a scale which ranged from 'daily' to 'never'. Again, what becomes evident is that each group has the highest level of communication between itself and its functional counterpart in the supplier. At the same time this frequency varies across the four groups. Those with the highest levels of communication are the purchasers and pre-series quality engineers, who on average exchange information with the supplier sales and quality managers respectively between once and twice a week. Next come the designers, who on average communicate with the design engineers of the supplier once a month, and lastly the series quality assurance personnel, who exchange information with their quality counterparts roughly once per quarter. What is also clear from Table 2.7 is that the purchasers and pre-series quality engineers have the highest level of interaction not only with their counterparts, but also with most of the other groups at the supplier, including design engineers, logistics personnel, and top management. Such a distribution of communication patterns mirrors the results presented in Table 2.4, the implication being that the designer and series quality assurance functions remain specialist, while the purchaser and pre-series quality engineers are called upon to be the generalists who tie the whole system together.

With differences identified in terms of with whom and how often each of the four Volvo groups communicate with the supplier, the last of the three communication dimensions to be analysed relates to the mode of communication used by each. Respondents were provided with a set of seven options, derived from previous research on communication in problem-solving,

TABLE 2.7. *Frequency of communication*

Supplier's personnel	Volvo personnel			
	Designers	Purchasers	Pre-series quality assurance	Series quality assurance
Sales manager	Bimonthly	Semi-weekly	Bi-weekly	Semi-annually
Design engineers	Monthly	Bi-weekly	Bi-weekly	Annually
Logistics personnel	Semi-annually	Quarterly	Quarterly	Semi-annually
Top management	Semi-annually	Semi-annually	Bimonthly	Semi-annually
Other (quality)	—	—	Semi-weekly	Quarterly

ordered hierarchically following a Gutman scale logic.[2] The options included were: (1) formal meetings, (2) informal face-to-face meetings, (3) telephone, (4) faxes, (5) e-mail, (6) electronic data exchange through the use of common CAD–CAM platforms, and (7) intranet. Respondents were then asked to rank each medium, with 7 being the most used and 1 being the least used medium. The aggregate results for each of the four Volvo groups is shown in Table 2.8.

Overall, the most common means of communication with the supplier is via the telephone and the least popular is through the use of CAD–CAM systems. Other forms such as formal and informal meetings, e-mail, and faxes fall in between these two others. In general, however, e-mail tends to be most popular amongst designers, faxes amongst purchasers, formal meetings amongst pre-series quality engineers, and informal meetings amongst series quality assurance personnel. These results can generally be explained by the nature of the interactions. In the case of designers, the exchange is most likely to be of technical information, for which e-mail is most convenient, while for purchasers contractual and order issues are best handled through fax or meetings. Finally, the series quality assurance personnel tend to interact with the supplier in most cases only when there is a problem, in which case informal meetings to resolve the issue quickly are most appropriate. However, as was mentioned earlier, previous work points to the importance of direct verbal contact in speeding up the learning and problem-solving processes. As such, the different groups within Volvo may not only be spending different amounts of time with suppliers and talking to different people, but their relative abilities to absorb information from the suppliers may vary as a result of differences in the mode of communication used.

6. Conclusions and Implications

As was mentioned in Section 1, this chapter sought to address three questions: Along what lines do supplier–manufacturer relationships in development differ from each other? Is there a fit between relationship type, management of the relationship, and performance? What does this mean in terms of the individual actors which make up the relationship? The answer to the first question is that they differ depending upon which of the two

---

[2] In Gutman scales the options are ordered so that any lower-rank option is included in higher rank ones. This is clearly the case for information media. The proposed ordering formalizes these observations, reflecting two assumptions derived from communication theory (Rogers 1983). First, higher-order options are richer ways of transferring information. Secondly, higher-order options are usually accompanied by several other lower-order ones. The richer the information-transferring media used, the wider the overall set of information media used.

Maurizio Sobrero and Omar Toulan

TABLE 2.8. *How different functions communicate, by communication means*

Functional area	Formal meetings	Informal face-to-face	Telephone	Fax	E-mail	CAD–CAM
Designers	5.2	1.9	6.1	2.9	6.3	1.6
Purchasers	4.7	3.5	6.7	6.6	3.5	1.0
Pre-series quality assurance	5.5	3.8	5.8	4.8	2.3	1.0
Series quality assurance	3.8	5.2	5.7	4.5	4.6	—

Notes: 1 = least used method; 7 = most used method.
None of the respondents claimed to use intranet as a means of communication.

parties takes the lead in the design and problem-solving activities. Through cluster analysis, two different groups of relationships clearly emerged: supplier- and OEM-led relationships.

Given that relationships can be classified into one of these two types, the question then becomes: When is it most appropriate to use which type of relationship, and is there a benefit to managing them differently? If not, one could simply ignore the distinction. However, as our results show, there is in fact an impact on performance of managing different relationships differently, depending on the task and partner characteristics. Specifically, we found support for the conclusion that when the part is not very critical or complex, results are maximized when the OEM takes the lead in development. On the other hand, when the part is critical or complex and the expertise lies outside the firm, performance will be worse if the OEM attempts to maintain the lead role. In this case it is best to outsource this role to the supplier. This conclusion poses a number of challenges for firms, as it implies giving up control and not just production of potentially critical components to entities outside the boundaries of the firm. However, failure to do so can result in micro-management and eventually poorer performance. The point is, one size does not fit all. Failure to recognize this will result in sub-optimization of resources, as well as missed opportunities.

Managing this process is complicated even more by the fact that these relationships are comprised not simply of one person on each side but rather of many. Through the analysis of communication patterns across different functional areas within Volvo it was shown that knowledge both about the supplier and about its relationship with Volvo is dispersed amongst a number of individuals. However, in general the purchaser tends to have the broadest breadth of knowledge of and communication with the supplier, and thus must play the role of relationship integrator and link between the various functions. As such, if supplier relationships are to be managed in a differential manner, the lead, in this case, must come from the purchasers. In other cases this role may be designated to another function. However, given that knowledge of the supplier and its relationship with the firm is not evenly distributed within the firm, the key is to identify that individual who serves as the node in the relationship with the supplier.

This chapter has not attempted to address the challenges of managing the supplier system implied by the above conclusions, and undoubtedly managers will face many obstacles in doing so effectively. The goal, however, was to highlight the importance of looking at relational 'fit', and not simply to identify universally appealing relational characteristics. Having shown the performance benefit of doing so, the next step is to address the issue of what one needs to do in order to maximize these benefits while controlling the costs associated with them.

APPENDIX 2.1. *Fit Index Formulation*

		Low						High
A Task characteristics	Criticality of part	1	2	3	4	5	6	7
	Complexity of part	1	2	3	4	5	6	7
		Volvo					Supplier	
	Design expertise	1	2	3	4	5	6	7

+

		Supplier					Volvo	
B Management model	Design lead	1	2	3	4	5	6	7
	Problem-solving lead	1	2	3	4	5	6	7

The fit index is defined as the absolute difference of each pair of scores from A and B.

3

Global Account Management: Linking External Demands with Internal Abilities

Julian Birkinshaw, Omar Toulan, and David Arnold

1. Introduction

As was highlighted in Chapter 2, the external linkages of a firm are not simple one-to-one interactions. Rather, each link is composed of multiple individual relationships. While the previous chapter addressed this issue from the point of view of managing supplier relations, the same is true of managing customers. Each customer relationship is composed of multiple contact points with the vendor, be it with different country or product divisions. This network or web of relationships becomes particularly extensive in the case of multinational firms serving other multinationals. The result is a dispersion of knowledge about the customer amongst a number of individuals in the firm.

In an attempt to better make use of this dispersed knowledge, and in part as a reaction to customer demands for better co-ordination across countries, many large multinationals are adopting one or another form of global account management. The commonality across the various forms of global account management is the presence of one individual, the global account manager (GAM), who is responsible for the needs of a specific customer on a global basis. This person then serves as the link or tie between the internal network of the company and its external network with the customer. He/she is responsible not only for integrating the two organizational networks at the corporate level, but also for co-ordinating the previously autonomous relationships in each country in which the two firms do business —in some cases, this can exceed 100 markets.

The objective of this chapter is to explore the role played by the GAM in bridging these two networks and making them operate more effectively. The guiding research question can be stated as: What systems or approaches for managing a specific global account relationship are associated with superior account performance? The basic premiss is that multinational firms need to develop new capabilities to operate effectively in a networked world. Global account management is a fairly recent innovation in the companies we have studied and represents an attempt by those companies to build the new capabilities needed to service their customers on a global basis. However, precisely because it is a relatively new approach, no consensus exists on the costs and benefits of global account management. This chapter will therefore attempt to provide some systematic evidence on the impact of various structural and strategic factors on global account performance.

The chapter itself is divided into four sections. In Section 2 we provide background information on the concept of global account management and how one theory in particular, information-processing theory, can shed light on the phenomenon. This section ends by proposing an organizing framework. Section 3 provides a brief description of the empirical research and the measurement techniques used. In Section 4 we present the findings from the research: both descriptive data about the sample and a multivariate test of the determinants of global account performance. Finally, we discuss the core findings from the research and their implications for capability management in network organizations.

2. Background

Very little research has looked specifically at global account management. There is a significant body of literature that looks at 'key account management' and the concept of relationship marketing in general (Morgan and Hunt 1994) but the focus of that work is much more on the vendor–customer relationship *per se* than on the organizational implications of the relationship. There is also work that acknowledges the increasing importance of the global customer (e.g. Prahalad and Doz 1987; Yip 1992), but stops short of examining the implications of global customer management for the strategy and organization of the multinational company.

George Yip and co-authors have done the only significant research into global acount management (Montgomery *et al*. 1998; Yip and Madsen 1996; Yip and Johansson 1993). Yip's focus has been primarily on the impact of global customer 'drivers' on the globalization strategy of the firm, and thus on the management of global accounts. He has also documented a number of cases of global account management. Other writings in this area are by the Conference Board of Europe (1995), Nahapiet (1994), and Galbraith (1997), but all these studies are anecdotal and/or conceptual. To date only the paper by Montgomery *et al*. (1998) has attempted to study global account management using a large-sample survey, and this paper focused on the firm as a whole and its use of global account management, as opposed to the individual account, which is the unit of analysis of this research.

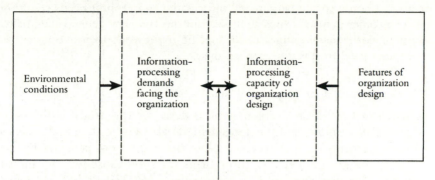

Effectiveness is a function of the quality of fit

FIG. 3.1. The information-processing approach to organization design.
Source: Egelhoff (1991).

2.1. *Information-Processing Theory*

Information-processing theory traces its roots back to the open-systems per-spective on organizations developed in the 1960s and in particular to the work of Thompson (1967), who argued that organizations need to 'buffer' certain core activities from uncertainties in the environment, which they do through the creation of 'boundary spanning activities' that monitor, soak up, and respond to those uncertainties. Galbraith (1973) elaborated on Thompson's ideas and developed the conceptual approach that has come to be called information-processing theory. Galbraith defined uncertainty as 'the difference between the amount of information required to perform the task and the amount of information already possessed by the organization'. Thus, he argued that the information-processing demands on the organ-ization (i.e. the uncertainty it faces) must be matched by the organization's capacity to process that information. Figure 3.1 illustrates this basic model (Egelhoff 1991). It should be clear, moreover, that this approach is one key variant of contingency theory, in that the appropriate organization struc-ture is a function of the environment in which it is operating (Lawrence and Lorsch 1967). High performance, according to this approach, is achieved through a close 'fit' between organization and environment.

How does information-processing theory help us to understand the topic under investigation here? The descriptive research available on global account management indicates that the main stimuli for its emergence are demands for greater information transfer throughout the multinational company network. The provision of globally uniform service contracts or a global price list, for example, requires the distribution of decision guide-lines throughout the multinational company's units as well as the monitoring of compliance and effectiveness. Thus, the function of the GAM and his/her team is one of increasing the information-processing capacity of the firm in response to the heightened information-processing needs resulting from customer demands such as these. But this is a very general statement, and it is worth developing a more specific framework to move from the conceptual level to specific propositions.

2.2. Development of an Organizing Framework

As stated earlier, the relevant unit of analysis for this study is the individual global account, and the dependent variable in the statistical analysis is the performance of that account. Note that we do not consider in this study the comparison between those firms with and those without global accounts. This was done by Montgomery *et al.* (1998). Rather, we work on the assumption that there is sufficient variance in the way that global accounts are run to be able to identify the impact of these different approaches on performance.

Building on the information-processing perspective, it is argued that the various systems and approaches associated with global account management will enhance the information-processing capacity of the multinational firm. This assumes that the information-processing requirements on the system are greater than its current capacity, a reasonable assumption given the shift from dispersed local responsiveness to co-ordinated global responsiveness. Thus, it follows that the extent to which such systems are put in place will be associated with superior performance in the global account. Or, to express it in layman's terms, well-co-ordinated accounts will outperform those that are weakly co-ordinated.

What are the relevant global account management mechanisms that will serve to enhance the information-processing capacity of the firm? Galbraith (1973) suggests an impressive list as follows: direct contact between individuals; individual liaisons; task forces; permanent teams to address frequently occurring issues; a specific manager with a co-ordinating role; a dedicated manager actively involved in decision-making; and matrix management structures. In pre-testing a questionnaire using these dimensions it became apparent that most GAMs use all of the above, implying that global account management itself places one at the high end of Galbraith's scale. As such, it was necessary to develop an even finer set of measures to discern differences across the accounts. We opted for an applied approach, by developing questions and measures that came out of the exploratory interviews. Three sets of factors, in particular, emerged as important.

Scope of relationships. In some global accounts the relationship between the vendor and the customer is only through the global account manager himself/herself. In others, relationships are established at multiple levels: top management, front-line managers, technical managers, and so on. Applying information-processing theory, it follows that the greater the scope of relationships between vendor and customer, the greater will be the information-processing capacity of the vendor, and thus the better will be the performance of the account. More formally:

(1) The greater the scope of relationships between the vendor and customer organizations, the better will be the performance of the account.

Frequency of communication with GAM. Obviously the frequency of communication between individuals does not help us figure out the quality of that communication, but it does give a sense of where the priorities lie. Thus, we asked GAMs to indicate how often they talked to a large number of different people in the customer firm and in their own firm. Again, the argument is that the frequency of communication is an indicator of where information is flowing, and that *ceteris paribus*, the greater the flow of information, the better the performance of the account. Research has shown that frequent contacts between the parties involved in problem-solving activities leads to faster and more effective solutions (Allen 1986; Bastien 1987; Carter and Miller 1989). Studies on project teams have also identified a significant positive correlation between group performance and the frequency and extensiveness of communication both within and outside the group (Ancona and Caldwell 1992). This suggests two propositions, as follows:

(2) The more frequent the communication between the GAM and other individuals in his/her organization on matters relating to the global account, the better will be the performance of the account.

(3) The more frequent the communication between the GAM and individuals in the customer organization on matters relating to the global account, the better will be the performance of the account.

It is important to note that propositions 2 and 3 are 'competing' with one another. Both sound somewhat self-evident and would expect to be supported. But a more interesting question is whether the information flow within the vendor firm (proposition 2) or between vendor and customer (proposition 3) is more important to the success of the account. Given that GAMs have limited time, and that they have to prioritize the time they spend with different parties, it is a matter of considerable importance to be able to distinguish between the relative predictive power of the two propositions.

Internal support systems. One thing that came out of the interviews very clearly is that there are a host of support systems that GAMs need to be able to do their jobs effectively. For example, information systems that enable the firm to determine the profitability of an individual customer are of great importance, as are internal seminars in which GAMs share ideas and connections with one another. All of these factors are again closely related to the effective flow of information within the vendor firm, and consequently they are proposed to have a link to the performance of the account. It is worth pointing out that even though these systems are typically developed at the firm level, the extent to which they are used depends on the individual GAM. Moreover, global account management units are usually structured to mirror the global structure of the customer, and so there can be considerable variety in their structure and processes within a single organization. Thus it is their specific answers to these questions that are relevant, not the question of what systems the firm has put in place. Thus:

(4) The better established the internal systems that support the specific account, the better will be the performance of the account.

Control variables. While the above propositions are explicitly concerned with the information-processing capacity of the multinational firm, there are many other important factors at work which are also likely to affect the performance of the account. Two in particular emerged from the interviews conducted during the study: the dependence of the customer on the vendor, in that a dependent customer is likely to work harder to make the account a success, and the autonomy of the GAM, in terms of whether decisions are made by the GAM or by the local sales manager. We would also expect certain firm-specific and individual-specific factors to have some effect on the performance of the account. Figure 3.2 provides a summary of these sets of factors and the four propositions developed above.

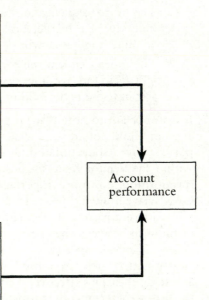

1. Scope of relationships between vendor and customer

2. Frequency of communication between GAM and internal colleagues

3. Frequency of communication between GAM and people in customer organization

4. Internal support systems

Mechanisms for enhancing information-processing capacity

Dependence of customer on vendor

Decision autonomy of GAM

Individual factors (e.g. tenure of GAM)

Firm-specific factors

Other factors proposed to affect account performance

Account performance

FIG. 3.2. Organizing framework

3. Research Methods

The research was conducted in two phases. The first phase was a series of exploratory interviews with approximately fifty managers in ten multi-national firms. All these firms were working to a greater or lesser degree with global account management, so the aim of the interviews was simply to understand the approaches being used, their apparent costs and benefits, and the major issues on these managers' agendas. Interviews were conducted both with senior managers responsible for overseeing the various global account management programmes and with GAMs themselves. Because of the exploratory nature of this phase of research no attempt was made to follow a pre-specified interview protocol. Thus, the output was a number of case-studies and a good understanding of the important issues, but no systematically collected data.

The second phase, which is being reported in this chapter, was a questionnaire administered to GAMs in ten multinational firms. The questionnaire was put together on the basis of issues identified in phase one and using concepts identified as important from theory. These questions were pre-tested with a small number of GAMs, and then amended.

Defining an appropriate sample was not a simple matter. No single company we spoke to had enough GAMs to do a single-company study, so we decided to work with a limited number of companies and survey all the GAMS in each. The final sample of fifty-eight GAMs came from eight companies, with between one and fourteen GAMs in each. Of course this design means that firm effects have to be explicitly factored in, but that is easily done in regression analysis. The companies were selected according to certain criteria: (1) annual revenue of more than $5 billion, (2) presence in ten or more countries, (3) an active global account management programme in place, and (4) not in direct competition with other companies in the sample.[1] Thereafter, the companies were selected on a convenience basis. The result is an interesting cross-section of companies, but one that should not be readily generalized to a particular population. There is a Swedish bias, because of the location of the researchers, but there are also several non-Swedish companies involved. Table 3.1 provides a summary of the companies involved and the number of respondents in each. The questionnaire was sent to all the GAMs in each participating company. The cover letter stated that their company had agreed to participate, and it gave the name of our lead contact in the company. Using this approach, we ended up with a very high response rate, as indicated in Table 3.1. Indeed, the only cases where the response rate is below 80 per cent are companies C and D.

---

[1] The participating companies requested this. Because of its perceived importance and novelty, many companies expressed strongly that they would only participate if none of their direct competitors were also involved.

TABLE 3.1. *Sample characteristics*

Company	Primary industry	Home country	No. of questionnaires	
			Sent	Returned
A	Electronics equipment	Sweden	14	14
B	Business solutions	Sweden	12	10
C	Telecommunications services	United Kingdom	13	8
D	Banking	Sweden	9	6
E	Insurance	Sweden	8	7
F	Electronics and consumer products	USA	7	7
G	Consumer durables	Sweden	3	3
Other			5	2
TOTAL			72	58

3.1. Measures

Many of the questions were about factual issues, such as the age of the GAM, the size of the company served by this account, etc. These data are reported in descriptive form in Section 4. However, to measure the main constructs discussed in the conceptual part of the chapter we used multi-item Likert scales. Details of the specific items used in each construct are as follows:

Account performance. In the course of the exploratory part of the research we identified thirteen different aspects of performance, related to such things as sales growth, better co-ordination, greater responsiveness to the customer, creation of a long-term relationship, and so on. However, a factor analysis revealed that twelve of the thirteen loaded onto a single factor. The one exception was sales discounts to the customer, which unlike all the other measures is an undesirable outcome. Thus, we created a single aggregate performance measure out of the other twelve. This scale had good reliability.

Scope of relationship with customer. GAM respondents were asked about the extent to which relationships with the customer had been established at four levels: senior executive, GAM, local account manager, and technical or front-line level, where 1 = no relationship and 7 = very strong relationship. Reliability for the scale was acceptable.

Frequency of internal communication. Five different groups of people were identified as important contacts for the GAM: other members of the global account team, senior executives responsible for overseeing the global account, country sales–marketing managers, other GAMs, and business unit managers. For each, the GAM assessed the frequency of communication, where 1 = daily, 2 = weekly, 3 = monthly, 4 = rarely, and 5 = never. Factor analysis indicated that these five measures should be combined into a single aggregate measure of internal communication frequency.

Frequency of communication with customer. In similar manner to above, GAMs were asked about their frequency of communication with the customer firm, including: the lead contact (e.g. head of global purchasing), country contacts, senior executives in the customer firm, and technical personnel. Here, factor analysis revealed that the four questions all loaded onto separate factors. It was therefore impossible to aggregate them to create a single construct, so instead we opted to focus on the frequency of communication with the lead contact.

Internal support systems. From the exploratory phase of interviews we identified six systems that were designed to support the global account management programme: information systems that monitor world-wide sales to customers, information systems that calculate profitability of global customers, global account 'executives' or mentors to oversee specific accounts, internal forums for all GAMs, specific evaluation or reward systems for GAMs, and specific career–development tracks for GAMs. These all loaded onto a single factor that we called internal support systems.

Dependence of customer on vendor. This was an aggregate measure of the extent to which the customer is dependent on the vendor. The questions were: (a) 'What percentage of the customer's inputs are provided by your company?' (< 1 per cent, 1–5 per cent, > 5 per cent); (b) 'How important is your company as a supplier to this customer?' (lead supplier, one of 2–5 certified suppliers, one of many); (c) 'We are a strategically important supplier to this customer' (disagree = 1, agree = 5), (d) 'The customer views us as one of its most important partners' (disagree = 1, agree = 5).

Centralization of decision-making with GAM. The GAM was asked who was responsible for making a series of decisions, where 1 = country sales manager, 2 = jointly by country sales manager and GAM, and 3 = GAM. The decisions were as follows: (a) frame agreement on world-wide customer sales, (b) price changes within a previously agreed band, (c) major price changes, (d) changes in volume of product or service ordered, (e) changes to delivery schedule, (f) modifications of product or service, (g) changes to local service agreement. These questions were aggregated to form a single construct.

Tenure of GAM. This was the number of years that the respondent had been in his/her current job.

Firm dummies. For each company we created a 1–0 dummy variable. In the models reported we have left in only those dummy variables that were significant.

4. Findings

The findings are reported in two ways. First, we discuss the descriptive data, using insights from the exploratory interviews where relevant, in order to shed light on the approaches used by the companies in managing their global customers. To our knowledge this is the first significant research study to survey GAMs, so the descriptive data should be of great interest. The second part of this section examines the relationships between variables, and specifically the four propositions developed earlier.

4.1. Characteristics of Global Accounts

Table 3.2 provides a breakdown of the key features of the global accounts. Several points are worth noting. First, there is no simple one-to-one

TABLE 3.2. *Characteristics of GAMs and global accounts* (no. of responses)

Tenure of GAM (years):	
0–1	15
1.5–2.5	15
3–5	16
6–15	6
No. of global accounts that GAM is responsible for:	
1	27
2–4	13
5–9	8
10–20	7
Age of GAM's main account (years):	
1–2	8
3–5	21
6–9	11
10–17	7
Percentage of GAM's time spent managing the account (%):	
5–10	8
15–40	13
50–80	15
90–100	16
No. of people working full-time on account:	
0	30
1–5	14
6–9	4
10+	3
No. of people working part-time on account:	
0	6
1–5	16
10–18	11
20–50	8
50+	2
Geographical scope of account:	
Global	44
Regional	9

correspondence between a GAM and a global account. Just over half the responding managers had two or more accounts to manage, and this is reflected in the amount of time spent managing the biggest account: anything from 5 to 10 per cent of the time (eight cases) to 90 to 100 per cent (sixteen cases). Most accounts also had more than one person working on them. Usually, this meant that the GAM had sales managers in multiple countries whose time they could 'borrow' for global account issues. In a few cases there was a dedicated account team who worked closely with the customer bidding for large projects. A second important point is that GAM systems are relatively new. Most were set up in the last five years, though some are over ten years old. And the GAM himself/herself has typically been in the job for between one and three years. Finally, these accounts are indeed global, with only nine respondents having an explicitly 'regional' (typically European) mandate.

4.2. Decision-Making Split between GAMs and Country Managers

Table 3.3 provides a summary of who makes the decisions on critical marketing decisions. Traditionally, most of these decisions would have been made in the local market-place by the national sales manager or the local account manager. What this table shows is that the GAMs have taken a considerable amount of that decision-making autonomy away from the national sales managers. Certain marketing decisions, such as the negotiation of frame agreements, are obviously the domain of GAMs. Other decisions, such as changes to price, product volume, and local service

TABLE 3.3. *Descriptive data on GAM autonomy* (no. of responses)

Decision	Decision made primarily by		
	National sales manager	National sales manager and GAM jointly	GAM
'Frame agreement' on world-wide customer sales	4	18	31
Price changes within a previously agreed band	13	22	17
Major price changes	9	21	19
Changes in volume of product or service ordered	22	17	10
Changes to delivery schedule	26	16	9
Modifications of product or service	14	22	12
Changes to local service agreement	26	20	3

agreements, are still for the most part within the domain of the national sales manager, but are increasingly influenced by GAMs. The reason for this is that GAMs have to be able to guarantee certain quality, price, and delivery standards on a world-wide basis, which involves reaching into a number of activities that are extremely local in nature. There is also a control aspect to this. If the local sales manager cannot do a deal for his customer on price (because of the frame agreement), he/she may be able to do the deal on the service agreement instead. Thus, GAMs have to become involved in all aspects of the customer relationship.

4.3. Patterns of Communication

Table 3.4 is a breakdown of the frequency of communication between the GAM and various groups inside and outside the firm. Not surprisingly the most frequent contact is with 'other members of the global account team' (daily or weekly). Other frequent communication inside the firm is with country sales–marketing managers (weekly on average), senior executives responsible for overseeing the global account (weekly to monthly), and other global account managers (weekly to monthly). In terms of the relationship with the customer firm, the lead contact is typically communicated with weekly, though as many as twelve respondents stated that they 'rarely' communicated with this individual. Technical and country-level contacts were made on a weekly or monthly basis, while the communication with senior

TABLE 3.4. *Descriptive data on frequency of communication* (no. of responses)

Partner GAM communicates with	Daily	Weekly	Monthly	Rarely	Never
Internal communication					
Other members of the global account team	19	16	12	3	—
Senior executive responsible for overseeing global account	4	16	20	8	3
Country sales–marketing managers	6	20	16	8	1
Other global account managers	7	12	15	4	1
Business unit managers	4	11	23	11	2
External communication					
Lead contact, e.g. head of global purchasing	6	22	13	12	—
Country contacts, e.g. purchasing managers	1	18	18	16	—
Senior executives in customer firm	—	12	23	18	9
Technical people in customer firm	3	23	18	9	—
Alliance partners working with us to serve the global customer	1	7	13	12	2

executives in the customer firm were less frequent—monthly on average, but with twenty-seven respondents answering 'rarely' or 'never'.

These patterns of communication confirm that the GAM sits in the middle of a complex web of internal and external relationships. He/she has a customer liaison role, which involves talking to many different individuals in the customer organization, and also has an internal co-ordination role that involves communicating with multiple interested parties at the local and global levels. While it is inappropriate to generalize too much, the broad pattern that emerges is that the GAM spends an approximately equal amount of time facing the customer and facing his/her own organization.

4.4. The Global Customer

Table 3.5 provides a breakdown of certain characteristics of the customers being served by global accounts. Several interesting observations can be made. First, the size of the global customer varies enormously, from revenues of less than \$2 billion to \$170 billion. In all cases, though, the firms are highly international, being present in at least twenty-four and as many as 150 countries. Furthermore, there is an enormous variation in the importance of the vendor to the customer. If one considers the percentage of the customer's input provided by the vendor, it is less than 1 per cent in twenty cases and more than 5 per cent in twenty-three. And while the vendor is the 'lead supplier' in nineteen cases, it is 'one of many' in seventeen cases. Finally, the last two panels of Table 3.5 provide some indication of the impact of global account management on prices and volumes. Most accounts have increased in volume sharply over the past three years (sixteen indicating growth of more than 20 per cent), but at the same time the average price of goods sold has decreased—'much lower' or 'slightly lower' in thirty cases. These two facts go hand-in-hand, in that the implicit deal in these relationships is often greater volumes in return for bulk discounts. Indeed, a surprising find is that ten of the respondents reported a 'slightly higher' price of goods sold compared to three years before, possibly due to a broadening of the products purchased to include ones with higher price points.

4.5. Statistical Analysis

The propositions developed in the earlier part of the chapter were tested using multiple regression techniques. Due to multi-collinearity problems and the relatively small sample size, each proposition was tested in a separate regression model, as reported in Table 3.6. The control variables were included in all four models.

Considering the control variables first, the dependence of the customer on the firm had a consistent positive relationship with account performance. This is as one would expect, in that the customer is likely to work harder

TABLE 3.5. *Characteristics of global account customers* (no. of responses)

Approximate annual sales revenues of the customer in 1997 ($USm.):	
0–2,000	17
2,001–10,000	8
10,001–25,000	10
25,001–50,000	6
50,001–200,000[a]	2
Number of countries where the customer operates:	
0–24	20
25–49	6
50–99	9
100–149	6
150–250[b]	12
Approximate percentage of the customer's overall input provided by your company:	
< 1	20
1–5	9
> 5	23
Importance of GAM's company as a supplier to the customer:	
The 'lead' supplier	19
One of 2–5 'certified suppliers'	16
One of many suppliers	17
Annual growth of sales to this global customer during the past three years (%):	
0 (or reduced)	5
5	11
10	8
15	6
20	6
> 20	16
Average price of goods sold to your global customer, relative to three years ago:	
Much lower	18
Slightly lower	12
No change	11
Slightly higher	10
Much higher	0

[a] The two highest are $US59,000 m. and $US170,000 m.
[b] The highest is 210.

TABLE 3.6. *Predictors of account performance*

Predictor variable	Model			
	1	2	3	4
Constant				
Dependence of customer on firm	0.433[a]	0.457[b]	0.438[b]	0.411[b]
Tenure of GAM	0.287[c]	0.314[c]	0.384[a]	0.316[c]
Centralization of decisions	−0.250[c]	−0.261[a]	−0.295[c]	−0.187[d]
Firm dummy (A)	−0.260[d]	−0.295[a]	−0.302[c]	−0.296[a]
Scope of contact with customer	0.183			
Frequency of internal contact		−0.263[a]		
Frequency of contact with customer-led contact			−0.234[d]	
Use of support operations				0.510[b]
Adjusted R²	0.317	0.359	0.335	0.546
ΔR²	0.023	0.061[c]	0.039[d]	0.321[b]
F Anova	6.103[b]	7.163[b]	6.547[b]	14.230[b]

[a] $p < 0.01$.
[b] $p < 0.001$.
[c] $p < 0.05$.
[d] $p < 0.10$.

to ensure the success of the global account in cases where it is depending on the vendor. The tenure of the GAM was a significant and positive predictor variable in each case. In other words, and not surprisingly, the longer the GAM had been in the job, the higher the performance of the global account. The centralization of decision-making with the GAM was also consistently significant and negative in the four models, the interpretation being that removing all authority from the country sales manager can endanger local buy-in and with it performance. Tentatively, this seems to suggest that the active and willing involvement of country sales managers is an important component of successful global account management. Finally, of the firm dummies, the one for firm A was included in the models because it was significant. This finding simply means that accounts in firm A generally underperformed those in other firms.

In terms of the propositions, we gained strong support for propositions 2 and 4, marginal support for proposition 3, and no support for proposition 1. Taking these in order, the scope of contact with the customer was not found to be a predictor of account performance. While directionally correct, the beta coefficient in the regression equation had a significance level of only $p = 0.182$.

The frequency of internal communication was significant at $p < 0.01$, meaning that the more frequent the communication inside the vendor firm, the greater the account performance. In contrast, the frequency of communication with individuals in the customer firm was only a significant predictor of account performance at $p < 0.10$. What does this finding mean? At face value one might conclude that internal communication frequency is more important to account performance than communication with the customer, but this is not necessarily the whole story.[2] Our interpretation is that many GAMs end up working extremely closely with their customers. Several acknowledged that they know their customer's strategy and organization better than they know their own firm. And in a few cases the GAMs actually had offices on their customers' premises. In this situation, it is not surprising that communication with the customer is easier for GAMs than communication with people in their own firm. Thus, we end up with the important finding that those GAMs that manage to continue to work effectively with both vendor and customer have the most effective accounts.

A second and related interpretation of this finding is that global account management is primarily an exercise in internal co-ordination. Given the complex organizational structures of the vendor firms we studied, it is no small matter to ensure that the disparate parts of the organization are working together to serve the customer. Moreover, it was clear from our field research that global account management units are supplemental to national sales organizations, rather than a substitute for them, and so add value by co-ordinating previously autonomous units. This interpretation is consistent with the information-processing perspective on global account management, and seems to be supported by the previously discussed finding that centralization of decisions (i.e. GAMs taking over from national sales managers) is associated with poor account performance.

The final proposition concerned the importance of internal support systems to account performance. Here the results were very strong, resulting in easily the highest adjusted R^2 value (0.546). This suggests that account performance is highly dependent on the development and use of internal support systems (remember that these systems are established at the firm level but the extent to which they are used will vary by GAM). This leads to a couple of observations. First, it strengthens the argument that effective global account management is about internal co-ordination. One common view hinted at earlier is that global account management is a 'new way' of handling global customers by putting the power in the hands of a centralized GAM. This result, coupled with the finding about decision-making centralization above, suggests that the value of global account management is much more as an internal enabler of co-ordinated action.

---

[2] Furthermore, the size of the two coefficients is roughly the same, implying that the impact should be roughly equal for both variables.

The GAM's view of the account's performance is therefore determined not so much by the quality of the relationship with the customer's executives, because much decision-making still lies with country sales managers, but rather by the internal communication and co-ordination systems that are developed as a result of the global account management programme. A second observation is that the importance of support systems as a predictor of performance may go down over time. Currently, many firms are still putting these sorts of systems in place, so the extent to which they are used is an important differentiator between accounts. If a few years from now all GAMs make use of these systems, then performance differentials will obviously end up being attributed to other factors.

5. Discussion and Conclusions

The findings from this research raise a number of important issues, both with regard to the specifics of global account management and with regard to the broader question of capability management in multinational firms.

Considering the implications for global account management first, the research suggests the somewhat surprising finding that it is effective internal co-ordination that discriminates between high-performing and low-performing accounts. Of course, global account management is fundamentally about the relationship with the customer, and it would be disingenuous to deny that this is central to its effectiveness. But what the research shows is that the internal co-ordination aspect to the relationship is also very important, and indeed appears to be the side that is less well managed in many cases. Although we know from current research that global account management is generally instituted in response to external customer-centred stimuli (Montgomery *et al.* 1998), our research suggests that its success depends not so much upon an external market-sensing capability as upon what Day (1994) identifies as the 'inside-out process' category of marketing capability, i.e. the ability of the organization to co-ordinate its actions among corporate and national units. For the marketing organizations of multinational companies, the successful establishment and maintenance of these processes represents a major challenge. Until now customer management has generally been delegated to local subsidiary organizations, on the grounds that it is an execution-sensitive rather than a strategic activity. The emergence of global account management is a major shift in the complexity of these marketing organizations, and our research suggests that it is towards organizational implementation, rather than business achieved with major accounts, that future research should be directed.

What does this research mean for the capabilities of the multinational firm? As indicated at the outset, global account management can be seen as a system that many firms have instituted to build a capability in managing their customers on a world-wide basis. Depending on one's theoretical perspective, this can be seen as an attempt to enhance the quality of net-work linkages within the firm and with the customer, or as a means of enhancing the information-processing capacity of the firm. Either way, it involves the creation of greater interdependencies between individuals in parts of the multinational firm that hitherto could work separately. Such a process clearly takes time, and it is important therefore to be aware that the research was conducted during the process of adjustment that all involved parties were going through. The firms involved were building the necessary capabilities to manage their customers on a world-wide basis, but none of them would suggest that they had really mastered this challenge. In particular, the support systems (such as IT systems for measuring the profitability of individual customers) were still being put in place by most firms in the study.

To conclude, this chapter should be seen as a first step towards understanding the complex and increasingly important phenomenon of global account management. Several previous studies highlighted the importance of global account management and described it in general terms. This is the first to focus on the level of the global account itself, and to examine the factors associated with the performance of individual accounts. Our focus, therefore, was on describing the data and developing some basic propositions regarding the information-processing capacity of the firm and account performance. Future research should examine these issues in much greater detail, in terms of both the internal- and external-network relationships of the GAM. There is also a need for research to consider the phenomenon of global account management in its broader context—in terms of why certain firms and certain industries have developed global account programmes, and how these programmes have evolved over time.

PART II

Innovation in the External Network

4

The Experience-Curve of Capability Management

Henrik Bresman

1. Introduction

The encompassing objective of the research presented in this chapter is to obtain a better understanding of how external knowledge is integrated by high-technology firms in a turbulent industry setting, and how the capabilities to do so are developed. The successful integration of knowledge from external sources—'external integration'—is a critical driver of firm performance in turbulent high technology (Burns and Stalker 1961; Lawrence and Lorsch 1967; Eisenhardt and Tabrizi 1995; Iansiti 1998; Leonard-Barton 1995; MacCormack 1998). Previous research has identified organizational mechanisms which enable firms to take advantage of knowledge emanating from their external environment. These include devices such as the nurturing of 'technological gatekeepers' (Allen 1977), encouraging 'informal know-how trading' (von Hippel 1987), and establishing organizational units dedicated to external integration (Granstrand *et al.* 1992). Previous studies, however, do not systematically address how firms can develop the capabilities needed to adopt the appropriate organizational mechanisms for external integration successfully in the first place. If these mechanisms were easily adopted, they would not be a valid source of sustainable competitive advantage. Still, studies show that some companies persistently outperform others due to a more successful management of external integration (Henderson 1994). Indeed, superior organizational mechanisms for external integration are underpinned by superior capability—'external integrative capability'—and this capability only develops slowly over time. Consequently, unless the forces that build external integrative capability over time are understood, we are not sufficiently equipped to generate suggestions of how to organize for successful external integration. My intention is to address this gap in our understanding of external integration. In doing so, I ground my research in organization theory.

The unit of analysis for this study is the external integration project, which involves the identification, evaluation, and internalization of knowledge originating from an external organizational member. The empirical arena chosen for this research is pharmaceutical drug development. This setting is deemed suitable for our purposes since pharmaceuticals is a high-technology industry that has been characterized by enormous turbulence for more than a decade, resulting in an urgent and industry-wide need for external integration and external integrative capability in R. & D. Furthermore, the focal technical entity of pharmaceutical drug development, namely, the chemical compound, provides a good basis for comparisons across projects and firms. The particular kind of external integration project that this study will investigate is the in-licensing of chemical compounds. The unmerciful and ever increasing pressures on pharmaceutical firms to keep a pipeline filled with compounds, with the potentiality of commercial success, have forced their researchers to go outside the firm boundaries in pursuit of compounds to license. The reason for this is that even if the science and technology of drug development evolve quickly, the lead times of in-house development still linger too long for the requirements of increased compound quantity to be satisfied through internal R. & D. efforts only. The practice of in-licensing involves a number of challenging management issues. Consider the case of the in-licensing of a compound involving a substantial component of novel and advanced knowledge, which to a critical extent draws upon external resources accessing this knowledge. The following dilemma emerges: in order for the project to be truly innovative, it has to be allowed independence from the established research unit, or else old thinking will kill new thinking; in order for the project to contribute to the knowledge base of the organization, however, it has to be 'in the loop'. How does one manage these seemingly paradoxical requirements? How does one develop a capability to integrate new knowledge without corrupting it? What should the linkage between the external novelty and the internal knowledge base look like? The answers to these questions are far from straightforward. The fact that variation in performance of in-licensing projects is wide reflects this. To find and analyse the sources of this variation lies at the heart of this study.

The research question formulated for this study is 'How is external integrative capability built over time?' My main finding is that organizations that have had a lot of variation in staffing over time, within as well as across projects, seem to perform better at any project. The reason for this seems to be twofold. First, since every compound that is brought in from the outside is by nature different from an internally developed compound in a unique way, a history of a variation of staffing solutions generates a multitude of organizational options to work with. Secondly, a history of variation helps to develop a dynamic capability to reshuffle the organizational options in a timely and effective manner. The logic is illustrated by the concept of the 'experience-curve of capability management'.

The methodology I have chosen for this research is inductive fieldwork involving one large pharmaceutical firm. An inductive research design is deemed appropriate since the central issues that emerged during the first interviews are not sufficiently addressed by existing literature. In order to investigate the evolutionary aspect of capabilities, I use a longitudinal design in which I research the use of compositions of project teams over time.

The chapter is structured in the following way. First, the conceptual context of the study is delineated. Secondly, a research question and a hypothesis are formulated. Thirdly, the methodology of the study is discussed. Fourthly, the findings are presented, and finally, the conclusions are summarized.

2. Conceptual Points of Departure

2.1. The Phenomenon: External Integration

The focal phenomenon of this study is the integration of external knowledge—'external integration'—in turbulent high-technology industries. The importance of the phenomenon has been stressed by many scholars (see e.g. Lawrence and Lorsch 1967; Tushman 1977; Eisenhardt and Tabrizi 1995; Iansiti 1998; Leonard-Barton 1995; MacCormack 1998). Its importance stems from the fact that in a turbulent high-technology environment it is not feasible to develop all critical knowledge in-house. External integration serves the additional purpose of counteracting organizational inertia. Properly managed, external integration tasks take the role of organizational 'feelers' towards the environment, ensuring that the organization stays abreast with developments outside its boundaries and retains the capability to act on and form these developments.

Scant prior research and theory-building exist that address the external integration in turbulent high-technology industries. In particular, having conducted a number of interviews, I found gaps in the literature with regard to how capabilities to manage external integration—'external integrative capability'—may be developed.[1] Broadly defined, conceptual guidance and empirical inspiration can be found in the 'open systems' tradition of organization theory, the eclectic collection of writings on capabilities, and the largely phenomenon-driven literature on the management of technological innovation. The purpose of the rest of this section is to craft a conceptual context for the study.

2.2. The Conceptual Foundation: An Open-Systems View of Organizations

My theoretical base is organization theory. More specifically, I take an open-systems view of organizations (see e.g. Thompson 1967). Scott (1998) defines this view in the following manner: 'Organisations are systems of

---

[1] It should be noted that Tripsas (1997) has already used the term 'external integrative capabilities' with a very different definition, namely, 'internal investments that develop absorptive capacity and an external communication infrastructure'. 'Absorptive capacity' (Cohen and Levinthal 1990) addresses both internal and external integration.

interdependent activities linking shifting coalitions of participants; the systems are embedded in—dependent on continuing exchanges with and constituted by—the environment in which they operate.' An open-systems view means that the interfaces between the organization and its various environments are viewed as complex. Among theories about how organizations and environments interact, 'contingency theory' is one of the most influential. The theory has often been criticized (see e.g. Schoonhoven 1981), but it has remained a dominant approach to the study of organizations (Donaldson 1985; Lawrence 1993). I believe the approach to be very fruitful in analysing external integration. I also believe, however, that some conceptual adjustments have to be made in order to make it appropriate for turbulent high-technology settings. This will be discussed next.

2.3. Contingency Theory Revisited

Contingency theory is a term that was originally coined by Lawrence and Lorsch (1967). For the sake of clarity in the following discussion, I will label as contingency theory those theories that are based on the following assumptions: (1) there is no one best form in which to organize; (2) any way of organizing is not equally effective; (3) the best way to organize is contingent on a number of external and/or internal factors.[2]

Although the sources of the contingencies vary—be it the type of work, technology characteristics, or the nature of the environment—a premiss of contingency theory is that in order to be functional the organization needs to adapt to characteristics of the internal and external environment. Successful adaptation results in good 'fit'. This notion of fit makes contingency theory compelling. As the environment becomes more turbulent, however, things get more complicated, and the notion of fit and adaptation conveys a rather non-dynamic and reactive view of organization. Chandler's (1962) seminal work on organization structure posited that structure will follow strategy, and that the fit between them will determine performance. What is less often quoted, however, is that he found a substantial time lag as well—approximately twenty years to be exact. That is a long time by any standard. In turbulent environments it means that the capabilities to manage the process will have to become at least as important as the organizational structure.

At this juncture it may prove fruitful to introduce the work of students of the modern multinational company who have confronted these issues for over a decade. They have found that in a thoroughly complex world with

---

[2] Lawrence and Lorsch (1967) had strong antecedents, however. This body of literature was pioneered by Burns and Stalker (1961), who were interested in the relationship between organization structure and the nature of innovative work. In the tradition of Burns and Stalker, Woodward (1965) and Thompson (1967) found that effective organization was contingent on the type of technology involved. Along the same lines, Lawrence and Lorsch (1967) found that differentiated organizations were suited for turbulent environments, while integrated structures worked well for stable environments.

a structure that is unstable over time manifested in differentiated subsidiary roles that are constantly shifting, the process not only becomes as important as the structure, it is no longer possible to separate from it (Hagström 1991). Capabilities become a crucial characteristic, and also an important source of competitive advantage (Hedlund 1986; Bartlett and Ghoshal 1989). A dynamic and proactive view of the organization emerges. Rather than finding fit and the optimal organization, choosing a structure may be interpreted as managing interdependencies over time. Hagström (1991) described the organization in this view as 'a meta institution constantly changing its interface with the environment as well as internal relationships as opportunities arise; it is continuously selecting new differentiated organisational forms within, at the edge of, and outside the firm boundaries'. We believe that students of innovation in turbulent high-technology settings—like students of the multinational company—need to go beyond the intuitively appealing but static notion of fit towards a dynamic and proactive view of organization.

A line of attack on the concept of fit related to that of the multinational company scholars may be derived from researchers concerned with organizational inertia (see e.g. Clark 1985; Henderson and Clark 1990; March 1991; Christensen 1997). The argument here is that a focus on one optimal way to do things may lead to inertia and can make a firm vulnerable to shifts in the relevant knowledge base. Continuous experimentation with ways to organize for its own sake may be the best way to stay quick on one's feet since it develops a capability for constant change. In support of this argument, Singh and Zollo (1998) found that while the integration of corporate acquisitions of operations with a high degree of relatedness were facilitated by a stock of codified procedures, the integration of acquisitions with less relatedness were obstructed by the same procedures. The explanation put forth by the authors was that generalizations of how to manage post-acquisition integration were wrongfully extended to operations that were very different from previous experiences. The implication for the present case is that if no variation in experience is proactively sought, inertial pressures will make attempts to integrate novelty fail.

I argue that the preceding discussion has far-reaching theoretical and practical implications. In particular, as we move from reaction to proaction; and, from the search of fit to managing interdependencies over time, the nature of contingencies changes. In addition to being constituted by environmental factors, contingencies come in the form of restrictions of choice (cf. Hagström 1991); namely, restrictions on how an organization can (successfully) choose to organize. This range of 'organizing options' is a function of the firm's capabilities, and these capabilities are developed over time.

Hence, I propose that success in dealing with a complex context is contingent not only on the structural conformity to the environment but also on the firm's capabilities. So what is a capability? Next, I will present my key working definitions.

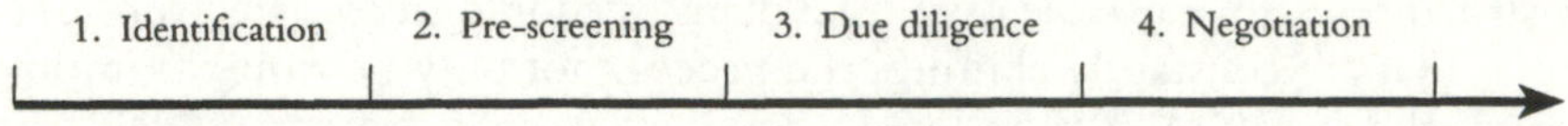

| 1. Identification | 2. Pre-screening | 3. Due diligence | 4. Negotiation |

FIG. 4.1. Phases of the external integration process

2.4. Definitions

Capabilities. I see an organization's capability pertaining to a given task as its ability to perform that task efficiently and effectively in a consistent manner over time. Drawing on the work of Leonard-Barton (1992), I see capabilities as residing in four interrelated dimensions: employees, technical systems, managerial systems, and organizational culture.

External integration. This is the identification, evaluation, and internalization of knowledge emanating from an external organizational member. Since the skills needed may vary over time, it may be fruitful to analyse external integration in terms of phases. Based on my interviews, I see the task of external integration as consisting of four phases. A point worth noting is that a number of studies have raised concerns of a sequential approach to problem-solving. The argument is that even if the plan may be sequential, in reality tasks are seldom managed in a linear manner.[3] As we will see, however, sequence is not central to the argument. The four phases are:

1. Identification. The task of finding a technology to fill a certain need.
2. Pre-screening. A preliminary investigation of the technology.
3. Due diligence. The full-scale technical investigation involving all crucial functions. Ends with a recommendation.
4. Negotiation. The pursuit of a final agreement with the party selling the technology. If agreement is reached, this phase ends with the setting up of an internal development team.

3. Research Question and a Hypothesis

3.1. The Research Question

The research question that guides this study may be formulated as follows: 'How is external integrative capability built over time?'

The conceptual discussion of the previous section together with intuition developed in early interviews resulted in one main hypothesis related to external integrative capability that will be discussed in some detail next.

---

[3] The most well-known conceptualization in this tradition is probably Cohen *et al.*'s (1972) 'garbage can model'.

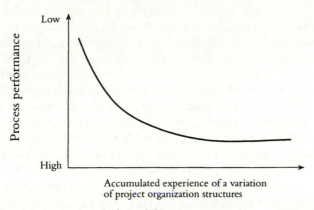

FIG. 4.2. The experience-curve of capability management

3.2. Hypothesis

My guiding intuition involves two components: one static and one dynamic. The static component is that any one way to compose a project team may not be suitable for any external integration project. This belief is rooted in traditional contingency theory as described above, and not very novel. The dynamic component is less intuitive. Over the years scholars have prescribed numerous ways to organize for success in the management of innovative tasks. An alternative to the belief that an appropriate organization structure is the most important driver of performance is that the success of managing innovative tasks is more a function of how organizational structures have been used in the past than anything else. In other words, the use of organizational structure not only produces results; more importantly it builds capabilities too.

The case for this argument is based on the critique of 'fit' as discussed in the previous section, but also on the empirical observation that competitors in the pharmaceutical industry have used essentially the same organizational structures in R. & D., but with very different results. From this observation we derive a conceptual cornerstone of our study: 'the experience-curve of capability management'.[4] The simple argument is that the success of any innovation project today is a function of the structures that have been used in the past. The reasoning is illustrated in Figure 4.2.

What pattern would be expected in terms of the use of organizational structures in the past? Will those that have consistently worked with one set of

---

[4] The experience-curve is a widely used concept in manufacturing management. The main idea is that as the people working on a given manufacturing process gain experience, they will get better and faster at what they are doing, and as they get better and faster, the production cost will fall (see e.g. Hayes and Wheelwright 1984). The idea to apply the concept to capability management came up in a discussion with Peter Hagström.

structures be more successful; or, will those that have experimented over time with many structures of different kinds be more successful? Figure 4.2 illustrates the hypothesis that those with experience of more variation will be more successful since they have more options to play with and since they will be 'quicker on their feet'. The argument is consistent with the findings of Singh and Zollo (1998) as discussed above. Since the environment is not consistently the same over time, and since there are important contingencies, it is not feasible to stick to exactly the same structures in exactly the same composition for every task. This is consistent with the static component of my argument. However, given that an organization has to be quick on its feet to adjust its arsenal of structures in response to the somewhat differing requirements of each task, those who have the experience of frequent reshuffling of its arsenal in the past may have developed a superior capability to manage any task in the present. The concept of 'architectural innovation' comes to mind. Henderson and Clark (1990) found that established firms in the photolithographic alignment equipment industry sometimes floundered since they failed to recombine existing components efficiently. The correct components were all there, but they were not reconfigured quickly enough. The components in this case are the components of organizational structure. The hypothesis is based on the idea that since speed and timely flexibility are all-important, and structures are in a state of constant change, the composition of specific structural components in each point in time, although by no means unimportant, is less important than the capability to manage constant change.

(Hypothesis) Organizations with a history of using a variety of organizational structures will be better at managing any given external integration project than organizations with a history of less variation.

Might an organization face too much variation? A powerful and commonly cited hypothesis is that of an inversely U-shaped relationship between variation and productivity. Translated into the context of this study this hypothesis would relate to the relationship between past experience of a variety of organizational structures and performance. The argument is obvious: too much variety as well as too little variety is bad; instead, 'requisite variety' should be maintained. This is conceptually appealing—so appealing in fact that scholars have invoked this proposition in virtually every context in which the words 'sufficient', 'appropriate', or 'requisite' occur. The proposition, however, remains largely unproven. In fact, I would argue that we do not know anything about the shape of the curve in between the two extreme points. It might be inversely U-shaped, but it might also be inversely V-shaped, or inversely any shape. In the context of a turbulent high-technology industry setting it proves useful to revisit the original notion of 'requisite variety' as expressed by Ashby (1956). He noted that an effective cybernetic system would show as much variety as its environment, and at this level variation would be requisite. This argument, however, presupposes that the level of external variety can be known and matched—which is true for cybernetic systems. I would argue that a turbulent industry environment is by nature so complex, however, that no organization can ever hope to match its level of variation. As a consequence, I would expect that the more variation the organization can accommodate internally, the better. 'Maximum variety', if one so wishes.

Obviously, since capabilities are sticky and develop only slowly over time, the notion of maximum variety does not mean that a more complex structure or process is better for every organization at every point in time. A central component of a more fruitful way to view the process is the continuous exchange between 'novelty' and 'confirmation'.[5] A fundamental problem with requisite variety when applied to turbulent environments is that it is a static concept. A more appropriate conceptual device, in my view, is that of a pragmatic bouncing between novelty and confirmation. This is not a linear process, but a circular process between the system and its environment. In this process novelty is continuously transformed into confirmation, and the system will be capable of working with an increasingly wide range of compositions of novel and confirmatory components. My analogy to external integration projects is that the more novelty and variation that the organization has confronted and transformed through various external integration projects, the better its capability in terms of compositions of structural components that it can master. Note that the term 'transform' is key here. It refers to the fact that experiences must be processed and useful knowledge retained. Thus, the usefulness of variation is contingent on learning from it. Granted, there is still some slippage in this theoretical argument. Please note, then, that it is a first attempt to conceptualize an observation that is in essence empirically grounded.

4. Methodology

4.1. The Research Process

Figure 4.3 illustrates the research process. Literature search and a number of exploratory interviews resulted in an inductive research design. Thereafter, a number of detailed case-studies were conducted. The unit of analysis of this study is the external integration project. To gain as full an understanding as possible I analysed the project level as well as the organization level.

---

[5] This concept was suggested to me by Paul Carlile.

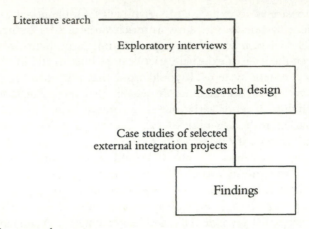

Fɪɢ. 4.3. The research process

4.2. Sample Composition

In the following I outline the empirical arena used in this study. It involves the selection of industry, function, companies, and projects.

The study requires a setting of high technology and turbulence. I believe that focusing on one industry is appropriate since I am particularly interested in organization-level and project-level issues. The industry chosen for this study is the pharmaceutical industry. This setting is deemed suitable for our purposes since pharmaceuticals is a high-technology industry that has been characterized by enormous turbulence for more than a decade, which has resulted in an urgent and industry-wide need for external integration and external integrative capability in R. & D. Furthermore, the focal technical entity of pharmaceutical drug development, namely, the chemical compound, provides an ideal basis for comparisons across projects and firms. An additional intriguing aspect is that the industry has seen a general 'conformism' evolve, with the result that with few exceptions major players use similar ways to pursue critical external knowledge. Yet, there is a significant variation in success across firms as well as projects. This is an intriguing setting, given our research question.

The function chosen is R. & D. As pointed out by Henderson and Cockburn (1994), several scholars have suggested that 'unique capabilities in R&D are particularly plausible sources of competitively important competence' (see e.g. Dierickx and Cool 1989; Nelson 1991).

The pool of firms possibly included in this study belongs to the group that is sometimes referred to as 'big pharma'. These are large, established pharmaceutical firms with sufficient resources and capabilities to manage the whole R. & D. process from discovery research to regulatory approval and marketing.

The research was focused on one firm, which for the sake of confidentiality I will call Pharma Inc. The impetus for focusing on one firm is the belief that deep understanding of the phenomenon is best gained this way. Furthermore, Pharma is the result of a recent merger. This provides a unique opportunity to compare and contrast two very different ways of managing external integration in two very different research organizations, which is a very desirable feature given our objectives. I will call the two R. & D. organizations Site A and Site B respectively.

I put two constraints on the definition of the external integration project for the purposes of this study. First, it has to be non-routine with the stated objective to create new knowledge related to technologies that are potentially of strategic value to the firm; secondly, the knowledge involved has to be complex. To operationalize this definition, I chose to investigate the in-licensing of compounds in drug development. This activity is appropriate for a number of reasons:

1. This is the most important integration task faced by industry participants, which ensures keen interest in this research on the part of the respondents.
2. The task involves a brief union of three to twelve months, which makes it easy to define.
3. It is not as straightforward an activity as it may seem. It entails substantial knowledge creation—even if some of the compounds licensed have already gone far in the development pipeline—and a host of problems that have created huge variation in success rates.

In co-operation with senior corporate R. & D. staff, three projects from each of the two sites were selected. Two selection criteria were employed. First, the projects should have been conducted in sequence or with just a little overlap so that possible learning could have taken place. This was crucial in order to perform the kind of longitudinal study that was necessary to test my hypothesis. Secondly, the sequence should be in the same therapeutic class so that they could be compared. The projects pertaining to Site A I will call A1, A2, and A3, whereas the projects performed at Site B will be called B1, B2, and B3.

4.3. Dependent Variable

The dependent variable of this research is project performance. Initially a subjective measurement of success with dimensions recommended by Hauptman (1986) and Ancona and Caldwell (1992) was chosen. The dimensions, rated in a questionnaire on a five-item Likert scale, were efficiency, technical quality, adherence to schedule, adherence to budget, and ability to resolve conflict. After piloting the questionnaire I revised the measure according to suggestions from respondents. I ended up using only two questions, efficiency and technical quality, since the respondents deemed the remaining dimensions less relevant and difficult to assess. In order to obtain data for the performance measure I asked two people to rate each project: the individual in charge of the project, and the most senior individual in charge of product development at the time of the project.

4.4. Data Sources

Three basic approaches of data-gathering were used. First, I conducted eighty-five interviews with researchers and managers. Secondly, questionnaires to be filled out by company respondents were used to measure performance. Thirdly, company data on past projects were used to help track the developments over time.

4.5. Team Composition as a Measure of Organizational Structure

There are a multitude of ways in which one can measure organizational structure. I will use the concept of team composition recommended by Ancona and Caldwell (1997). They observed product development teams and noted that in managing the boundaries of the project organization external linkages changed over the course of the project. They concluded that in fast-changing environments there is a need to create more fluid and changing team boundaries. The importance stems from the need to cope with the high degree of environmental complexity. They identified a number of dimensions of team composition, four of which I use here: (1) organizational tenure, (2) use of internal and external experts, (3) full versus part-cycle membership, (4) core versus peripheral membership.

The concept of team composition as a measure of organizational structure seems to be particularly appropriate when analysing external integration projects since every project involves a high degree of novelty and dependence on the environment, and thus a lot of complexity. I will use the symbols shown in Figure 4.4 to help map the composition over time.

5. Findings

As I started to map the compositions over time in the six projects, distinct patterns emerged for each of the two sites (see Figures 4.5 and 4.6). Site A projects were clearly much more fluid and changing in their team compositions compared to Site B projects, within as well as across projects. More internal and external experts were retained, more part-cycle members were involved, tenure was more diverse, and more peripheral members participated. Furthermore, in Site A projects there were staff overlaps between the technical investigation of the due diligence phase and the negotiation phase.

So how did the projects perform? Since the sample is too small to achieve any statistical power, I chose simply to illustrate the results by plot-

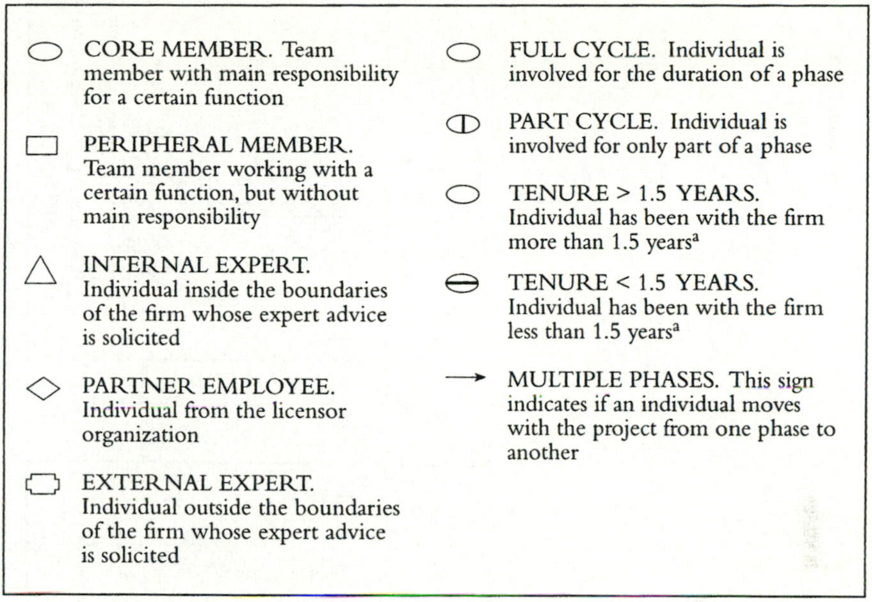

○ CORE MEMBER. Team member with main responsibility for a certain function

☐ PERIPHERAL MEMBER. Team member working with a certain function, but without main responsibility

△ INTERNAL EXPERT. Individual inside the boundaries of the firm whose expert advice is solicited

◇ PARTNER EMPLOYEE. Individual from the licensor organization

⬭ EXTERNAL EXPERT. Individual outside the boundaries of the firm whose expert advice is solicited

○ FULL CYCLE. Individual is involved for the duration of a phase

⬭ PART CYCLE. Individual is involved for only part of a phase

○ TENURE > 1.5 YEARS. Individual has been with the firm more than 1.5 years[a]

⊖ TENURE < 1.5 YEARS. Individual has been with the firm less than 1.5 years[a]

→ MULTIPLE PHASES. This sign indicates if an individual moves with the project from one phase to another

FIG. 4.4. Symbols for mapping team composition over time

[a] Katz and Allen (1982) found that the Not Invented Here attitude started to manifest itself in R. & D. personnel with a tenure of more than 1.5 years in the organization

ting the performance assessments on a graph (see Figure 4.7). As the graphs show, all of the projects at Site A performed as well as or better than the projects at Site B. Moreover, there is an experience-curve effect at Site A—which is consistent with my hypothesis—whereas no such effect is evident at Site B. Why would this be? In light of the hypothesis, two things stick out. First, ample experience of variation at Site A seems to have created a capability to handle different projects. Secondly, as will be evident from the detailed description below, Site A has enabled transformation of new experience into knowledge that can be used in later projects. It is important to point out here that the sample size is obviously far too small to draw any firm conclusions. Nevertheless, next I will describe some of the actual processes that occurred in more detail. As we will see, there are concrete reasons to believe that the relationships illustrated above are no coincidence.

5.1. Project Management at Site A

When project A1 started, it was the first time that Site A attempted to bring in a drug of this particular therapeutic class. Early on the project members ran into problems related to evaluation of the selectivity of the compound.

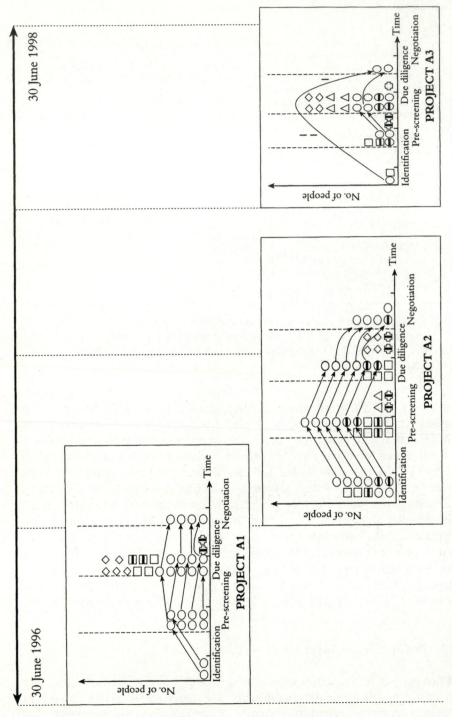

FIG. 4.5. Team compositions of Site A projects

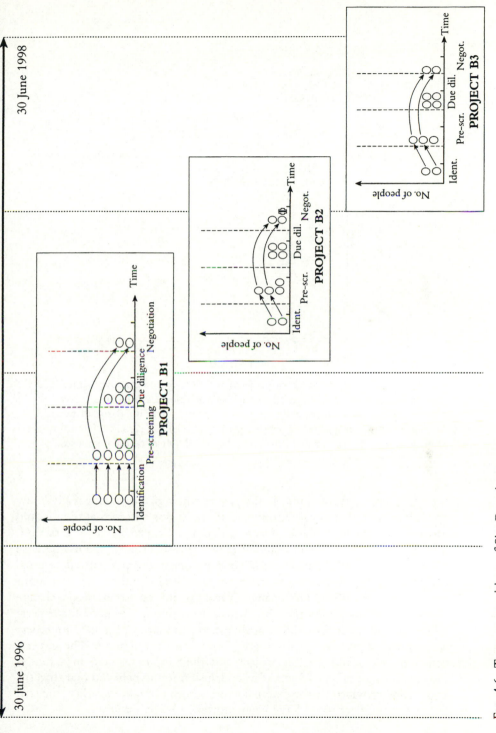

Fig. 4.6. Team compositions of Site B projects

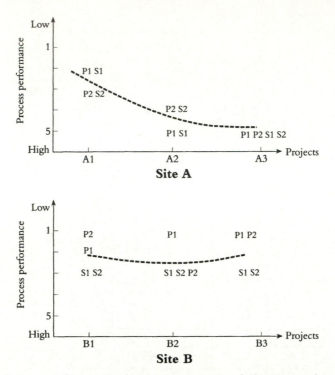

FIG. 4.7. Process performance of projects at Site A and Site B over time. In accordance with the discussion of dependent variable measurement, I have coded the data points in the following way: senior officer in charge of product development (S), project manager (P), project efficiency (1), and technical quality of project (2). The dotted line illustrates the simple mean of the responses

Internal expertise was lacking. In the pre-screening phase, no one really knew enough about how to deal with the issue, but it was agreed that they would move on to the next phase. It was a decision largely based on intuition. The possibility to bring in external expertise was decided against because of the sensitivity of the matter and since no one knew any trusted external experts. In the next phase a number of peripheral members were brought in to support the effort. This change of team members also induced a change in the external networks that the project drew upon. The need for expertise became all the more evident at this stage, and two of the new members recommended two external experts, who were brought in. The experts contributed crucially to the project and their input resulted in a fundamental redesign of its course. After conclusion it was believed that, had the knowledge provided by the external experts been brought in earlier, the lead time of the project could have been shortened by half a year.

Shortly before project A1 concluded, project A2—pertaining to a compound in the same therapeutic class—was started. This project was enhanced by the experience of A1 in two important ways. First, the team members of A2 could interact freely with the members of A1, which greatly enhanced their effort to avoid reinventing the wheel. A prerequisite for this to work was that the members of A1 were encouraged by management to spend time advising their colleagues. Secondly, the two experts retained in A1 were brought in early on in the A2 project, which facilitated the process greatly. Furthermore, the policy of associating many people with the due diligence phase again had the effect that a great number of personal networks could be drawn upon. In particular, valuable formulation experts were brought in this way. When project A3 was started—yet another compound of the same therapeutic class—many of the procedures were already routine, and a number of experts were brought in again. The project concluded in record time.

5.2. Project Management at Site B

At Site B a very different pattern emerged. There had been projects pertaining to the same therapeutic class as the compound of project B1 previously. However, no one thought that any significant experience had been retained. No project reports had been written, and many experienced people had left the organization. In fact, this lack of feedback continued throughout the sequence of projects studied here.

As a policy of secrecy, external experts—or even internal experts from other parts of the organization—were not retained. Furthermore, people were not brought in as peripheral members or as part-cycle members. No new hires were made in the in-licensing function, and therefore all the people involved had been with the organization for a long time. A consistent effect of this model was that the people involved in the identification and pre-screening phases typically lacked the knowledge to anticipate the problems encountered by the technical personnel in charge of the due diligence phase. These members, in turn, typically did not have enough knowledge either. But since they were discouraged from using external expertise, the work was often poorly done. Furthermore, since management often set deadlines without taking the project-specific issues into consideration, people involved in the due diligence phase were less than motivated to do a good job. As one member in charge of toxicity in the due diligence phase of project B1 put it: 'They think that a consistent one-size-fits-all type of organisation of in-licensing projects facilitates efficiency. Well, they forgot about effectiveness.' In short, no slack and autonomy was given for the project organization to adapt to the unique characteristics of every individual project. In addition, no technical personnel were present at the negotiation table. Therefore, critical aspects were often not considered. For example, after the contract was signed with the licensor of project B1, it emerged that twice the amount of the very expensive active ingredient initially calculated was needed, which greatly diminished the drug's commercial viability.

6. Conclusions

The results of this study challenge the conventional wisdom that a lean and structured project organization is good for efficiency and effectiveness. In environments characterized by speed and constant change, flexibility is needed that cannot be provided with such a form of organization. Arguably, this has implications for most product development in turbulent environments, but in particular for product development involving external integration. An approach to team composition which allows for variation is the cornerstone in this context. It was found that an organization which allowed the numbers and the types of team members to fluctuate over the course of the project, and provided incentives for its members to retain experience from this, consistently outperformed an organization with a more structured and closed approach. The reason for this to hold true in the case of external integration seems to be twofold. First, since every technology that is brought in from the outside is by nature different from an internally developed technology in a unique way, a history of a variation of staffing solutions generates a multitude of organizational options to work with. Secondly, a history of variation helps to develop a capacity to reshuffle the organizational options in a timely and effective manner. The findings are illustrated by the concept of 'the experience-curve of capability management'.

This approach suggests a change in mindset. In particular, a higher tolerance for loose and unpredictable structures is needed. An important stumbling-block here is that many R. & D. organizations are naturally concerned with matters of confidentiality. This study suggests that this secrecy mindset has a tendency to work at the expense of crucial openness to external actors, such as external expertise and partner firm personnel. Yet another important implication of these findings is that they imply that external integrative capabilities are built over time. External integrative capabilities are not merely a structure to be put in place, but are contingent on personal networks, flexible procedures, and attitudes that are shaped only slowly over time.

I believe that these findings may have important implications for management of innovation in settings other than pharmaceutical R. & D. Consider the case of the auto industry. Conventional wisdom has it that efficient car development project teams be clearly defined. The widely used approach with a 'heavy weight project team' (Clark and Fujimoto 1991) is a case in point. Our research suggests that rather than being an obstacle, an approach with blurred and less well-defined project team boundaries may facilitate performance. In particular, as mega-mergers and international markets induce cross-border and cross-organizational car development projects, permeable team boundaries and flexible staffing solutions may be an important means to deal with multifaceted internal and external environments and to build distinctive capabilities. The same logic holds true for fast-changing high-technology consumer goods industries, such as mobile phones, which need to combine frantically evolving state-of-the-art technologies with sophisticated aesthetic design for increasingly choosy consumers. This task of combining cutting-edge competencies from very different and relentlessly changing disciplines, I would argue, may be greatly facilitated by the more fluid team structures that this study found to be so successful in pharmaceutical in-licensing.

It is important to point out that this study has too many limitations for us to draw any definite conclusions. The sample size is far too small to generate any statistical power. Furthermore, there are many variables at work here that it has not been possible to control for. I will challenge the tentative findings presented here and pursue further understanding of the phenomenon of external integration intensely in my continuing research.

5

Strategy in the Periphery: The Role of External Linkages in Strategy Creation

Patrick Regnér

1. Introduction

Contemporary strategic management models appear to include two striking paradoxes. First, strategies are assumed to emanate from the centre of firms (most often referring to the upper echelons). However, in reality the centre often opposes strategy change and creation and peripheral sections play the active and primary role. An examination of successful strategies in several Swedish multinational corporations (MNCs) reveals that peripheral sections were decisive for the strategies, while the corporate centres opposed them. A case that illustrates this is the development of the block-buster drug Losec by Astra (Johanson and Vahlne 1992). It was developed by a peripheral section of Astra against the will of corporate management. A second anomaly is that factors peripheral to and outside a company's traditional industry and resource spheres often play a crucial role in the creation of new strategies. This can be illustrated by the great achievements of Absolut Vodka by Vin och Sprit AB (Hamilton 1994). The brand was developed through the assimilation, integration, and combination of marketing and advertising competencies outside the state-owned monopoly's industry and resource spheres. Some other cases where both paradoxes are distinguishable are examined and described later in this chapter. The anomalies become particularly apparent when strategy-making involving complex foresight horizons is evaluated through the lenses of the two most influential strategic management theories of the last two decades. One research tradition stresses the importance of positioning and collusion within a given industry (e.g. Porter 1980, 1981). The other emphasizes the role of resources and capabilities within a particular firm (e.g. Barney 1991; Rumelt 1984; Wernerfelt 1984). However, there is little indication of how the industries and resources discussed in these two strategy content traditions emerge and how they are created in the first place. The perspectives seem to take the industry and resource scope more or less for granted and build explicitly or implicitly on a strategy formulation or planning view of strategy. In brief, it seems as if they cannot provide a comprehensive explication regarding strategy creation, the creation of entirely new industry and resource positions.

This chapter attempts to examine strategy creation and discusses theoretical as well as practical aspects of strategy-making. It illustrates and explains strategy creation in four Swedish MNCs and proposes suggestions for new approaches regarding strategy theory and strategy-making. The findings illustrate that peripheral actors, resources, and industries are important in strategy creation. It is concluded that external linkages and networks play a pivotal role. The integration and co-ordination of external resources and knowledge in external networks by peripheral organizational sections and actors seem to be crucial. At the same time it appears that strategy content theory disregards the role of resources and industries outside prior ones in the development of new strategies and underestimates the role of peripheral organizational sections and actors in strategy creation. The detailed examination of strategy creation reveals alternative strategy paths, apart from industry- and resource-embedded ones. Customer- and entrepreneurial-embedded strategy creation paths are illustrated and discussed.

The chapter proposes a reassessment of prevailing conceptions of strategy-making. It is divided into three parts. Section 3 discusses strategy creation in relation to strategic management theory and some possible reasons for strategy creation's exclusion are illustrated. In Section 4 the observations from a study of strategy creation in four Swedish MNCs are illustrated and discussed. In Section 5 the findings are debated in relation to contemporary strategic content research, industrial organization perspectives, and resource-based views. Finally, conclusions regarding strategy theory, alternative strategy models, and avenues for future research are suggested. Before turning to strategic management theory, methodology is briefly discussed in Section 2.

2. Research Design

This chapter is based on a broader study of MNC strategy creation and the link between strategy content and process (Regnér 1999). Owing to the pre-paradigmatic status of strategy theory, strategy creation, and, in particular, the strategy process–content connection, a case-based qualitative study method was used. Studies focusing specifically on strategy creation and the relationship between and characteristics of strategy process and content are limited. It was therefore difficult to know in advance specifically what kind of constructs, relationships, and causations to focus on in this particular respect. The research design was supported by the fact that processes involving communication and action between individuals and groups of individuals were studied. The sensitivity of the study object contributed to the methodological choice as well. It is a highly sensitive matter to collect information about the way managers develop strategies, inform themselves about them, and make decisions in them (in some instances it was even out of the question to tape interviews). The method used is suitable for descriptive purposes and theory-building (Eisenhardt 1989) and it is the most appropriate method for the purpose here, where how and why questions were under consideration (Yin 1989). The method was guided by writings on grounded theory (Glaser and Strauss 1967; Strauss and Corbin 1990), case-study design (Yin 1989, 1993), qualitative data-analysing techniques (Miles and Huberman 1994), scientific inference in qualitative research (King *et al.* 1994), and strategy process research methods (Pettigrew 1985*b*, 1987*b*).

A dual methodology was used; an in-depth single case-study was combined with a retrospective multiple case-study about the same phenomenon (cf. Leonard-Barton 1990). Through the single in-depth case-study detailed patterns of the strategy creation process were investigated. The major advantage with this more longitudinal case was that the strategy creation could be more specifically examined, including participant observation, and it enabled the researcher to improve cause-and-effect tracking. The multiple retrospective case-study design lowered the risk of observer biases and augmented external validity compared to the single in-depth case-study. All cases concern the creation of and entry into new businesses. The single in-depth case-study focused on Couplet's entry into non-mechanical track coupling systems (electromechanical and electrohydraulic systems) and development of a truck trailer surveillance business.[1] The multiple retrospective study included strategy creation processes in three Swedish MNCs: Ericsson's entry into mobile telephony communications systems and creation of a mobile telephony business, Pharmacia & Upjohn's entry into smoking cessation products and creation of a consumer healthcare business, and AGA's entry into Eastern Europe and creation of an East European industrial gas industry business. Interviews were conducted with CEOs, presidents, senior vice-presidents, vice-presidents, and other corporate, divisional, and subsidiary managers involved in the strategy creation processes. In Table 5.1 is a description of the cases examined in the study (all company figures are based on 1998 annual reports). Next is an evaluation of current strategic management theory and its relevance regarding strategy creation.

3. Strategy Creation and Strategic Management Theory

3.1. *Strategy Creation and Strategy Content Research*

Strategy content research, highly influenced by economic theory, has contributed significantly to the development of the strategy field during the last two decades. The two main areas in strategy content research provide two distinct explanations as regards strategy-making. Industrial organization (IO) based strategy theories (e.g. Porter 1980, 1981) explain how companies use

---

[1] All names, figures, dates, locations, and companies regarding this case have been disguised.

TABLE 5.1. *The cases*

Company	Industry	Sales ($USm.)	Employees (no.)	No. of markets	Strategy creation	Interviews
Ericsson	Telecommunication equipment	22,843[a]	103,667	140	Mobile telephony/mobile communication systems	22
Pharmacia & Upjohn	Pharmaceuticals	6,758	30,000	>100	Consumer healthcare/smoking cessation	16
Couplet	Truck-trailer coupling	5,234	31,000	42	Trailer surveillance systems/Electro-hydraulic coupling systems	15[b]
AGA	Industrial gas industry	1,895	10,203	38	East European business/Eastern Europe	5

[a] SEK 184.438m. The figure has been converted into $US. The rate of exchange $US1 = SEK 8.0740 per 31 Dec. 1998 has been used.

[b] The single in-depth study was based on participant observation, interviews and examinations of internal strategy and strategy related documents. Interviews were conducted prior to, during, and after participant observation.

collusive reductions in competition of various kinds in order to strengthen their positions. Resource-based views (RBV) (e.g. Rumelt 1984; Wernerfelt 1984) show how firms use their resources and capabilities to build a competitive position. Both sides have provided extensive arguments and evidence for their models. One side provides explanations regarding industry positions and has an 'outside-in' perspective, and the other explains resource positioning and takes an 'inside-out' view. They present foundations for explaining and guiding companies' strategic postures, but from different perspectives. However, it seems as if the strategy content theories focus on the industry manœuvres and entry barriers or company-specific resources and capabilities respectively that have been dominant and that currently predominate, rather than explain how they emerge and how they are discovered. It seems as if it is more challenging for these theories to determine how industry and resource positions appear, change, and develop over time. In particular, the role of external networks, outside prevailing industry and resource settings, and the co-ordination and integration of peripheral resources and industries tend to be left out. In summary, strategy content theories seem to be weaker at explaining how a specific entry barrier or resource is identified or created in the first place. What seems to be an exaggerated concern with present and historic industry and resource positions can partly be explained by strategy content theories' base in economics with an accompanying focus on economic equilibria rather than on economic development and evolution. The inherent economics assumptions of equilibrium, rationality, organizational flexibility, etc. leave out processes, bounded rationality, uncertainty, inertia, instability, etc., which are vital ingredients in the formation of strategies, often characterized by complex foresight horizons. Rumelt (1995) has highlighted some of the erroneous assumptions borrowed from economics. The foundation in economics can possibly explain why strategy creation appears to be overlooked in contemporary strategy content research. There are difficulties in terms of modelling strategy creation in economics terms since it includes different rent characteristics, level of analyses, and processes. These three factors are outlined and discussed below.

First, the inherent rent concepts[2] used in economics-grounded strategy research of IO and RBVs appear to be less useful in the investigation of strategic change and strategy creation. Monopoly rents, or rather profits, arise as a result of a deliberate restriction of output through various market power mechanisms (Peteraf 1993) such as raising entry and mobility barriers. Ricardian rents in RBVs are returns on an asset in fixed supply, given that the rent determined by the factor is 'insufficient to attract new resources into use' (Rumelt 1987: 142). These rent concepts are, in the first case, based on collusive behaviour within given industries and, in the second, based on

---

[2] The concept of economic rent has been given various meanings. Peteraf (1994) defines it as 'the excess return to a factor over its opportunity cost'.

the productivity of given resources or their different applications respectively. The focus is on the scarcity value of given assets owing to their being protected from market entry or being in fixed supply. Hence, the point of departure is given industry and resource positions rather than the discovery and creation of new positions or new combinations of them.

Entrepreneurial or Schumpeterian rents are alternative rent concepts, which, in contrast, are returns due to discovery and innovation of new combinations of resources in uncertainty.[3] It is the excess of a venture's returns over the *ex ante* cost of the combined resources (Rumelt 1987). Uncertainty is important for this rent concept since the *ex post* value of the particular combination is uncertain *ex ante*. Essentially, then, entrepreneurial or Schumpeterian rents are the difference between the *ex post* and the *ex ante* value of the resource combination (Knight 1921; Rumelt 1987). It might be argued that the difference in comparison with other forms of rents is subtle, once discovered and established rents may be determined in terms of monopoly or Ricardian rents. However, in the determination of a suitable theory for strategy creation and change it is of importance. It takes the scarcity value of innovation and combination of new knowledge in uncertainty into consideration, rather than the scarcity value arising out of protection from market entry or resources in fixed supply. Monopoly and Ricardian rent concepts principally become *ex post* definitions of returns in a strategy creation context. They are possible to identify once they are established, but their discovery is downplayed. Entrepreneurial or Schumpeterian rents seem more appropriate for strategic management theory, especially as regards strategy creation and change.

A second possible reason why current strategic management theories have had difficulties in providing an understanding of strategy creation and change might be their level of analysis. The theories focus on industry and resource levels rather than specific firms, individuals, and interactions among firms and individuals. Ironically this appears to leave out a detailed analysis of the specific interaction and relationship which strategic management concerns, the one between firm and environment. It seems especially critical if the assimilation and integration of external information and knowledge in the organization is left out. Inter- and intra-firm processes of learning are largely underrated owing to too close a focus on industry and resource levels of analysis. This focus risks neglecting more peripheral organizational sections and peripheral resources and industries outside historic and present ones, which might play an important role in the combination of new knowledge and creation of new strategies. It seems that entrepreneurial integration, co-ordination, and learning in external networks

---

[3] Note that rent here refers to quasi-rents (Peteraf 1994) or t-rents (temporary rents; Schoemaker 1990), rents due to factors whose supply is fixed in the short run. Hence, this differs from pure economic rents (Peteraf 1994), which persist in long-term equilibria.

need to be considered in strategy change and creation. Strategy processes and learning practices on the level of firms, groups of individuals, and individuals seem crucial.

A third explanation that could possibly clarify why strategy creation is not more thoroughly investigated in contemporary strategic management theory might be the neglect of management and organizational processes, as highlighted by Rumelt (1995). This has isolated strategy content research from strategy process research. If strategy creation is to be explained, it is necessary to include strategy process characteristics in the examination. Internal as well as external processes need to be investigated. On the other hand, it seems as if strategy process research has not provided any definite answers regarding strategy-making or strategy creation either. One direction, which recognizes some of the strategy creation aspects discussed above, must be acknowledged before discussing strategy process research. It is the dynamic capabilities approach (Teece *et al.* 1997), which includes management and organizational processes that are more applicable in the context of strategy creation. This approach explicitly recognizes Schumpeterian rents, processes, and alternative levels of analysis, and it is discussed in the last section.

3.2. *Strategy Creation and Strategy Process Research*

Strategy process research, like strategy content, has grown considerably in volume during the last two decades, but it has provided less in terms of theoretical structures and parsimonious answers. It is not particularly controversial to assert that the classical and traditional view of strategy as an in-advance controlled and conscious plan including a clear separation of formulation and implementation (Andrews 1971; Ansoff 1965) has been demonstrated to be erroneous (Mintzberg 1978, 1990, 1994; Quinn 1980). Strategy is rather an adaptive, but purposive, process where piecemeal strategic decisions are taken based on continuous feedback between formulation and implementation in an emergent pattern over time (Mintzberg and Waters 1985; Quinn 1980; Pettigrew 1985*a*, 1987*b*). These characteristics seem applicable to strategy creation, and the process views provide detailed descriptions of various contextual factors influencing strategy. However, these perspectives do not seem to explore where strategy emanates from, how strategy content is changed, and what the implications are for managers; strategy content and specific managerial mechanisms appear to be underrated. Some political and cultural views (Pettigrew 1985*a*; Johnson 1987) specify strategic change to a larger extent, but it is still not quite clear what the specific change mechanisms are and how they work. It is often indeterminate what the underlying logic in the strategy process is, how it is discovered, and from where it develops. It is not entirely clear what the source and foundation for the strategy process and content is. Many process perspectives stress environmental restrictions in strategy development, but it seems as if they need to consider individual firm and management action in response to these bounding forces. There is one direction within strategy process research that defines strategic change mechanisms more specifically and that explicitly recognizes the role of peripheral organizational sections: the Bower–Burgelman model of strategic change (Bower 1974; Burgelman 1983; Noda and Bower 1996). Burgelman (1983*a,b*, 1991) divides incremental strategic decision-making processes into 'induced' and 'autonomous' ones. Induced strategic behaviour refers to strategic initiatives within the scope of the company's current strategy and serves as a variation reduction mechanism. Autonomous behaviour, on the other hand, develops outside the prevailing strategy and functions as a variation enhancer. This approach combines a selection-orientated view with an adaptive one in an attractive way for strategic management theory and strategy creation in particular, and it is discussed in the last section.

In summary, strategy creation, and the role of external linkages and networks in its development, appear to be insufficiently examined and explained by strategy content and process research. Strategy content theories seem to focus more on prevailing and historic industry and resource positions than on the combination and integration of entirely new kinds of resources and industries. In general strategy process is neglected in these theories or, in the normative interpretations, explicitly or implicitly assumed to be of a strategy-planning character: first analysis and planning, then implementation. Strategy process theories, on the other hand, are imprecise as regards the specific strategic change mechanisms, how they arise, and how strategy content develops, and they seem to focus too closely on environmental restrictive factors. Next is an examination of strategy creation in four Swedish MNCs.

4. Four Strategy Creation Cases

4.1. Introduction

The single in-depth case-study concerns Couplet's entry into non-mechanical truck trailer coupling systems (electromechanical and electrohydraulic systems) and the subsequent development of a truck trailer surveillance business. Couplet, formerly part of the specialty mechanics company Scanmeck, started out as a mechanical trailer coupling assembler and manufacturer in Sweden more than forty-five years ago. The company first led the consolidation of the Swedish mechanical trailer coupling industry and subsequently moved into Europe in the mid-1980s, and has since expanded globally.

The multiple retrospective study includes strategy creation processes in Ericsson, Pharmacia & Upjohn, and AGA. Ericsson is a global supplier of telecommunications equipment and systems. The company produces wired as well as mobile telecommunications in public and private network systems. It was founded in 1876 and entered automatic switching in the early 1920s. From then on it has been dominated by telephone exchange and switch design. Since its home market was limited, Ericsson expanded internationally at an early stage. Today 97 per cent of its sales are outside Sweden, and it has subsidiaries in over 140 countries on all continents. The strategy creation case studied is Ericsson's entry into mobile telephony communications systems and creation of a mobile telephony business.

Pharmacia & Upjohn is a Swedish–American pharmaceutical company which has grown out of a series of mergers and acquisitions during the last twenty years. Pharmacia grew out of a consolidation process of the Swedish and later European pharmaceutical industry. In 1995 the company was merged with the American company Upjohn. The strategy creation process studied is Pharmacia & Upjohn's entry into smoking cessation products and the subsequent creation of a consumer healthcare business. The process started prior to the merger between the companies, but the company will be referred to as Pharmacia & Upjohn throughout.

The last of the multiple retrospective case-studies is AGA's entry into Eastern Europe and the creation of an East European industrial gas industry business. AGA is a Swedish industrial gas manufacturer established in 1904. It is the fifth largest industrial gas company in the world, with manufacturing and distribution in about thirty-six countries in Europe, Latin America, and the USA. AGA initially focused on acetylene gas and its use in lighthouses. The company subsequently grew into a conglomerate, but began to refocus on the gas business during the 1970s and 1980s. Since then the focus has been on industrial and medical gases, with an increasing emphasis on special gases. Below is a description and examination of each of the cases. They are described and analysed in terms of Pettigrew's (1985*b*, 1987*b*) framework for strategy research (i.e. strategy content, context, and process).

4.2. Outer Context: Complexity

The strategies in the examined companies emerged and evolved in a context distinguished by high uncertainty. When Ericsson thought of replacing fixed telephone networks with cellular ones, and when Pharmacia & Upjohn had the idea of marketing a smoking cessation product and subsequently of building a consumer healthcare business, there were genuine uncertainties concerning markets, legalistic structures, and/or products involved. The situation was the same when Couplet started to look into non-mechanical systems and electrohydraulic systems and when AGA first envisaged Eastern Europe as a potential market. All cases involved complex foresight horizons. The market potential in the cases was highly unclear, and market predictions were extremely difficult even after the strategies had taken some form. The respective industries were highly sceptical regarding the ventures in question. Ericsson's mobile systems and Couplet's electrohydraulic systems were at first considered to be, at best, products for a limited, more affluent sector of the market, if marketable at all. Pharmacia & Upjohn's consumer healthcare concept, with its main smoking cessation product, was really not thought to be part of the pharmaceutical market, and it was doubtful if smoking cessation was marketable in any case. The East European markets were at first virtually non-existent, and later unpredictable in all aspects, ranging from who and where the customers were, to if or when they would buy industrial gases. Uncertainty regarding regulations and legal structures played an important role in all cases. Various governmental regulating bodies considerably increased Ericsson's, Couplet's, and Pharmacia & Upjohn's uncertainty regarding the potential products and markets. In AGA's case it was even unclear whether there was a government regulator, and, if so, where it was and what its regulations were. The technologies in the Ericsson and Couplet cases were far from developed, and there was much doubt about the direction in which the technology would proceed. The smoking cessation product in Pharmacia & Upjohn was the first of its kind in the world and naturally involved technological uncertainties. Hence, in all cases the unpredictability regarding products and technologies was very high, except in AGA's case, where those problems rather concerned the customers' and partners' technologies. In sum, the outer contexts were uncertain and ambiguous in marketing, legal, and technological terms and, hence, were characterized by complexity.

4.3. Strategy Content: A Puzzle

The strategic issues in the companies involved such complex circumstances that they were at first met with more or less total confusion. They were very imprecise and indefinite, hardly defined as specific 'issues' at all, and certainly not as 'strategic'. There was no clear direction, and little sense of how to move forward. It was impossible to sketch a strategic plan, and traditional strategic planning and formal strategy processes characterized none of the strategies. Moreover, except in the AGA case, the strategies did not solely involve competitive manoeuvring, where at least the industry direction is clear, and there were no well-defined resources to build upon.

In the single in-depth case-study non-mechanical systems (electromechanical and electrohydraulic systems) were not at the outset considered by Couplet to be a strategic issue, although they were around as one among many other industry developments. Couplet had no idea where their various moves regarding the potential new products and technologies would take them. Furthermore, they did not really know what they wanted to achieve with those moves, which illustrates that there was not only high uncertainty and complexity regarding the outer context, but high ambiguity as regards the strategic issue itself. The various actors were unsure about the issue and what role it would play for the company and industry, if any. The strategy situations were similar in the multiple retrospective case-study regarding Ericsson and Pharmacia & Upjohn. What later evolved as major strategic issues in the companies were at first quite imprecise general considerations among many others. Traditional strategic planning processes certainly did not characterize the strategies. Ericsson had no strategic plan for mobile systems or telephones at all in the early stages. A peripheral section of the corporation had an idea about mobile terminals, but there was considerable confusion regarding the project and its potential. Corporate management was puzzled and quite negative towards the idea. Similarly the consumer health-care issue in Pharmacia & Upjohn was rather a puzzle than a well-defined strategy. It was discussed and supported by a few, but it was highly uncertain if it was of any importance, and corporate management was sceptical. In AGA there was also confusion rather than a determined strategy. A 'skunkwork' looked into the East European markets and started their own strategy creation process, but others were sceptical. To sum up, strategy content was not identified from the start. It took an indistinct shape during the processes and then gradually became clearer, but it was not completely apparent even towards the end. The strategic issues were not specified in terms of content, planning, or competitive manœuvring issues, but were more like puzzles to the companies and managers involved. The term 'strategic puzzle' seems to be more appropriate than 'strategy content', since the strategic concerns first arose as loosely defined issues of confusion and ambiguity rather than specific problems or ordered and framed inquiries.

4.4. Inner Context: Two Sub-Groups and Processes

Essentially the strategy processes were divided into two sub-processes. This was apparent in Ericsson and Pharmacia & Upjohn. In Ericsson a small and peripheral radio communications unit, SRA (later ERA), fought for their mobile communications idea in conflict with corporate management. In Pharmacia & Upjohn another peripheral unit battled with corporate management and other divisions regarding smoking cessation and consumer healthcare. In Couplet corporate and divisional management were not particularly interested in the passive restraint or airbag question, even if they thought it might have some impact on more exclusive long-haul truck models, although later Couplet's technical departments and a new president, recruited from another industry, became more and more active in the area. The strategy was essentially developed within this latter group and in close co-operation with buyers, primarily the Swedish truck manufacturer Roadstar. External links to customers and actors in other industries played a primary role. Similar observations were made in AGA, where a skunk-work consisting of a couple of managers together with local subsidiaries worked with the East European entries in an unconventional and entre-preneurial way, partly against opposition from corporate management.

Senior and/or corporate and/or divisional management dominated one sub-group within each company, and the other consisted of more peripheral actors or skunkworks. The two sub-groups were at odds in their approach to the strategic puzzles, handling them quite differently and in conflict with one other. At the beginning the first group ignored the puzzle altogether, while the other group started to sort out the first pieces and do the strategic puzzle through various means. When it came to solving the puzzle, the two groups used quite different approaches in terms of picking out the pieces and interpreting the patterns. There were two distinct and separate strategy processes at work. In brief, two separate strategy motors dominated the inner context.

4.5. Strategy Process: Diverse Knowledge Assimilation Practices

The two sub-processes or strategy motors were fundamentally different in character. From the very start and throughout the process they differed in style and were in conflict with each other. The way the two sub-groups and individual actors acted towards and informed themselves about the strategic puzzles seems to have influenced their position regarding them and their development over time. They acted differently and used diverse mechanisms for assimilating knowledge, which resulted in different positions regarding the strategy developments. In Ericsson the peripheral SRA unit co-ordinated and integrated different technologies via various co-operations, consultants, and acquisitions. They successively learned about how to develop, manufacture, and sell mobile systems and later mobile telephones. External networks were important in all cases. In Couplet it was primarily external knowledge assimilation and actions related to customer relationships by the strategy motor outside corporate and divisional management that developed the strategy. This customer-based strategy development was in sharp contrast to the other strategy motor's industry-based perspective, emphasizing and examining existing technology and industry positions. The tendency to rely on diverse knowledge in the two strategy motors prevailed in the AGA and Pharmacia & Upjohn cases as well. In AGA the 'skunkwork' assimilated and combined market, technology, and institutional knowledge and in Pharmacia & Upjohn knowledge about the pharmaceutical industry was combined with consumer market knowledge by the peripheral unit. In summary, the knowledge framework and the assimilation, combination, and integration mechanisms in the two strategy motors differed considerably. It seems as if the conception and creation of the strategies in the two motors was a function of diverse knowledge assimilation practices. These included various forms of experiences, experiments, scanning activities, etc. which integrated, combined, and transformed activities and knowledge.

Externally focused knowledge assimilation practices or learning dominated one group, while learning was more orientated towards the current

industry and resources in the other. In general it was externally orientated knowledge assimilation practices within the peripheral group, such
as informal scanning, experiments, and trial and error, which developed
the strategies. The focus was externally directed towards industries and
resources outside the prevailing and traditional ones. The strategy motor
in this peripheral group involved knowledge assimilation and combination
from entirely new technology and market sources. This 'creative motor'
emphasized the resolving of the new strategic puzzle, and had its main attention centred at the opportunities for it and its development. It was more
directed towards external networks at the periphery of and outside current
industry borders, in the direction of entirely new resources and new resource
combinations. Its knowledge assimilation practices were more explorative
and actively developed and created the strategy by probing the environment
and building external networks. The other strategy motor was more focused at adaptation within the borders of the prevailing strategy. This 'adaptive motor', involving the group that first resisted the strategic puzzle, focused
on the prevailing strategy, its planning and manœuvring, and its relationship to the new strategic puzzle. It worked within the borders of the
historic industry and resource spheres and its knowledge assimilation practices were more aimed at exploitation than exploration. In summary, the
knowledge framework and the assimilation, combination, and building
mechanisms in the two strategy motors differed considerably.

4.6. Summary

The short overview above shows that extremely high uncertainty and
ambiguity or complexity, in terms of technology, legislation, and markets,
dominated the outer strategy context. Strategy content was highly ambiguous and was characterized as a strategic puzzle. As regards the inner context, two sub-groups with accompanying sub-processes or strategy motors
developed the strategy in sharp conflict with each other. Diverse knowledge
assimilation practices, and ways of acting towards and assimilating information about the evolving strategy, were used in the strategy motors in order
to inform each sub-group regarding the strategy development and to
develop the strategy. One set of knowledge assimilation practices operated
within the traditional industry and resource field for knowledge accumulation—the adaptive motor. The other directed its attention externally,
outside this established sphere, towards the external network of resources,
industries, technologies, and markets—the creative motor. The strategies
developed within the creative motors, and essentially built on resources peripheral to and outside the companies' own resource spheres, and stretched
into industries beyond the original. Hence, external knowledge assimilation
mechanisms and external resources and industries seem to have played a
pivotal role in the development of the strategies.

It seems as if many of the assumptions inherent in economically orient-ated strategy writings of IO and RBVs did not apply. The case-study com-panies did not smoothly respond to the complexity involved, and did not easily identify and select various industry and resource positions or change their strategies, selecting various market and resource positions—far from it. In fact, it is difficult to determine exactly what role IO and RBV factors played in the strategies developed by Ericsson, Pharmacia & Upjohn, AGA, and Couplet. At the least it is clear that the economics assumptions inherent in economically orientated strategy research such as IO and RBVs were not entirely applicable. This is discussed below, where the findings are debated in relation to strategy content research.

5. Strategy Creation: A Blindspot in Strategic Management

5.1. Strategy Creation and Strategic Planning Views

It came as no surprise that the strategies did not follow a planning scheme. Traditional models of strategic planning and management where strategies are first planned and then implemented clearly did not apply. In no case did traditional strategic planning play a significant role in the development of the strategies. Instead the strategies developed in an evolutionary fashion from peripheral sections of the companies. The complexity in the outer contexts in each case was much too intricate to be planned for. It was evident that the strategies exhibited an incremental, but purposive, character (e.g. Mintzberg 1978; Mintzberg and Waters 1985; Pettigrew 1985a; Quinn 1980) where peripheral actors (Burgelman 1983a,b, 1991) rather than man-agers and strategic planners at the centre played the pivotal role. This is in sharp contrast to the explicit or implicit strategy formulation or planning character of strategy content theories (e.g. Porter 1980; Barney 1986). Strat-egy content theories of IO and RBVs do not specifically address the process issue. They do not explicitly take into consideration the process of building industry or resources positions. The process is rather taken for granted and explicitly or implicitly rests on strategic planning approaches with top management and planners at the centre.

5.2. Strategy Creation and Peripheral Resources and Industries

5.2.1. Strategy Creation and the Resource-Based View In AGA's case resources and capabilities were clearly available to build on. In the other cases it is problematic to use RBVs in explaining the strategies developed. In Ericsson no one knew what the important resources and capabilities would be in the mobile telephony systems industry. Similarly, they were highly undefined for Pharmacia & Upjohn in smoking cessation and the consumer healthcare business. In particular, technological and other core competencies were unidentified. Couplet in the electrohydraulic and truck trailer surveillance industry had no clue what the important core competencies were, even when the strategic issue was quite well defined. Was the critical element the electronic sense devices? Was it the hydraulic pump? The cylinder coupling itself? The integration of the entire system? Or perhaps competencies as regards testing equipment and simulations? Or old relationships with the truck industry? Or was it something else?

Ex post it might be possible to analyse which specific resources, capabilities, and competencies became decisive for the development of the strategies. Certain technological and market competencies played determining roles in the strategy developments, and the case-study companies brought resources and capabilities with them into the strategy processes. However, there are also problems in doing this analysis after the fact. It is difficult to identify specifically what resources and capabilities made Ericsson a world leader in mobile telephone systems and telephones. They certainly did not have many of the core technological resources to build on. They had no base stations and had inferior mobile stations or telephones. Their switches were clearly over-dimensioned and much too expensive to fit mobile networks adequately. In terms of capabilities, much of the radio and all the cellular planning competencies were attained through co-operations, acquisitions, and external recruitment of consultants. When it comes to marketing competencies Ericsson certainly had capabilities to market to the old monopoly operators and governments, but most customers in the developing mobile telephony industry were new operators of a completely different character. Furthermore, end consumers played an increasingly important role, especially on the telephone side, which subsequently developed into a mass consumer market. Similarly, Couplet started without any particular resources or competencies for electrohydraulic trailer coupling systems. They too turned to external knowledge sources, outside their own corporation and industry. Most of the resources were acquired or built. For Pharmacia & Upjohn it was also a case of progressively building resource and capability positions and acquiring them externally, rather than building on existing ones.

It seems clear that there were no specific core competencies in the different cases. However, even if there were no 'hard' or articulated technological or marketing competencies that determined the strategies, RBV proponents might suggest that there were 'soft', tacit, or subtle competencies and capabilities which are less identifiable. In the Couplet case, for example, it seemed as if relationships to customers and their competencies might have been a resource base. However, when the resource definition is stretched as far as that, it seems to lose much of its meaning within a traditional RBV framework. A common capability in all the cases was integration and co-ordination of external resources and competencies. In the

Ericsson and Pharmacia & Upjohn cases this kind of capability seemed to dominate over any others. In these cases there was no particular industry, resource, or customer base to anchor the strategies in. Integration, co-ordination, and combination capabilities seemed to be determinant. And even if there were resources and capabilities available in AGA, and customer relationships and their competencies in the Couplet case, the capabilities to integrate and co-ordinate them with those in external networks seemed to be equally important in these cases. It may be suggested that an integration and co-ordination capability was decisive—an ability to acquire, integrate, and co-ordinate resources and capabilities. However, this is, again, quite far from the traditional RBV and comes closer to the dynamic capabilities approach (Teece *et al.* 1997), which is discussed in the last section.

5.2.2. Strategy Creation and Industrial Organization   IO concepts of scale, concentration, and entry barriers appeared to have little meaning *ex ante* since there was no mobile communications system industry, no non-mechanical coupling or electrohydraulic system industry, and no smoking cessation or well-defined consumer healthcare industry around at the outset. Even more clearly, there was no well-defined industry in AGA's case, since industry borders, buyers, suppliers, etc. were undefined. However, in that case the strategy process could, perhaps, be interpreted as a competitive game in terms of moves and counter-moves within an industry (Knickerbocker 1973), but this was not until the strategic issue had been clearly framed and some order had emerged. When it comes to explanations after the fact it is difficult to determine specifically which and where the experience and scale effects were in the companies examined. Ericsson had no experience or scale advantages in manufacturing radio base stations, a central part of the mobile telephone system. In contrast, Motorola and other competitors had much longer experience of this technology. The situation on the mobile station or telephone side was similar: competitors were ahead of Ericsson. On the switching side Ericsson was on a par with competitors in terms of mobile telephony applications. Couplet's position was similar. A number of competitors were far ahead on the electrohydraulic system experience-curve, and manufactured on a bigger scale. Concentration moves and raising barriers did not seem to be determinant. Even in the AGA case it is difficult to discern any production economies in the early strategy creation process, since they started out small and in bottled gases, which is essentially a small-scale local business; but clearly organizational and managerial scale advantages might have been important. It seems as if the companies penetrated external networks and industries external to their own in order to gain resources and experience rather than positioning themselves and using collusive behaviour within existing industries. Certainly, some advantages in the form of experience and scale effects could be identified after the strategies had been instituted. Similarly, Ericsson made some minor acquisitions after some years, when the strategy was more defined, but they were aimed more at gaining technology competencies and engineers than at raising entry barriers.

5.3. Summary

The analysis of strategy content in the strategy creation processes indicates that strategy content developed over time, hand-in-hand with strategy processes, rather than being specified in terms of industry and resource positions from the start. It was a process of incrementally building resources and competitive positions, rather than choosing among given resource and industry positions. It seems that, if strategy processes had been different, the strategy content would have differed as well. The process of linking to and assimilating external resources and capabilities, outside the realm of the MNCs and their industries, in external networks, was important in determining the strategies. It was difficult to identify either critical resources and capabilities or scale and experience effects early on in the strategy creation processes. Even after the strategic issues were identifiable and had taken some form, it was laborious to specify what specific resource and industry factors to build on. Moreover, it is even difficult to determine exactly *ex post* what specific industry and resource factors propelled the strategy developments in terms of strategy content theories. The findings far from rule out the importance of strategy content theories in explaining strategy development, but they indicate that strategy content needs to be closely linked with a theory of strategy process in strategy creation. Industry and resource factors naturally played a role in the strategy creation processes, but an analysis solely in terms of IO and RBV factors runs the risk of involving rationalizations after the fact. Specific experience effects and resources might be identified in retrospect, but they were impossible to determine at the time. There is potential for the conclusions to become almost tautological: specific industry and resource factors are outlined as important in strategy development because they are and have been important historically.

In summary, external networks including peripheral actors, resources, and industries played an important role in the creation of the strategies. External knowledge assimilation processes, external resources, and industries were important in determining strategy content. The findings indicate that strategy content theories have some limits when it comes to explaining strategy creation and strategy-making involving complex strategic foresight horizons. In these cases the role of strategy process and peripheral industries, resources, and organizational sections becomes apparent. Once industry borders and resources have been sufficiently determined, content theories seem to be of greater importance.

6. Summary and Conclusions

6.1. *Adaptive and Creative Strategy Logic*

Before moving into the concluding remarks it can be established that the strategies examined had several characteristics that seem to counter some aspects in strategy content research. First, in contrast to the explicit or implicit planning views of strategy content, the strategies developed incrementally and from the periphery of the companies, with planning and implementation essentially co-evolving. Secondly, collusive behaviour, concentration forces, and entry barriers seemed to play a limited role in the initial development of the strategies. Instead, external networks in related and completely different industries were important, and in the end industry borders were changed and entirely new industries created. Thirdly, external resources, outside the companies' own resource spheres, played a central role in the strategy developments. The combination, co-ordination, and integration of external resources and industries were decisive for strategy content. In sum, the strategies were created in the periphery in terms of both process and content. Industry and resource positions separate from historic ones were leveraged through peripheral sections, and their external networks and linkages played the pivotal role in the creation of the strategies.

The findings in the study come close to two alternative strategic management views presented recently, the dynamic capabilities view (Teece *et al.* 1997) and the relational view (Dyer and Singh 1998). The process of incrementally building resources and competitive positions rather than choosing among given resource and industry positions determined the creation of the strategies. It included the linking to and co-ordination and transformation of external resources and capabilities, outside the realm of the MNCs and their industries. Knowledge assimilation practices or learning played a significant role in this process. Many of these findings parallel the organizational and managerial processes described by Teece *et al.* (1997) in their dynamic capabilities view (i.e. co-ordination–integration, learning, reconfiguration, and transformation). The importance of external integration and co-ordination of various resources and competencies was observed in the creative motors of the cases. It was established in the analysis that various knowledge assimilation practices or learning mechanisms determined the understanding, attitude towards, and development of the strategies. In terms of transformation there was a reconfiguration of the asset structures in all companies. In other words, the observed probing of environments, and acquisition, integration, and combination of resources and capabilities in external networks, corresponds well with the dynamic capabilities view. The emphasis on external networks resembles the relational view as well (Dyer and Singh 1998). The relationship between the companies and external actors was important in the development of the strategies. The created capabilities were embedded in inter-firm and inter-group resources and competencies. However, there is an important difference: while prior customers played an important role in the case of Couplet, external inputs in that case, as well as in the others, was related not so much to actors within the existing industry as to actors from other industries and external consultants and individuals. The reason was that the potential new industries were simply not formed at the outset of strategy creation. There were no industry partners or natural alliances to turn to. This is in contrast to the relational view, which seems to refer primarily to prevailing trading partners. The relationships observed in this study did not relate as much to prior and present suppliers or competitors as to the creation of entirely new relationships outside or at the periphery of the industry. The same reasons that distinguish the findings from the relational view distinguish them from many network views (e.g. Nohria and Eccles 1992). Network perspectives seem to be primarily concerned with supplier relationships (Håkansson 1987; Johanson and Mattson 1988), competitor relationships (e.g. Doz and Hamel 1997), or outsourcing within existing industry borders.

The observations in the study signify the completely distinct character of strategy creation as compared to strategic management within the domain of present industry and resource practices. The findings indicate that strategy creation involves an entirely different logic from that previously discussed in strategic management theory. It is concerned with creating new combinations of knowledge, resources, and capabilities in completely new relationships (i.e. creative motor). Prior strategic management and strategy content research appears to focus more on an adaptive form of strategy-making (i.e. adaptive motor). The dual character of strategy-making observed in this study has earlier been observed in strategy process research by Burgelman (1983*a*,*b*, 1991), who has identified 'induced' and 'autonomous' strategy types, corresponding to the adaptive versus creative strategy motors observed in this study. The identified motors relate to Schumpeter's (1947) adaptive and creative response towards economic change. Adaptive response refers to changes within the realms of existing traditions and practices, while creative response pertains to solutions outside the existing range of practices. The observations indicated that strategy creation was triggered and developed within the creative motors. It seems as if strategy content theories have exaggerated strategy expansion within current industry borders and growth on the basis of prevailing resources and capabilities. Of course these are conceivable strategy paths, but they underestimate paths external to these domains.

6.2. *Alternative Strategy Creation Paths*

Strategy creation and growth was conducted into an entirely new product area and, in terms of technology, a completely new industry in the single in-depth case of Couplet. Furthermore, it was not primarily a resource-based growth, since the company did not possess any of the core technologies. In other words, none of the traditional content theories seemed to apply completely and properly. *Ex post* it was possible to delineate and describe that the industry structure changed and that certain resources and capabilities had become important. However, this does not explain Couplet's strategic management in terms of strategy creation. The outer context was dominated by true complexity in technological, market, and legalistic terms. Internally there was genuine uncertainty and no strategy content: it was, rather, a puzzle, and not even defined as 'strategic'. The inner context consisted of two diverse and opposing strategy motors: an adaptive and a creative strategy motor. The strategy motors included various knowledge assimilation practices with conflicting interpretations of the puzzle. In this setting Couplet initially exhibited inertia via the adaptive motor, but subsequently the creative motor actively penetrated and interacted with the environment. Relations to customers and their knowledge bases played a significant role in this process. Couplet probed into the complex environment, learned about it, built resources and capabilities, and positioned itself in the end as a global leader in the truck trailer surveillance industry. In contrast to strategy content explanations, strategy-making was based on new combinations of resources outside the company and on privileged access to customer knowledge. The entrepreneurial combination of external resources and the interaction with customers, primarily Swedish Roadstar, provided for strategy creation. It was a customer- and entrepreneurial-embedded strategy creation more than an industry- or resource-embedded one. The other cases showed a similar pattern. Externally directed knowledge assimilation practices in the form of informal scanning, diverse experiments, and subsequent acquisition and creation of resources and capabilities were decisive in the cases. Hence, entrepreneurial activities in terms of actively discovering, creating, and combining knowledge from various directions drove the strategies. Even in the AGA case, where the prevailing resources did play a crucial role, and in the Couplet case, where former customers were of importance, knowledge assimilation practices in external networks aimed at integration and combination of activities and knowledge were as important. In fact, co-ordination, integration, and combination skills played an important role in all strategy processes. In the Ericsson and Pharmacia & Upjohn cases these kind of factors played the dominant role. There was no specific resource or customer base to build on in those cases.

The findings indicate that knowledge assimilation practices which probe the environment and integrate and combine internal and external resources and capabilities solely, or jointly with a base in either resources or together with customers, provide a foundation for strategy creation. It might be suggested that strategy creation is a function of various knowledge assimilation practices or learning dynamics, exclusively or in conjunction with a resource or a customer base. Accordingly, two alternative strategy expansion

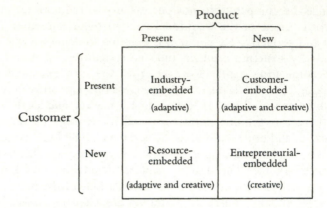

FIG. 5.1. A strategy creation framework

paths can be suggested, besides resource-embedded strategy creation, entre-
preneurial- and customer-embedded strategy creation. Given the suggested
focus on entrepreneurial rents rather than monopoly and Ricardian rents,
entrepreneurial-embedded strategy creation implies entry into new markets
which match the entrepreneur's or firm's new combination of resources or
their new insight into these combinations. Similarly, customer-embedded
strategy creation implies entry into markets which match the entrepreneur's or firm's privileged access to customer knowledge and needs
(cf. Zander and Zander 1998). In that case rents are returns due to privileged access to customer knowledge and needs. These alternative strategy
creation and expansion paths have not been sufficiently discussed earlier.
They are illustrated in terms of Ansoff's (1965) product–mission matrix
(see Figure 5.1). The various paths reflect the firm's privileged access to
customers, resources, or the firm's new combinations of resources and
capabilities via external and peripheral networks. In this respect they also
reflect different foundations for knowledge assimilation or learning. In
customer-embedded strategy creation technologies and products are most
uncertain, while there is a certain stability in relation to customers, which
can be used as a base for knowledge assimilation. Customers constitute a
learning base. It is primarily market aspects that are unpredictable in the
resource-embedded case, while resources are clearer and, thus, determine a
base for learning. The third path is purely entrepreneurial-embedded: the
product and technology as well as the customer side are uncertain and ambiguous. This is a pure entrepreneurial path where knowledge assimilation and
learning are entirely anchored in peripheral external networks.

The overview specifies various strategy paths in terms of contemporary
strategic management theory, industry, and resource-based perspectives
(industry- and resource-embedded paths). In addition, these paths are complemented with two alternative forms of strategy-making: customer- and

entrepreneurial-embedded strategy paths. In particular the framework distinguishes between two generic forms of strategy. One is purely adaptive and conducted within the realm of existing industry practices: the industry-embedded path. The other is purely creative and conducted outside existing industry, customer, and resource practices: the entrepreneurial-embedded path. The remaining two paths are combinations of these two. One is based on existing resources, but involves new applications of those resources via certain knowledge assimilation practices in external networks: the resource-embedded path. The other is grounded in relationships to customers, but involves the development of new products for and in co-operation with those customers and others in external networks: the customer-embedded path.

The industry-, resource-, and customer-embedded paths all involve path dependency and the potential for lock-in or risks for becoming trapped into a certain strategic direction. This has been illustrated for each of them, in terms of industry or market myopia (Levitt 1975), resource or core competence rigidities (Leonard-Barton 1992), and the risk of being held captive by customers (Christensen 1997). On the other hand, the entrepreneurial-embedded path is no guarantee of success, and returns to more experimental and entrepreneurial activities are clearly less certain than the further development of the industry-, resource-, or customer-embedded paths. This exploration–exploitation balance between the creative and adaptive motors is reflected in many theories of organizations and firms in the past (Holland 1975; March 1991; Penrose 1959; Schumpeter 1942; Wernerfelt 1984).

In summary, strategy creation and expansion can be explained in terms of privileged access to knowledge due to an existing resource and capability base or a customer base. Furthermore, it can develop solely out of explorative knowledge assimilation aimed at integration and transformation in external networks without being anchored in resources or customers. Depending on the dominant learning base, the strategies develop along various paths. Couplet's strategy creation process was primarily customer-based. Strategy creation was a function of the privileged access to customers and co-ordination, integration, and knowledge assimilation practices in external networks. Strategy creation in AGA was primarily a resource-embedded learning combined with co-ordination, integration, and learning in external networks, while the strategy creation processes in Ericsson and Pharmacia & Upjohn were purely based on these latter mechanisms and, thus, entrepreneurial-embedded. The cases are outlined in the strategy creation path framework shown in Figure 5.2.

The analysis and evaluation of the single in-depth and multiple retrospective case-studies essentially illustrates the two anomalies mentioned in Section 1. The strategies did not emanate from the centres of the firms, not from its core actors or competencies and resources, nor from their central positions in their industries. They developed from the outer periphery and border of the organizations and industries. External networks, linkages, and

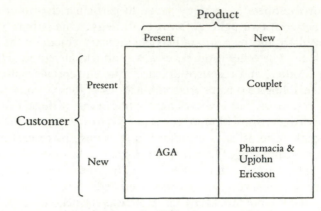

FIG. 5.2. Strategy creation paths at the different companies

external-orientated knowledge assimilation mechanisms played the decisive role on the strategy process side. External resources and industries, outside the traditional resource and industry spheres, were determining on the strategy content side. The alternative strategy creation paths, customer- and entrepreneurial-embedded paths, have not been captured earlier since strategy content and process research have essentially developed separately. Once they are combined it is evident that strategy creation and new industry and resource positions might emanate from peripheral organizational sections and from more peripheral industries and resources.

It can be concluded from the reasoning in this chapter that alternative theories need to be considered when examining strategy creation and change. The findings in the single in-depth and multiple retrospective case-studies indicate that strategic management theory needs to be complemented as regards strategy creation. Alternative rent concepts, levels of analyses, and process conceptions need to be considered when examining strategy creation. The complexity of strategy creation is likely to benefit from a variety of theories. It is through an integration of more dynamic economics-based perspectives and behavioural and cognitive strategy formation views that strategy creation and strategic management theory can make progress. Schumpeterian economics seems more relevant than prior directions in economics-based strategy research, since creation, discovery, and entrepreneurial rents emanate out of uncertainty and complexity. In addition, economics-based views need to be complemented with other social sciences. This seems especially relevant as regards strategy creation and change, since organizational and individual beliefs and values, perceptiveness, and knowledge play an important role. Researchers in the economics-based tradition seem to share this view: 'Where the co-ordination and accumulation of knowledge is key, and where patterns of belief and attitude are important, other disciplines will have more to say' (Rumelt *et al.* 1991: 27). More dynamic RBVs offer an opening for other disciplines and a potential merger between economics and behaviourally orientated strategic management research, since it recognizes, in some sections more than others, that the practice of strategic management matters. Research on strategy creation can make progress in the intersection between the economics-orientated dynamic resource-based models, emphasizing the mechanisms of capability creation, and the behavioural-based organizational learning models, focusing on the firm as a cognitive entity. It might seem to be an exaggerated eclectic approach. However, at this pre-paradigmatic stage in strategic management, especially as it relates to strategy creation and strategy content and process relationships, and because the area by definition is an applied one, parsimony has to give in to realism. Moreover, these perspectives have a common denominator in that they all involve aspects of organizational learning. Various organizational learning mechanisms seem especially appropriate for future research in strategy creation and strategic management. The observed difference in terms of knowledge assimilation practices between the adaptive and creative motor provides a foundation for further research.

6

Innovation in the Networked Firm: The Need to Develop New Types of Interface Competence

STEFAN JONSSON

1. Lean and Innovative?

There are several reasons why outsourcing and being networked is beneficial to firms. This chapter investigates the relation between outsourcing, capability development, and innovation. Increased networking (expanded use of the external market) is assumed to be a result of outsourcing certain capabilities and thus introducing changes into the innovative system. It is argued that when the balance of internal to external sources of inputs to innovation changes, firms need to beware of and manage three interrelated issues:

1. the absorptive capacity of the firm is likely to change with the reduced set of activities and thus vicarious capabilities may need to be developed;
2. as the value system is made more complex (in case of vertical outsourcing) the recombination task of the innovator can become complicated and greater integrative capabilities are needed;
3. the innovative system that the firm is part of can be affected by introduction of market-type relations driving out slack.

This chapter will first discuss the relationship between learning by doing, external capabilities, and innovations. Following this is a discussion of the potential effects of outsourcing on capability formation and how these effects can be mitigated. Lastly, there is a case-study illustrating these concepts and a discussion extending and generalizing the ideas.

2. Where do Innovations Come From?

Innovation is seen as the combination of new or recombination of existing capabilities in ways new to the market-place (von Hippel 1988; Gallouj and Weinstein 1997). 'Capabilities' is a broad term which encompasses both technology (technical–production capabilities: how to produce something and the means to produce it) and processes or capabilities based only on knowledge (with no intermediating technology). The ability to combine capabilities is in itself a meta-, or second-order, capability (Argyris and Schön 1978). There are thus two important inputs to innovation in a conceptual sense: productive capabilities (skills and routines) and, on a meta-level, recombinative capabilities.

There are many factors affecting the level of innovation of a firm: inputs provided (e.g. R. & D.), the internal creative climate (e.g. slack), the external environment, such as the market structure, competitive climate, and even regional effects (Porter 1990). This chapter will differentiate only between internal and external inputs to innovation, where internal inputs are capabilities coming from within the legal boundary of the firm and the rest are external. Both internal and external inputs are necessary for the innovative process, and they can both be of varying types, from arm's-length market type (Simon 1991) to socially close networks. Introducing an internal market increases the market-type relations in a similar sense as outsourcing (increasing dependence on external markets). For the sake of simplicity this chapter will use the terms 'internal' and 'external' inputs in a mutually exclusive sense.

There are also difficulties in defining what constitute 'inputs' to innovation. Along the lines of von Hippel (1988) a distinction can be made between invention (the discovery of something new) and innovation (a marketed invention). An innovation thus includes an element of market adaptation, or requires market knowledge and capabilities. Both internal and external inputs can serve in the invention as well as the innovation process of a firm. The focus of this chapter is on inputs to the innovation process of firms, and sources of inventions will be dealt with in less depth.

A recent survey of service industries (Table 6.1) by Statistics Sweden (SCB 1998) indicates the importance of customer contacts and internal sources of innovation in relation to, for example, universities and competitors. Unfortunately the survey did not differentiate adequately between invention and innovation, which renders it impossible to know whether the respondent meant that a source was important to the innovation or invention process of the firm. However, it is interesting to see how important customers and internal sources are considered to be to service firms. Customers (external) and internal sources are considered by far the most important by responding firms. Outsourcing could change the balance of these two inputs to the innovation process of a firm. How this can be expected to change is investigated by looking deeper into the relation between these sources and innovation. Capabilities of a firm are not static but change continuously, and innovative capacity depends on the internal generation and adoption of external capabilities (Cohen and Levinthal 1990). The next section delves more deeply into how internal capabilities are generated and their relation to the innovation process.

TABLE 6.1. *Sources judged 'extremely important' for innovation in service industries*

Source of innovation	Percentage that judged source 'extremely important'
Customers	57
Internal	56
Corporate	24
Other (patents, fairs, universities, etc.)	22
Suppliers	21
Competitor	16
Consultants	7

Source: SCB (1998).

2.1. Internal Inputs

2.1.1. Routines, Skills, and Capabilities   According to the SCB survey, 56 per cent of the innovating service firms judged internal sources as 'extremely important', second in importance only to customers. This indicates the importance of the internal stock of knowledge to innovation. Without becoming too philosophical, this stock of knowledge can be divided into knowledge of how to *do* something (production or process routines) and how to *learn* how to do something (search and adaptation routines) (Cyert and March 1963; Argyris and Schön 1978; Nelson and Winter 1982; Kogut and Zander 1992).

Research on organizational learning asserts that organizational routines are generated mainly by what the organization does (Nelson and Winter 1982; Dierickx and Cool 1989; Kogut and Zander 1992; Cohen and Levinthal 1990; Levinthal and March 1993)—activities carried out in the 'normal course of business'. A number of individually held skills which are developed for, and needed in, a particular activity are blended with, and incorporated in, interpersonally shared routines—formal and informal rules for 'how things are done around here' (Nelson and Winter 1982). A firm knows by what it has done, and therefore managerial discretion can influence the learning and capability formation patterns by choosing what markets to serve and how to serve them (Levinthal and Myatt 1994; Deephouse 1999).

The concept of routines has become more widely known in popular management of late through the work on intellectual capital (e.g. Edvinsson and Malone 1997; Stewart 1997) using the terms 'structural', 'organizational', and 'human' capital. In strategy literature the resource-based view (Wernerfelt 1984; Barney 1991; Peteraf 1993) carries the understanding of the firm as a repository of routines (termed 'resources', 'capabilities', or 'knowledge'). A main finding is that resources central to creation of competitive advantage tend to be firm-idiosyncratic (Penrose 1959; Dierickx and Cool 1989) or tacit (Spender 1996) and in essence a result of the specific history and developmental path of the firm. Choosing the activity set of a firm is thus a strategic task, setting the developmental path for learning and capability development.

Historical activities can also guide the search for new solutions, or innovations. Firms develop search routines—routines for identification of new opportunities and ways of doing things based on prior experience (Cyert and March 1963; Levinthal and March 1993). As these are based on historical experience they are 'path-dependent'. Patterns of innovation have been found to be closely related to a firm-specific experience, technology trajectory, or development path (Barras 1986; Dosi *et al.* 1988; von Hippel 1988; Hauknes 1996). In other words, firms tend to 'stick to their knitting' in innovative terms. There are several reasons for this related to learning and learning effects: learning myopia—learning is responsive to immediate (in time) feedback (Levinthal and March 1993); returns to doing—the more a firm does of a certain activity, the better it becomes and the higher is the relative expected pay-off to the firm of further deploying this activity (March 1991). These and other learning effects together lead to development of path-dependence.

Internal capabilities develop through activities performed by the firm. What a firm does also affects search routines for new (external) capabilities and solutions through focusing effects of learning. The stock of internal capabilities, in particular recombinative capabilities, underlie innovation and thus there is a relation between what a firm does and its innovative capabilities. In service (or more generally in process-intensive) industries the relationship can be argued to be stronger than in production industries because of a higher degree of tacitness of the capability which will tend to render it more sticky (Zander 1991; Kogut and Zander 1992; Szulanski 1996), leaving the innovating firm more dependent on what it already knows (as acquiring external capabilities is difficult).

2.2. External Inputs

Customers and suppliers are, according to the SCB survey, the most appreciated external inputs to innovation–invention. How are external sources different from internal in relation to the innovative process of the firm? Both can provide input to inventions as well as innovations; both can influence the learning and development of routines in a firm. The difference, it is argued, is based on the assertion that the legal boundaries of the firm make a difference to control over and transferability of capabilities (Zander and Kogut 1995; Szulanski 1996; Chesbrough and Teece 1996). While it is recognized that the legal boundary of a firm does not ensure full homogeneity of knowledge or capabilities within a firm, even so social interaction, common sense-making, and the creation of a common history through joint activities and routines is thought to affect positively the capability of internal transfer of knowledge. A corollary is that external capabilities will be relatively more difficult for the firm to utilize as they may represent a different knowledge base than the internal capabilities. Thus the conjecture is that capabilities within the legal boundaries can be expected to function differently as compared to external capabilities in the innovation process. Explaining how firms integrate external knowledge, Cohen and Levinthal (1990) introduce the concept of absorptive capacity.

2.2.1. Absorptive Capacity   Absorptive capacity is the ability to *recognize, understand,* and *internalize or use* new external information. It is generated by what a firm does, and through R. & D. Recognition of new valuable external information is not self-evident as the valuation of external information tends to become biased (narrower) by what the firm does and its market position and customers (Cohen and Levinthal 1990; Henderson and Clark 1990; Christensen 1993; Greve 1994). Adoption depends on the ability of a firm to transfer capabilities across the firm boundary and also within the firm. Cross-boundary adoption (outward absorptive capacity) is controlled by 'gatekeepers'—individuals in the interface with the environment, and their relation and shared knowledge base with the external environment. The closer the relationship and the more shared the knowledge base between the gatekeeper and the external environment, the better the absorptive capacity of the firm. Adoption within a firm (inward absorptive capacity) is contingent on the homogeneity of the knowledge base and culture of the firm: the more homogeneous, the easier to share knowledge within the firm. There is thus a trade-off between the 'inward-' and 'outward-'looking absorptive capacity; the more specialized (smaller set of activities) a firm is in a certain field, the more homogeneous its knowledge base and the better its inward-looking (but worse the outward-looking) absorptive capacity (Abernathy 1978; Cohen and Levinthal 1990; Levinthal and Myatt 1994).

Absorptive capacity is thus seen as essential to the innovative capability of a firm; it is generated through R. & D. and by doing, and can induce specialization and rigidities to change. More importantly to the argument of this chapter, it provides an explanation of how external capabilities differ from internal in the innovative process of firms.

2.3. Innovations Come from Routines and Customers

Summarizing the argument this far: firms are highly dependent on their internal and external capabilities for innovative activities. Internal capabilities are largely a result of historical choices of activities. External capabilities need to be recognized and adopted to be included in the innovation process; a firm needs to know what to get externally: absorptive capacity is what determines how well a firm recognizes and integrates external capabilities. The absorptive capacity is affected by what the firm does. Internal and external capabilities differ in their relation to the innovative process in that external capabilities are mediated through the absorptive capacity of the firm, which is dependent on what the firm does and the type of relationship between the firm and the environment. Thus the activity set and the types of external linkages chosen for the firm can be expected to have implications for the innovative process of the firm.

3. Outsourcing and Innovation

3.1. Relation of Routines and Innovation

Firms learn from what they do and thus innovations are dependent on what firms have done. What they do affects their ability to integrate external capabilities. What then is the effect on innovation of outsourcing? One obvious effect is that the scope of activities performed in-house shrinks. The total activity set performed by the firm is thus reduced and with that the variety of its experience base. This is not necessarily bad. Presumably the activities outsourced are those where value was not added but destroyed by the firm. What happens, though, is that the balance of external to internal inputs to the innovation process changes (unless only very peripheral activities are outsourced). Based on the above discussion of the difference in the role of internal and external sources of innovation, this change in balance brings on the following three issues to be managed:

1. the absorptive capacity of the firm is likely to change with the reduced set of activities—higher capacity in terms of the reduced set of activities but a greater risk of rigidities;
2. relatedly, as the value system is made more complex (in the case of vertical outsourcing) the recombination task of the innovator can become complicated;
3. the innovative system of which the firm might be a part can change with a change in type of relation of participants.

These three issues are elaborated on below.

3.1.1. Absorptive Capacity.
The absorptive capacity of a firm can be affected in two ways; by outsourcing the width (scope) and complexity of the knowledge base and by the multitude of external relations.

Width of knowledge base. The knowledge base effect is dual. On the one hand, a reduced scope of activities would lead to a focus on activities still carried out and possibly an increase in inward absorptive capacity by allowing a more focused and thus more shared internal knowledge base (Cohen and Levinthal 1990; Levinthal and Myatt 1994). On the other hand, an increase in the focus of absorptive capacity could lead to a lessening of its width and decrease the outward absorptive capacity, increasing the risk of developing 'core rigidities' or informational 'blindness' (Cohen and Levinthal 1990; Henderson and Clark 1990; Leonard-Barton 1992; Christensen 1993). There is thus a risk that outsourcing capabilities emaciates the absorptive capacity of the firm, forcing it into a narrower development path than before; hence management needs to consider measures of maintaining outward absorptive capacity when increasing outsourcing.

The task of recombination. Another issue concerns the learning interdependencies in the web of different routines and capabilities comprising a firm's total activity system giving rise to potentially complex linkages in the generation of routines in a firm which underlie innovative capabilities (Nelson and Winter 1982). Service firms are often process-heavy, especially in the financial and insurance sectors. The process can be said to be the service. To handle this the industry is characterized by large information technology investments and extremely large and complex systems for managing the fund accounting, fund administration, and transfer agency functions (Levinthal and Myatt 1994). The service or product the customer purchases can be described as the orchestration and packaging of these fundamental functions. In orchestrating and packaging these functions managing the interdependence of the different functions becomes crucial. These cross-dependencies feed into the process of learning and development of routines. Chesbrough and Teece (1996) differentiate between autonomous and systemic types of innovation, where the first type is rather independent of other complementary resources and the second is heavily interlinked with complementary resources. They argue that it is the location of the capabilities underlying the innovation and the extent to which the innovation is autonomous that together determine the degree to which an innovative firm should integrate to enable appropriation of rents from the innovation (Figure 6.1).

Actually determining the effect that innovation or change in one function will have on the other functions is not a trivial matter. Process management is often a separate (and sizeable) unit with the specific mandate to untangle the routines and processes and harmonize the effects of innovations in different functions (in-house). A process management department has a tough time understanding all the inter-linkages within the boundaries of the firm. If some routines develop through interaction with other routines, it can be detrimental if activities are outsourced without ensuring continued close interfacing.

3.1.2. Effects on the Firm's Innovation System   Outsourcing can mean externalizing part of the innovation process and thus introducing market forces

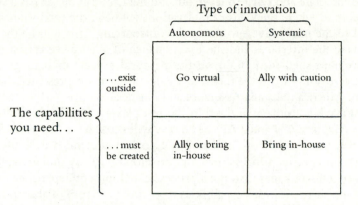

FIG. 6.1. Matching organization to innovation.
Source: Chesbrough and Teece (1996: 73).

into the process (cf. Chapter 2). The effect of externalization on innovation is complex. On the one hand, increased emphasis on market-type relations (Simon 1991) could kill potential innovations that in the innovation system are not considered viable in the short run (but might be so in a longer perspective). This reasoning is analogous to the problem of markets optimizing locally (and sub-optimizing globally) by only communicating with prices. An integrated firm (or 'planned' market) can serve as an 'island of innovation in the sea of market forces' (Zander and Kogut 1995). On the one hand, market-type relations drive out slack and can enhance the flexibility of partners, but can also lead to an emphasis on evolutionary or incremental innovation (owing to path-dependencies), whereas closer relations can increase the slack in the system, or increase the rigidity of the system, but encourage revolutionary innovation.

The issue essentially boils down to a strategic decision by the innovating firm as to where it considers the locus of innovation to be in the 'value system' (Porter 1985); (Normann 1993); the decision of what to integrate within the boundaries of the firm follows from this (Teece 1985).

3.2. Summary: Interface Management

Summarizing the argument so far: outsourcing reduces the scope of activities of the firm, which can lead to a progressively slimmer experience base. As resources and routines of the firm are path-dependent and interrelated, this reduction in scope can lead to impoverishment of capabilities for innovation (a more restricted development path). On the other hand, outsourcing increases the number and variety of contacts and thus potential innovation inputs to the firm, which can be valuable if the firm possesses the requisite absorptive capacity to manage the interfaces. Furthermore, the decision on what to integrate and what to leave outside the firm can be seen as a strategic decision as to where the locus of innovation will be in the total value system. Crucial to the innovative success of the outsourcing firm will be the ability to manage the interfaces and the maintenance of absorptive capacity.

In order to shed some light on the practical aspects of managing these issues a case-study from the financial services industry is presented. The case is that of American Skandia Assurance and Financial Services (AFS), the hugely successful US subsidiary of the third largest player in the global unit-linked insurance industry: Skandia AFS. The case will show how American Skandia has dealt with the tensions of being networked and innovative by articulating the integrative process (product development), by understanding the capability inter-linkages through a process development department, and by developing three vicarious capabilities to ensure the depth of absorptive capabilities and integration of customer feedback.

4. Skandia AFS: Slim and Creative

4.1. Why Case and Case Method

The case method is useful for exploring new research ideas and capturing complex relations that might not manifest themselves in more quantitative research methods. Where the quantitative research question is strict and defined to test the validity of a hypothesis, the case method leaves room for a wider exploratory approach and a less defined research question. This makes it suitable to research on new and untested ideas, which this chapter is about. This case is a 'rich', or detailed, case aimed at an in-depth understanding of one particular phenomenon in a particular firm. Naturally this severely limits any generalizability of findings; however, the main aim is to explore new issues and stimulate continued thinking on the subject.

Over a period of five months fifteen interviews were carried out within Skandia AFS in Stockholm, American Skandia at Shelton, Connecticut, and the Process Development Centre in Berlin. Interviewees ranged from the director, intellectual capital, to process analysts and product development officers. Each of the interviews lasted about one hour and was taped and transcribed. Interviewees were selected by recommendation by the top official in charge of the function investigated. Additional information has been elicited through the internal magazine of the AFS (*New Horizons*), other case-studies of Skandia AFS (Bartlett 1996; Oliver 1996), and a review of all the articles concerning Skandia AFS in the Swedish press from 1994 to 1998.

4.2. American Skandia: A Success Story

Even though this case will specifically deal with the innovative activities of the US subsidiary of Skandia AFS, American Skandia, the 'AFS model' will

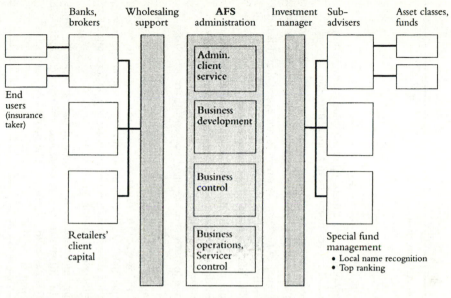

FIG. 6.2. AFS organization.
Source: Adapted from Bartlett (1996).

first be described and discussed, as it is a novelty in the insurance industry and a thorough understanding of it is necessary to understand the issues regarding the innovative activities of American Skandia.

4.2.1. The AFS model   Skandia AFS is one of the most networked organizations in its industry. Their organizational model has served as a textbook example of the virtual corporation (Hedberg *et al.* 1994; Edvinsson and Malone 1997; Stewart 1997; Ghoshal and Bartlett 1997). The basic structure is depicted in Figure 6.2, but this structure is a theme on which the different subsidiaries vary according to local history and taste.

The history of Skandia AFS can be traced back to the International Life Operations (ILO) division of Skandia. ILO had over 90 per cent of its business in the high-risk reinsurance sector and was losing money. In 1988 the reinsurance business was sold off, leaving a 50 per cent share in a Spanish primary insurance company and a 60 per cent share in an entrepreneurial life assurance venture in the UK (Skandia Life). The UK operation moved into unit-linked annuities.[1] Skandia soon acquired 100 per cent of Skandia Life and began to change it.

---

[1] A form of life assurance in which the policy holder can choose from a number of investment alternatives offered by the insurance company for the savings portion of paid-in premiums (Skandia annual report, suppl. on intellectual capital, 1994).

TABLE 6.2. *Competitors' views on the Skandia AFS concept*

Competing firm	Percentage of Swedish market (1997) for:			View on AFS concept
	Unit-linked	Life assurance	Individual pension scheme	
Wasa	13	18	—	They do not believe in a break-up of the value system as the market is too small for specialization in administration
Trygg Hansa	20	13	—	Long-term savings is moving towards a commodity market with smaller margins, which necessitates keeping activities in-house
SPP	—	—	—	Outsourcing of fund management is not essential as it is not a critical activity to attract customers (price is). There is a possibility of a break-up of the value system
Sparbanken	1	—	43	They are impressed by the rapid international expansion of AFS but doubtful about the profitability. A break-up of the value system is considered unlikely as it is seen as too expensive to outsource sales and no benefits are seen from outsourcing asset management
Svenska Handels Banken	—	6	13	No external fund managers are needed as it is provided in-house, and it would require expensive new systems to handle it. The profitability of AFS is doubted and as the long-term savings market is a mass market, no benefits are seen in focusing on one part of the value system
Skandinaviska Enskilda Banken	6	—	8	They are impressed by AFS's rapid global expansion but think it will be difficult to be profitable in a small niche. Profits will come from asset management. The profitability of AFS is questioned

One problem faced by Skandia Life was that the best in-house fund managers often left for higher pay elsewhere, as did the best-performing dedicated sales agents. In order to deal with the problem of (negative) factor mobility, Skandia Life decided to externalize both the fund management and sales function. Skandia then entered into alliances and co-operative set-ups with local retailers (banks, brokers) and local and global high-profile mutual fund managers, effectively focusing Skandia on providing the administration and product development of financially linked insurance services. In effect they broke up the traditional value system in the industry, where the competitors had both asset management as well as sales force in-house. Skandia calls the organizational structure 'specialists in collaboration'. This step was a radical divergence from industry standard, which still is one of heavy vertical integration—from a captive sales force to in-house fund managers.

Even though the Swedish business press (*Affärsvärlden*, 22 October 1997) and several business scholars (Ghoshal and Bartlett 1997) have hailed the breaking-up of the value system as an important part of the AFS success story, the rest of the industry remains sceptical, mainly doubting the profitability of outsourcing fund management and the loss of control over sales forces. Analysing the Swedish market for long-term savings products,[2] Hedberg and Randel (1997) interviewed the CEOs of the main competitors of Skandia on the 'AFS concept' (Table 6.2). As can be made out from the table, none of the competitors call the AFS concept a positive competitive innovation that they would like to imitate; in fact most of the CEOs expressed doubt about the profitability of AFS[3] and about the value of outsourcing (focusing on one part of the value system) in a small market. Whether a full-scale break-up of the value system is desirable or not, several of the competitors have now (five years after the introduction of the AFS model) begun offering the option of external fund management to customers of their unit-linked products.

The generic product offering of American Skandia is the combination and administrative solution of a combination of financial instruments satisfying a customer's particular preference for risk, yield, cash flow, purchase channel, and conforming with the options available in the financial market and the legal system. Their role can, at one level, be seen as that of the intermediate—the archetype arbitrator (see Figure 6.3)—between the market for savings and the market for fund management. On one level they mediate and manage the interface between the market for fund managers and the market for financial investors and make a profit on having better information than either actor, key information being customer preferences and financial market possibilities–capabilities. However, given the complex

[2] e.g. unit-linked, life assurance, individual pension schemes, and various combinations thereof.
[3] As the contract sold to the customer costs Skandia money up front (commissions to the broker) but yields a stream of revenue over an extended period of time, the 'profitability' of a contract is not clear at the outset of a contractual time period.

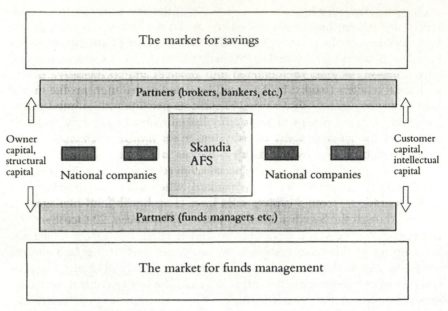

FIG. 6.3. AFS business model.
Source: Homepage Imaginära organisationer

structure of many of the financial instruments and the multitude of options available to the customer, the mere record-keeping function is in itself a complex task requiring complex procedures and information technology systems.

In short, Skandia develops the product, markets it to the brokers, and administers it. The premium paid by the end customer is split between the broker, Skandia, and the fund manager.

4.3. *American Skandia: An Innovative Powerhouse*

> American Skandia was unknown at the start of 1988. We decided to compete on the basis of product innovation . . . We see ourselves competing with product innovation and are in a sense a [service] packaging company.

> (Senior officer, product development)

American Skandia was established in 1988 and rode through a couple of tough first years as a single product line, single-outlet company until it had developed into a full-fledged successful financial service provider by 1997. The growth of American Skandia has been exceptional, with premiums up from virtually nothing in 1989 to close to $US10 billion in 1997, and it is described as one of the powerhouses in the AFS federation.

American Skandia defines itself as an innovative company where the capacity to develop and market new products faster than the competitors is key to competitiveness. Product innovation is considered vital to the competitive advantage of American Skandia, and consequently they have had a cycle of three product launches a year, where in the variable annuities industry most competitors have launched new products once a year. This clearly innovative firm is at the same time extensively networked. It is essentially structured along the lines of the AFS model, with no in-house sales force or fund managers. Yet it has thrived on being innovative in a mature industry. A closer look at the product development process yields some insight as to how this has been achieved in American Skandia.

4.3.1. Four Phases of Product Development at American Skandia   Initially, product development at American Skandia meant some of the vice-presidents coming together and brainstorming around the variable annuities product line. The result of a high-powered group focusing on one product line was prolific and successful product development. American Skandia employed three cycles of product roll-outs during the year, while competitors normally had one. American Skandia have the largest number of variable annuity products in the industry and have gained a reputation for being an innovative company.

With the rapid growth of the organization, the introduction of more product lines (mutual funds, variable intermediate annuities, etc.) and more channels (wire houses, banks), product development could no longer be carried out in the old 'simple' high-powered way but had to be routinized to allow the responsibility for product development to be pushed down from the level of vice-president. The problem was how to enable an organization where 60 per cent of the employees have less than two years' firm or industry experience to develop successful products. The solution involved formalization of the product development process into a four-stage process (Table 6.3) and extension (through coaching) of product development competence.

New product managers are phased in at the development stage, where the task is relatively well defined, issues and problems are more analytical and less political, and there is a picture of the whole—the intended result. Senior management oversees and participates extensively in the conceptualization and the planning and design phases. Articulation of the product concept is used to transfer it effectively to less experienced team members.

The project management department is responsible for 'driving' the process and for 'filling the gaps'—taking the lead in issues that are not directly the responsibility of any one department as well as fulfilling a co-ordinative role. This role is crucial in terms of integrating the different types of capability that go into development of a new unit-linked insurance product.

In terms of development resource inputs the distinction between the four phases of development is not clear. Rather, there is a continuous

TABLE 6.3. *The four phases of product development at American Skandia*

0. Concept	1. Research	2. Design and planning	3. Development	4. Implementation
Actions	Capability research: Can we do this? Is this legal? Can this sell? How big is this? Go/no go?	Assemble team. Specification: product architecture. Plan: who does what?	Set target date. Co-ordinate meetings with departments. Iteration back to design	Hand over to sales, service personnel: training, transfer of knowledge
Main departments involved	Legal; actuarial; product development; sales and marketing	Product development; information technology	All	Product development; sales and marketing; customer service
Approximate time share (%)	5	45	45	5

development characterized by tapering in and tapering out of resource bases over a period of time (see Figure 6.4).

The role of the product development department might seem strange as it does not possess any of the production skills of the other line departments (e.g. information technology). However, it is essential in the role of brokering knowledge between the departments and utilizing the knowledge in the vicarious capabilities developed by AFS to support innovation while outsourcing.

4.4. Vicarious Capabilities at AFS

To counter the potentially negative effects on learning from outsourcing, AFS has developed a number of vicarious capabilities in the interface with the activities which are normally kept in-house in this industry. The three main vicarious capabilities are:

1. key account management;
2. investment manager management;
3. whole sales support.

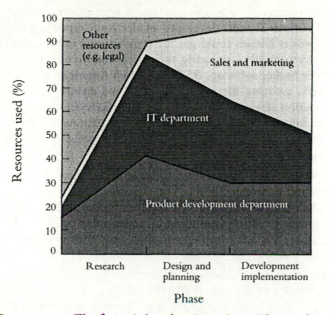

Fig. 6.4. Resource use. The figure is based on interviews. The numbers are not accurate, but serve only as an illustration of the concept

In essence these are capabilities which might not have existed had American Skandia been a normally integrated firm, with less outsourcing. These three capabilities in conjunction with the integrative capabilities provided by the product development department will be described below and analysed in relation to the support they provide to the innovative capabilities of AFS.

4.4.1. Key Accounts Management at American Skandia: Capturing Knowledge and Fostering Customer Loyalty

> It is our responsibility to go out and learn exactly how our customers do business. Whether they are doing it today or not, it is how they want to do business with us and bring that information back to American Skandia and use that information in our development process.
>
> (Senior officer, key account management)

American Skandia has a small key account management team exclusively working with their seventy largest broker dealers. The key account management function is responsible for the development of customer competence but at the same time it has a two-way relationship to product development: to confer client competence and client wishes and to maintain a balance between customer competence and the rest of the product system. The team learns the business of the customer and works to increase the 'ease of business' between the customer and American Skandia. As an example, American Skandia developed an electronic reporting format so that the largest broker houses could get the transactional information (commissions etc.) electronically—reducing their administrative overheads. Another example is the broker software, ASSESS, which American Skandia distributes to its brokers, assisting them in their work and ensuring compatibility of their information stream with American Skandia systems.

There are four main roles (in relation to innovations) of the key account management group, which makes them a more useful tool for innovations than the normal sales force:

1. to interface with lead users (to acquire knowledge to feed into the innovation process);
2. to include lead users in the AFS business model to encourage synergies;
3. to test new products (sounding out customers on new ideas);
4. to engineer system complementarities (and thus customer loyalty, or 'lock-in') in trading systems and processes.

The last function and the system interaction with the client is really what distinguishes the key account management team from the customer focus teams which deal with the individual brokers and financial planners. Normann (1993), Wikström *et al.* (1994), and Gallouj and Weinstein (1997) emphasize the role of the customer in the service production function, and the need for management and education of the customer as a vital part in service management and development. Similarly von Hippel (1988) emphasizes the role of lead users in successful innovation, and this function serves as an interface with the lead users of American Skandia.

4.4.2. Investment Management

> . . . yes, it can be a disadvantage not to handle the process [of fund management] in-house but we do it like that in Germany: one fund specialist, not a hundred analysts . . . We are only in on the margin. It is a change in the product to add or take away a fund . . . fund analysis is part of our product and we must have competence in that area.

> (Senior officer, Process Development Centre, Berlin)

Some of the most significant innovations in the unit-linked value system take place with the investment managers. New financial instruments are developed which have distinct risk–reward profiles and perhaps new legal implications if included in insurance products. Development of new fund-linked insurance products builds on intimate knowledge of innovations in financial instruments. Furthermore, knowing the fund managers is crucial, as part of the information that the end customer is paying Skandia AFS to 'package' into the product is a screening of suitable investment options for a specific product. Not having the fund management in-house is naturally a step down in level of knowledge of the fund management market, and the absorptive capacity of AFS could potentially suffer from not being a player in the investment management market. To compensate there are special fund manager managers who monitor and evaluate fund managers and their performance, and learn what is new on the market. The interaction of the broker managers with the product development team is not as intensive as with the key account team, but it forms a backbone capability that Skandia AFS must possess to be a player in the market. It is a skeleton capability, in essence the same as if they took part in the market, but on a much smaller scale.

Broker management enhances the absorptive capacity of a critical capability for innovation—fund management.

4.4.3. Whole Sales Support: Broker Management   Not having a sales force can be a disadvantage when it comes to knowing the customer. The key account management team deal with the seventy largest clients—which corresponds to a sizeable part of the total business generated. However, the largest number of the clients (95 per cent) are small or medium-sized. Valuable feedback from these customers must be fed into the innovative process.

To support this American Skandia has 'whole sale support', organized as specialized customer focus teams of nine members dealing with all issues that brokers might raise. These teams service the brokers, update them on new products, and listen to their comments and problems. The teams are locally based and are in contact with one internal whole selling organization at American Skandia headquarters. In essence this is a set-up to provide product support and to be able to absorb customer feedback into the innovative process.

5. Discussion

5.1. The American Skandia Case: Development of New Absorptive and Integrative Capabilities

The three vicarious capabilities help American Skandia keep the innovative process alive while being extensively networked. Broker management enhances the absorptive capacity, whole sale support channels customer competence into the innovation process, and key account management interfaces with lead users. Product development is taken seriously and there is a department in charge of co-ordinating and marrying the diverse capabilities that go into the development of a new insurance product. Apart from this there is also the process management team, who sort out the ripple-through effects that innovation in different parts of the service production process has. Taken together this forms a functioning innovative system which relies extensively on networking the functions it feels other actors can do better. It is not one of these aspects in isolation that makes the innovative

TABLE 6.4. *Resources and effects of outsourcing*

Innovative resources	Description	Possible effect of outsourcing	Advice
Internal			
Routines, capabilities	Developed through learning by doing. Managerial discretion in choosing what the firm does. Sets the base for innovative capability	Scope of activities reduced, potentially reduced variety of input, and impoverished set of routines leading to constraining innovative capability	Ensure breadth of set of capabilities by developing vicarious capabilities in lieu of outsourced ones. Work strategically, choosing how and what markets to serve in the long term as it has ramifications for innovative capacity
Absorptive capacity	Ability to understand and incorporate new external knowledge generated by R. & D. and by doing	Focus of absorptive capacity to activities still being undertaken, encouraging further specialization owing to returns to specialization	Develop vicarious capabilities that maintain breadth of absorptive capacity
External			
Customers	Feedback from customers and the market in general. Also possibility of customer participating in production	If sales–support function is externalized, customer feedback can be severed. Customer participation can be hampered	Develop/engage vicarious capability ensuring customer–market feedback and ensuring functioning product support. Engage in process development to understand effects of outsourcing
Suppliers	Contact with potential sources of innovation and invention in the value system	Outsourcing can increase the number and variety of supplier inputs, which can be beneficial if handled correctly	Develop absorptive capacity to handle increased interface more efficiently. Consider *nature* of relation in terms of impact on innovative capability. Ensure safety of some new ideas or capabilities (maintain slack)

powerhouse, but the orchestration of them all. The message of this chapter can be summarized in Table 6.4.

Innovation is dependent on access to and control over capabilities. These can be internal or external. If the capabilities are external, their usefulness to the innovative process of a firm is mediated by the absorptive capacity of that firm. Outsourcing changes the balance of internal to external capabilities in a firm's innovation process and this gives rise to issues that need management. The first issue is to maintain absorptive capacity, both in terms of technical and processual capabilities (to be able to understand and adopt external innovation) and in terms of relation to the external environment. Maintaining the absorptive capacity is essential to utilization of both internal and external capabilities, and this can be achieved by developing special vicarious capabilities in lieu of outsourced capabilities.

In relation to internal capabilities in particular it is essential to work strategically with the long-range implications for capability generation of the choice of markets and how to serve them. With respect to customers the possibility of including them in the production is, especially in service industries, an important area for innovation (Normann 1993; Gallouj and Weinstein 1997). This possibility can be hampered by outsourcing and must be managed. Suppliers are more often considered part of an innovative system. The nature of the relationship to them—social closeness, degree of market forces—will affect the behaviour of the innovation system as a whole and needs to be managed. Close networking can be beneficial to certain types of networking while proving to breed inertia, while arm's-length relationships can drive out slack but constrain innovative activities.

6. Conclusion

Firms learn by what they do and they know by what they have done, and their innovative behaviour will be partly guided by the activities they choose to undertake. Outsourcing (or networking) in this light necessitates a long and hard look at the competencies and capabilities that underlie the innovative dynamics of the firm and how this will be affected by discontinuing some activities. There can be both direct and indirect effects on innovative capabilities from outsourcing.

Once the competence development dynamics of the firm, and its relation to the innovative process, have been understood, a decision can be taken as to whether new vicarious capabilities need to be developed to keep innovative power or whether the outsource activities truly are unrelated to the innovative dynamics of the firm. Vicarious capabilities often need to be developed in the interface between the current core activity and the activities that earlier were carried out in-house. In essence development of vicarious capabilities is a way of capturing the learning of the earlier 'thicker' activity system in an activity system which is 'thinner' in implementation.

7

Communities of Practice in a High-Technology Firm

ROBIN TEIGLAND

1. Introduction

This chapter offers the opportunity to explore the themes of the book in the exciting new world of the internet. One of the major motivations for undertaking this study was that most organization theory was developed during the pre-internet era. However, since the mid-1990s we have seen an explosion in the use of internet-based media such as e-mail, electronic communities and bulletin boards, intranets, etc. Research has had a difficult time keeping pace with this new world based on 'internet-time' and, as such, we have little detailed understanding of the ways in which the internet is affecting the networks of social relationships or of the ability of management to create and leverage valuable capabilities within high-technology firms.

With this in mind we set out to perform a study of Icon Medialab (Icon). Icon is considered to be on the 'bleeding edge' of New Age knowledge-intensive companies since it specializes in technologically complex digital communications solutions for large multinationals, e.g. websites, intranets, and e-commerce solutions. A major management objective for Icon is to ensure the development, use, and reuse of the latest internet technology, a difficult challenge since much of the technology becomes outdated within six months of its development. In addition to leading the technological development within its field, Icon also focuses on rapid global expansion. Thus, within two years of its founding the company had grown to 240 employees with offices in eight countries.

In a New Age company such as Icon where success is based on the development of breakthrough, complex internet solutions, one of the most important capabilities is the leveraging of the knowledge that is distributed throughout the firm while at the same time staying abreast of developments in the market-place. In order to understand the knowledge flows into and within Icon, I decided to focus on the individual as the unit of analysis.

After more than thirty interviews I administered a detailed questionnaire to every employee in the firm aimed at developing an understanding of the sources of knowledge that each individual used in the course of his or her work. I was then able to build a rich picture of an individual's knowledge networks both inside the firm and reaching outside the firm. The next step involved linking these knowledge flow patterns to individual performance on various dimensions in order to provide clear evidence regarding the value (or not) of such knowledge flows.

This chapter is organized as follows. The next section provides a brief review of the knowledge management literature, followed by a more detailed discussion of the communities of practice literature. Section 3 provides a conceptual model and the specification of five hypotheses linking knowledge flows to individual performance. Section 4 describes the research methodology and provides a brief description of Icon Medialab. Section 5 reports the results of the empirical study. Section 6 is a discussion of the results. Finally, the last section discusses the implications of this research for theory and practice.

2. Background

There is a vast and growing literature in the field of knowledge management. I will not provide a review here, but it is important to consider briefly the factors contributing to the emergence of this literature, and the various sub-fields that exist, before focusing on the communities of practice literature as the particular angle that is developed in this chapter.

Peter Drucker predicted the emergence of the 'knowledge worker' back in the 1950s. Over the past forty years his vision has become a reality as work continues to become increasingly complex, non-standardized, and dependent on the combination of multiple sources of knowledge (Quinn *et al.* 1996; Wenger 1998). At the level of the firm, we see shrinking product life cycles, the need for integration across an increasing diversity of technologies, and increasing levels of competition from new competitors (Boland and Tenkasi 1995; Purser *et al.* 1992). All of this puts pressure on firms to do a better job of gaining access to new knowledge in their business environment and leveraging their existing knowledge within the boundaries of the firm (Bartlett and Ghoshal 1989; Doz and Hamel 1997; Drucker 1990; Hedlund and Nonaka 1993).

While there may be some level of agreement around the importance of this set of economic, technological, and social drivers of change, there is no such consensus around the goals of, or boundaries around, the field of knowledge management. My approach in this chapter is to define knowledge management as the systems and structures that exist within the firm that facilitate the acquisition of new knowledge from outside and the leverage of existing knowledge inside the firm, in such a way as to enhance the competitiveness of the firm. This definition is not intended to be one that all scholars in this field could agree upon. It is simply put forward as a way of clarifying my own approach. Thus, I focus primarily on knowledge flows, not stocks; I am interested in the flow of knowledge into and within the firm; and I am concerned about the systems and structures that have an impact on firm performance. In taking this approach I am consistent with much of the current literature in the field (e.g. Grant 1996; Hedlund 1994; Kogut and Zander 1992; Nonaka and Takeuchi 1995; Spender 1996), but perhaps not with the related bodies of work on intellectual capital (e.g. Edvinsson and Malone 1997) and organizational learning (e.g. Fiol and Lyles 1985; Huber 1991; Levitt and March 1988).

One of the basic distinctions in the knowledge management literature is between tacit and articulate knowledge. The 'hardware' side or the articulate form of knowledge is that which is represented explicitly in physical or material objects such as a patent. It is the know-what or information (Kogut and Zander 1992). Tacit knowledge (Hedlund and Nonaka 1993; Polanyi 1962), the 'software' side, is intuitive, non-verbalized, and not yet articulated. It is the know-how and know-why, or the practical skills or expertise, that allow someone to work smoothly or efficiently (Kogut and Zander 1992; von Hippel 1988). While this distinction is well understood, management in many organizations seems to be caught in the time warp of Tayloristic routine work. To exaggerate somewhat, it is still believed that employees need only be taught how to perform their tasks through training courses involving manuals in which the individual steps required to complete the task are listed. However, this training only develops the cognitive knowledge dimension of an employee, and the development of the remaining skills often falls by the wayside (Brown and Duguid 1991; Quinn *et al.* 1996).

Such training represents a heavy focus by management on the development and transfer of explicit knowledge within the organization. However, this focus on only the explicit side of knowledge presents quite a challenge in a knowledge-based economy since research has shown that the majority of knowledge and an even greater portion of the valuable knowledge within an organization is tacit or implicit (Reber 1993; Snyder 1996). It is argued that this tacit knowledge is bound by both a physical and a social context, embodied in the language and behaviours of those using it, and, as a result, it is not receptive to being made explicit or codified through commodification or packaging. Thus, this tacit knowledge is locally specific and harder to get access to from across space or time (Westney 1993). As a result, it is more costly and more difficult to transfer it to other parts of the organization.

How then is it possible to transfer or disseminate tacit knowledge? It has been argued that the most effective means is actually not to codify it, but rather to transfer it through an implicit mode. According to Reber (1993), transfer through implicit mode means that 'the acquisition of knowledge takes place largely independently of conscious attempts to learn and largely in the absence of explicit knowledge about what was acquired'.

Researchers have observed employees solving work-related problems, skirting the formal organization by relying on informal organizing processes. Individuals collaborate with each other through an emergent and fluid structure of relationships and engage in patterns of exchange and communication to reduce the uncertainty of tasks (Pava 1983; Purser *et al.* 1992). Thus, the procedures required to fulfil the task are developed as the worker performs the task, demanding the creation and use of knowledge along the way (Purser *et al.* 1992; Stebbins and Shani 1995). As a result, it is argued that the most effective means to develop and transfer tacit knowledge is not through formal systems and structures but through informal interactive learning activities (Schön 1983; Snyder 1996, 1997).

2.1. Communities of Practice

One conceptual lens through which knowledge transfer can be studied is the evolving community of practice body of research. This research is based on the ethnographic study of Xerox service technicians during the late 1980s, when it was observed that there was a variance between the organization's formal description of work and the actual work performed. When the technicians were faced with problems for which the formal structure often did not provide solutions, they relied on the organization's informal systems for help, such as storytelling, conversation, mentoring, and experiential learning (Brown and Duguid 1991; Snyder 1997; Wenger 1998). This research has sparked considerable interest among academics in recent years, with many heralding the importance of communities of practice to the success of an organization.

Communities of practice are ethereal, with no real boundaries, and we are all members of numerous communities, both at work and in our social life. Communities are in a constant state of evolution as members come and go and commitment levels fluctuate. This fluidity creates difficulties when management wants to pin down communities of practice, determine their boundaries, and develop some form of recipe to manage them. Indeed, it is argued that this is not possible, owing to the pure informal nature of communities of practice (Wenger 1998). Thus, we must satisfy ourselves at this point with a definition that captures this fluidity and intangibility:

> a group of people informally and contextually bound who are applying a common competence in the pursuit of a common enterprise. (Brown and Duguid 1991; Lave and Wenger 1991; Snyder 1997; Wenger 1998)

To begin by explaining this definition, I will start with a simple definition of community and practice. A community implies a form of collaboration or collectivism, a group of people bound together. Practice can be thought of as the sustained pursuit of an enterprise or an undertaking that is contextually bound in a historical and social sense. Within an organization individuals belong to several communities of practice. Thus, an individual may belong to one community of practice that performs the same job (e.g. Xerox technical representatives), one that works together on a shared task (e.g. software developers), or one that develops a product (e.g. engineers, marketers, and manufacturing specialists) (Brown and Gray 1997). It is also important to point out here that communities do not exist only within the traditional boundaries of the firm. Rather they extend beyond these boundaries to include members who may be working on a similar type of problem at another firm.

Through three aspects, 'narration, social construction, and collaboration', employees become members of and build communities of practice within their organization (Brown and Duguid 1991). First, through the narration of stories, employees help each other to make sense of non-canonical or unexpected circumstances. Used in this manner, stories are more flexible than strict documentation such as training manuals since they provide the ability to interpret each new situation (Brown and Duguid 1991). The second aspect of a community of practice is the collaboration that occurs between its members. With knowledge-intensive tasks, often no one individual can solve the problem on his or her own owing to the inability to know everything. By relying on the community, individuals can perform their work without needing to know everything. In addition, many employees are confronted with information overload. Through asking someone in the community for help, time does not have to be spent sorting though piles of information for relevant documents (Wenger 1998). Through collaboration and storytelling, the members of a community of practice socially construct their world, the third aspect of a community of practice. Both a tacit and explicit means of communication and working are developed that enable the community to perform its practice in a satisfying manner. The explicit includes its own language and vocabulary, codified procedures, documents, regulations, etc. But more interestingly, the tacit is the invisible, the implicit relations, cues, unarticulated etiquette, etc.—the invisible glue that holds the community together (Boland and Tenkasi 1995; Brown and Duguid 1991; Wenger 1998). Thus, the members become bound together by the context of the situation and in an informal manner, creating the social fabric of the organization (Brown and Duguid 1991).

In order for narration, collaboration, and social construction to be supported within a community of practice, researchers argue that it is important to build identity and trust. To obtain access to the community and its knowledge, it is necessary for an individual to become an 'insider'. This occurs through a process of legitimization, primarily through storytelling, during which the individual learns the language and values of the community, while, most importantly, how to function as a community member (Lave and Wenger 1991). In addition, research has shown that when members of a community of practice did not feel a high level of shared trust and commitment, their capacity to share knowledge and skills was reduced (Snyder 1997).

2.2. *Operationalizing Communities of Practice*

While the amount of papers and articles focusing on communities of practice continues to grow, few researchers have attempted to understand the relation between communities of practice and performance. This is understandable because they are—by definition—extremely hard to pin down. Any individual can potentially be involved in numerous communities of practice both within the firm and crossing the firm's traditional boundaries. Moreover, the process of defining the membership of communities of practice apparently takes away their very essence because they thrive on their informal nature. Bearing this in mind, it is not surprising that the community of practice literature is populated with ethnographies and case-studies rather than surveys or experiments.

My approach in this chapter is to bring community of practice thinking down to the level of the individual. Rather than attempt to define the communities of practice within and outside of the firm's boundaries, I work instead on the basis that an individual's performance at work is associated with the extent to which he or she is a member of various communities of practice. Thus, by measuring the patterns of communication of the individual with various groups of people, and through various different forums, one can predict to some degree his or her performance. In the next section I formally develop this idea into a series of testable propositions.

3. Conceptual Framework and Propositions

As defined earlier, knowledge management involves both the acquisition of new knowledge from outside the boundaries of the firm and the leverage of existing knowledge within the firm. This definition, however, is deliberately vague on the level at which the knowledge acquisition and leverage occur, because it can potentially occur at all levels—the individual, the group, the business unit, and the firm. As suggested by Hedlund (1994), it is the ability to transfer knowledge between levels of analysis (e.g. from the individual level to the firm level and vice versa) that is valuable, and indeed one of the major characteristics that make the firm unique.

This chapter is concerned with two levels of analysis: the individual and the community of practice. The logic here is that individuals are able to draw from their communities of practice to solve problems they encounter in the course of their work, and that they also contribute back to these communities in a reciprocal manner. Thus, the extent to which an individual is actively involved in communities of practice will *ceteris paribus* be associated with superior performance at work.

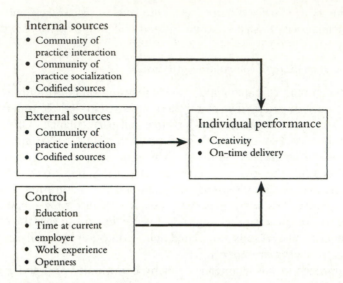

Fɪɢ. 7.1. Conceptual framework

But, as I have already noted, there are significant methodological problems in studying communities of practice. My primary concern is that the concept is typically defined in such a way that all informal interactions, inside or outside the firm, could represent participation in communities of practice. If this broad definition is accepted, then the concept becomes very difficult to research in a rigorous manner because nothing is excluded. The theory, in other words, cannot be falsified.

The approach taken here, as hinted above, is to move down to the level of the individual, and to examine the way in which that individual acquires new knowledge to address work-related problems. Some knowledge, as we will see, is gained through access to 'codified' sources such as the internet or company databases, but most is gained through interaction with other people in the firm and outside. My premiss, in other words, is that the frequency and quality of the interaction an individual has with specific groups of individuals is a manifestation of the communities of practice with which he or she is involved. And that such interactions will have a positive impact on his or her individual-level performance.

The conceptual framework in Figure 7.1 illustrates my approach. Individual-level performance, I argue, is a function of the various ways knowledge is acquired by the individual, and the sources of that knowledge can be divided into (1) internal versus external sources, and (2) community of practice relations versus codified sources. In addition there are many other factors contributing to individual-level performance, some of which are empirically examined as controls.

3.1. Proposition Development

The first proposition follows directly from the discussion about the nature of communities of practice inside the firm. As stated above, individuals within organizations are thought to be members of numerous communities of practice. Researchers claim that the creation and exchange of tacit knowledge occurs in the interaction between the individual and other community members when solving work-related problems. Being an active member of communities within the organization implies a high degree of collaboration and interaction with other members through primarily face-to-face but also non-face-to-face interactions. A high degree of interactions with other community members should therefore lead to a greater individual development of task-related knowledge and thus higher performance.

(1) The higher the level of individual personal interaction with communities within the firm, the higher the level of individual performance.

For an individual to become truly a member of a community of practice and access the community's knowledge, it is argued that he or she must not only have a high degree of interaction, but also become an 'insider' through the development of trust with other members of the community (Lave and Wenger 1991). Through a high level of trust, the member learns of other members' mistakes and breakthroughs through storytelling and narration of work-related happenings. While trust is difficult to measure, and particularly so when the community in question is not clearly specified, one manifestation of it is in the existence of social contacts outside work. Thus:

(2) Social contacts with community members from work leads to a higher level of individual performance.

The two propositions above are concerned with an individual's participation in communities of practice within the boundaries of the organization. However, it is central to the concept of communities of practice that they also spread across organizational boundaries, through professional or technical relationships. These communities may involve members from the suppliers, customers, or even friends working on similar tasks in other companies. A high degree of interaction with members of communities that cross organizational boundaries can be expected to broaden the individual's knowledge through the exchange of knowledge from outside the firm. Thus, much in the same manner as proposition 1, proposition 3 becomes the following:

(3) The higher the level of individual personal interaction with members of communities that spread across organizational boundaries, the higher the level of performance.

Propositions 4 and 5 are concerned with the acquisition of knowledge through codified sources. The spread of the internet and the development of intranets are factors that have led to this explosion of rapidly accessible codified knowledge. While communities of practice are understood to be the channels for the development and exchange of primarily tacit knowledge, the use of codified sources of data such as company documents facilitates an individual when solving work-related tasks. For example, access to an internal document can help an individual to avoid reinventing the wheel, thus facilitating the completion of a work-related task. This codification and documentation of knowledge within the firm is one of the main thrusts of management in organizations in order to ensure the transfer and application of knowledge throughout the firm.

(4) The higher the use of internal codified sources of information, the higher the level of individual performance.

In addition to company-specific codified knowledge, individuals also have access to numerous sources of codified knowledge outside the firm. In today's fast-changing world, the knowledge required to solve a new, challenging task may not exist inside the firm, thus the individual may have to search outside the firm for help.

(5) The higher the use of external codified sources of information, the higher the level of performance.

Many other factors are also expected to be associated with individual performance. In this study I measured the education level of the individual, the amount of time he or she has spent with Icon Medialab, and his or her general work experience. In addition I measured individuals' perceptions of how open the work environment was at Icon because it is a factor that is likely to affect their propensity to exchange information with others.

Finally, I would like to make a few comments concerning the dependent variable of individual performance. First, it is worth observing that individual-level performance is not a uni-dimensional construct. At the very least, we would expect to see a split between 'exploration' and 'exploitation' (March 1991), where exploration would be manifested as creativity or the development of novel solutions, while exploitation would be manifested in the ability to get work done on time and on budget. However, given the exploratory nature of this research, I have not specified any a priori expectations regarding the type of performance associations I expect to see. Secondly, I would like to point out that I am only making observations about individual performance and not trying to make any great leaps to firm performance. To give an example, an individual may feel that he has a high level of creative performance; however, this might not necessarily be beneficial to the firm's performance. Also, as will be discussed below, the measures of performance did not work out as clearly as I would have liked.

4. Research Method

4.1. Sample and Analysis

The research was undertaken in a single firm, Icon Medialab. As already mentioned, the choice of Icon was motivated primarily on the basis that it is a quintessential 'IT-intensive' firm, in which a large proportion of the employees are working on a day-to-day basis with the latest internet technology. Many of these employees, it turns out, are interacting frequently with communities of 'techies' whom they have never met. As such, this setting represents a fascinating test of the communities of practice concept.

It should be noted that Icon is based in Stockholm. This was convenient for me, but it is also quite an opportune location for studying such a firm because Sweden is at the forefront of digital communications technology. The country has one of the highest penetration rates in the world of mobile telephones and internet subscriptions per capita, and Stockholm is a recognized high-technology 'cluster'. Icon is one of many recent start-up internet firms in the area (founded 1996), and one of the world's best 350 small companies, according to Forbes (1998). A description of the company follows the discussion on measures.

Two phases of data collection and analysis were conducted. The first phase was conducted at the Swedish office, in which thirty in-depth field interviews were held from May 1998 to June 1998. People at different areas of the company, e.g. corporate management, business development, sales, and different production competencies, were interviewed for one-and-a-half to two hours each. Interviews with management were conducted first in order to understand the formal structures that had been put in place to facilitate knowledge acquisition mechanisms. Extensive written material was also collected from the companies. At the end of this phase it was decided to focus primarily on the technically focused competencies (techies), the programmers and web designers, owing to their heavy use of explicit sources of information and storytelling.

The second phase of the data collection involved a questionnaire sent to all eighty-eight techies of Icon Medialab at their local offices. Questionnaires were then sealed in individual envelopes and returned to us by mail. Of the eighty-eight questionnaires, seventy-two usable questionnaires were collected, an eighty-two per cent response rate. Throughout the data collection process, individuals were assured that their responses would be kept confidential and that all results would be presented on an aggregated level. In addition to these individual questionnaires, each of the managing directors of the eight subsidiaries and seven managers at the Stockholm office were asked to complete a questionnaire relating to the performance of the individuals at their office. The average age of the respondents was 26.8 years with an average of 363 days employed at Icon and 3.1 years' experience in their competence. The sample was 17 per cent women.

4.2. Measures

Dependent variables. Several different approaches exist for measuring performance, including both subjective and objective measurements. For the purposes of this study I used two different dependent variables that measure individual performance.

1. Creativity. Individuals were asked to answer three questions that created a creativity scale (Sjöberg and Lind 1994). These were based on a seven-point scale from 1, 'strongly disagree', to 7, 'strongly agree' (three items, $\alpha = 0.63$).
2. On-time performance. The second performance measure asked respondents to answer to what degree they felt they delivered their work on time on a seven-point scale from 1, 'strongly disagree', to 7, 'strongly agree' (two items, $\alpha = 0.71$).

In addition, I asked the managers in each of the offices to rate the performance of each individual reporting to him or her on two different items: ability to meet superior's objectives and to develop creative solutions. The two items were strongly correlated with each other ($\rho = 0.71$), while the correlation with the various self-reported performance measures was weak to moderate (between 0.25 and 0.42). After discussing this matter with several of these individuals, it became clear that the managers often had remarkably limited contact with many of their direct reports, and that they could not easily assess their performance. I therefore concluded that the self-reported performance measures were more valid, an observation that is consistent with a number of previous studies (e.g. Heneman 1974; Wexley *et al.* 1980).[1]

Independent variables. These variables included the different dimensions of the knowledge acquisition processes, and I have chosen to split them on the external versus internal dimension. The external mechanisms consisted of two measures. The first measure which relates to proposition 5, codified—external, asked respondents to answer on a seven-point scale the frequency of use of external knowledge sources. These sources included traditional sources such as externally produced books or journals in addition to sources such as internet web pages or internet discussion forums (five items, $\alpha = 0.66$). The second measure, external community interaction, was measured on a four-point scale relating to the degree of interaction on work-related matters with customers and friends. Respondents were asked

---

[1] It is worth noting in passing that the significant correlates with manager-rated performance were (*a*) age of employee, and (*b*) *lack of* socialization with other people outside work. In other words, managers believe that older employees without social contacts with colleagues are the better performers!

how often they initiated the interaction as well as how often the external party initiated the interaction (four items, $\alpha = 0.76$). This measure relates to proposition 3.

The second group of variables, internal mechanisms, consisted of three different measures. The first measure relating to proposition 4, codified—internal, asked respondents to answer on a seven-point scale the frequency of use of internal knowledge sources. These included using the company's intranet as well as materials such as documents that were produced internally by Icon (three items, $\alpha = 0.73$). The next measure, interaction with internal community, relates to proposition 1 and was based on a four-point frequency scale on two dimensions. The first one was based on whether it was the respondent who initiated the interaction and the second one based on whether the other party initiated the interaction. This measure was built upon the interaction with others within the same function, others within one's work group, and others outside of one's work group (three items, $\alpha = 0.77$). For example, the work group of a programmer included art directors and web designers, as these three functions comprised the production team for each project. Those outside of the programmer's work group included those in support functions, e.g. sales, or those in management functions, e.g. human resources. The final measure, social contact, was measured through the level of social contact outside work with any individual throughout the organization. This was measured on a simple 1–2 scale, 1 for no and 2 for yes (three items, $\alpha = 0.90$) and relates to proposition 2.

Control variables. These variables included level of education (1–5 scale), time employed at Icon (number of days), related work experience (years),[2] and openness. Openness was created to measure the level of openness at Icon perceived by the individual on a seven-point scale from 1, 'strongly disagree', to 7, 'strongly agree' (eleven items, $\alpha = 0.68$). Summary statistics for the control variables and the other variables are presented in Table 7.1.

The propositions were tested through a series of stepwise regression models. The stepwise approach was chosen primarily because of the small sample size and the relatively large number of independent variables. Also, the exploratory nature of the study made it appropriate to work with a rather larger number of independent variables than would normally be the case.

4.3. Company Description

Icon Medialab was founded in March 1996 in response to the rapid growth of the internet.[3] The company's mission is to provide digital communication

---

[2] In order to avoid multicollinearity problems, I decided not to include age as it correlated highly with related work experience.

[3] The digital communications market is among the fastest-growing markets ever. In a report by the International Data Corporation the market for internet services is predicted to grow from $US2.5 bn. in 1996 to $US13.8 bn. in 2000.

TABLE 7.1. *Descriptive statistics and correlations for all variables*

Variable	Unit	Mean	Standard deviation	1	2	3	4	5	6	7	8	9	10
Self-evaluated performance													
1. Creativity	1–7 scale	4.83	1.04										
2. On-time performance	1–7 scale	4.80	1.38	0.19									
Control													
3. Education	1–5 scale	2.85	1.11	0.07	-0.21								
4. Related work experience	Years	3.08	2.77	0.32[a]	0.16	0.27							
5. Employed at Icon	Days	362.51	271.32	0.12	0.10	0.10	0.45[b]						
6. Office openness	1–7 scale	5.03	0.65	0.42[c]	0.29[a]	-0.14	0.29[a]	0.10					
External													
7. Codified	1–7 scale	4.00	1.25	0.17	-0.09	0.14	0.35[c]	0.06	0.12				
8. External community interaction	1–4 scale	2.46	0.84	0.23	0.12	0.07	0.27[a]	0.31[a]	0.37[c]	0.43[b]			
Internal													
9. Codified	1–7 scale	3.20	1.38	-0.06	0.24	0.04	0.04	-0.25[a]	0.21	0.26[a]	0.04		
10. Interaction with internal community	1–4 scale	3.07	0.60	0.31[a]	0.41[c]	0.07	0.26	0.22	0.20	0.16	0.24	0.06	
11. Social contact	1, no; 2, yes	1.34	0.46	0.43[c]	0.07	0.20	0.30	-0.07	0.20	0.10	0.01	0.22	0.41[c]

Note. Range of N is 49–72.

[a] $p < 0.05$.
[b] $p < 0.001$.
[c] $p < 0.01$.

services and products to its customers, e.g. internet homepages, intranets, extranet, and e-commerce. Icon Medialab's clients range from the Swedish Postal Office and Compaq to British Petroleum and Volkswagen. The company posted sales of SEK 65m. for the fiscal year ending April 1998 (SEK 13m. in 1997) and at the time of this study had 242 employees with 46 per cent of these in Sweden. The remaining employees were spread throughout offices of ten to twenty-five employees in Spain, Finland, Denmark, Germany, Belgium, England, and the USA, with new offices planned for France and Norway.

A strategy of rapid global growth was developed by the founders at the company's inception. One of the means by which Icon hoped to achieve profitable growth was through the reuse of knowledge developed throughout its different projects. In fact, management set a target that more than 50 per cent of all projects should include already proven successful products or services. Thus, Icon Medialab invested heavily in building its structural capital, with the key objectives to transfer and reuse knowledge complemented with follow-up and reporting.

In addition, Icon Medialab was unique in its representation of a mixture of competencies under the same organizational umbrella. These disciplines included technology, design, usability engineering, statistics and analysis, media and entertainment, and business strategy, representing the six sides of the 'Icon cube'. Thus, Icon Medialab brought together art directors, behavioural scientists, copywriters, journalists, scriptwriters, animators, TV producers, software programmers, management consultants, and web designers, with accounting, personnel, and administration completing the organization.

5. Results

The propositions were tested using multiple regression analysis. Because there were two different performance constructs, creativity and on-time performance, the analysis for each was conducted separately.

Results for self-reported creativity. As shown in Table 7.2, I received support for propositions 2 and 5. Thus, the higher the level of social contact and the higher the use of external codified sources, the higher the level of individual creative performance. In addition, there was one significant control variable: openness ($p < 0.05$). Overall these three predictor variables explain 45 per cent of the variance in self-reported creativity.

Results for self-reported on-time performance. Again looking at Table 7.2, proposition 4 is supported. In other words, use of codified internal sources of knowledge is positively related to on-time performance ($p < 0.01$). Propositions 1–3 did not receive support, while proposition 5 received support but in the opposite direction to that which was expected. In other words, the higher the use of external codified sources of knowledge, the lower

TABLE 7.2. *Results of regression analysis of the relationship between knowledge acquisition mechanisms and individual performance*

Variable	Propositions	Self-reported creativity		Self-reported on-time performance	
		Variables included	Variables excluded	Variables included	Variables excluded
Control					
4. Education			−0.00		−0.11
5. Work experience			0.10		−0.04
6. Time at Icon			−0.22		−0.09
7. Office openness		0.42ᵃ		0.28ᵇ	
External knowledge					
8. Codified external	5	0.35ᵃ		−0.31ᵃ	
9. External community interaction	3		−0.22		−0.06
Internal knowledge					
10. Codified internal	4		0.11	0.55ᶜ	
11. Internal community interaction	1		0.06		0.26
12. Social contact outside work	2	0.30ᵇ			0.08
R^2		0.51		0.48	
ΔR^2		0.45		0.42	
F for ΔR^2		8.31ᶜ		7.43ᶜ	

ᵃ $p < 0.05$.
ᵇ $p < 0.10$.
ᶜ $p < 0.01$.

the level of individual on-time performance. In addition, the perceived level of openness was also a significant predictor of on-time performance ($p < 0.10$).

6. Discussion

Table 7.3 provides an overview of the support for the different propositions from the different regression models. Altogether we can see some support for propositions 2, 4, and 5, but of course what is interesting here is the fact that we see such different results for the two dependent variables. Following is a discussion of the regression findings related to our qualitative findings.

6.1. Creativity

Taking creativity first, we see social contact outside work and the use of external codified sources of information (internet communities and the like) as the significant predictors. Building on our qualitative findings, the impression one gets is that technical employees attach great importance to their external internet-based relationships as sources of ideas and as ways of solving tricky problems. Several programmers even stated that they preferred to go first to their internet community or use their private e-mail list for help instead of asking someone at their own company even if he or she was sitting at the next desk. This appeared to be for several reasons. The first was that by posting a question in an open forum, people were not obligated to help. Instead those who wanted to help could do so in a voluntary fashion. By reaching out to the community for help, one did not disturb a colleague at work who had his or her own schedule and deadlines to meet. Another reason was that people could access a much broader source of expertise than at their own company. Members of the communities worked at different types of company all over the world; however, they worked on the same type of problem. Thus, it was felt that this enabled one to gain access to the latest thinking within one's field.

Another quite interesting reason for the use of electronic communities that I uncovered during the qualitative phase was that prestige played a significant role in which source one turned to for help. Several commented that programmers feared making mistakes or making themselves look stupid by asking others at Icon for help, so they turned to the internet, where 'no one knows if you're a monkey'. Another aspect was that it was seen as prestigious if one belonged to some of the closed internet communities.

To turn the discussion to the second predictor, social contact, individuals became members of a tightly knit community of practice through extensive social contact outside work. During this social contact these individuals discussed the difficult problems encountered during the day, the responses

TABLE 7.3. *Support for propositions*

Proposition	Creativity	On-time
(1) Interaction with internal community		
(2) Social contact outside work	0.30[a]	
(3) Interaction with external community		
(4) Codified internal		0.55[b]
(5) Codified external	0.35[c]	−0.31[c]

[a] $p < 0.10$.
[b] $p < 0.01$.
[c] $p < 0.05$.

received from the electronic community, and how they then attempted to solve the problem. The latest solutions or tips from both the outside communities and one's own work were passed between the members of the community. In this manner, these community members socially constructed their world through the narration of stories, turning incoherent data into coherent information. This enabled them to gain insights into the work they were performing, allowing them to be more creative in their daily work.

6.2. On-Time Performance

In terms of achieving on-time performance, a very different picture emerges. Here, the use of internal codified sources of information is a predictor of performance, while the use of external codified sources is a negative predictor. This is entirely in keeping with our intuitive expectations. Building relationships with external communities and creating unique or 'elegant' solutions on the basis of those relationships works well when creativity is the objective, but it is a strong negative when on-time delivery matters. Gathering information from the outside takes time because first either the sources must be located or one must wait for someone to help voluntarily. And once the information or help is received, it must be assimilated into the context of both the problem and the company's way of doing things. This may take considerable time depending on the complexity of the information and the problem. In addition, reciprocity within these electronic communities is necessary in order to become a true member. In other words, to be able to ask the other internet community members for help, one must prove that one also gives back to the community through providing help to others when these members ask.

Thus, on-time performance can best be achieved by reusing existing solutions that can be accessed through the firm's intranet or company documents. To give an example from Icon, the company's intranet included a programming module database that included both a description for the sales force and a technical description for the programmers. Programming modules were building-blocks of programming code that could be reused in a number of customer projects, such as a discussion forum, telephone book, and conference room booking system. In addition to a technical description, the module list also specified how many hours were required to develop the module. This information was added to help determine the pricing and planning of future projects.

7. Implications for Theory and Practice

This study raises a number of very interesting theoretical and practical issues. First, what do we make of the concept of the community of practice in the light of these findings? Some support was clearly found, in terms of the importance of work-related and social interaction with other community members. But there were also some surprises, notably the importance of so-called 'internet communities' as sources of knowledge for technical employees. This is a curious discovery because these 'communities' exhibit many of the characteristics of communities of practice—reciprocity, identity, and so on—but the individuals involved have typically never met, and they work through what is by definition a codified exchange of information, which goes against other aspects of the theory. One programmer commented,

I've been really active in the internet community for a long time. I'm in contact with a group of about 20 people who are experts at what they do. But I have never met them physically. But it doesn't matter because on the internet we have always been friends. It's just like when you used to go snowboarding 10 years ago. If you were somewhere and saw another snowboarder, you said hi and then you would hang out together in the evening. Just because we snowboarded and there were so few who did it. We were on the same level. . . . we knew where we were with one another.

The development of these electronic communities has added a spoke of a new dimension to the wheel of network relations. As a result, we need to revisit certain aspects of community of practice theory as well as other theories within the network of social relationships field to understand better which theories are still valid and which need to be adapted to the new empirical contexts.

The second implication from these findings is that the building of the capability to manage these knowledge flows presents a considerable challenge for a company's management on several dimensions. First, as I found in my research, on-time performance was negatively correlated to the use of external codified sources. Too much external knowledge leads to missed deadlines. Opportunity cost may be partly the reason for this finding; however, based on my qualitative findings, the aspect of prestige including the 'not-invented-here' syndrome—the desire to develop one's own solutions rather than reuse existing solutions—plays a significant role in the choice of knowledge sources.

While it was found that this matter of prestige was strong within Icon, it may have its roots outside Icon's borders in the global community, primarily among the programmers. One programmer explained that he started working on one project because he really wanted to show Silicon Valley that other areas of the world could produce 'bleeding-edge' products as well. While, on the one hand, programmers were inspired to make Icon the world's best company, on the other hand, programmers were pressured by their global community to produce the latest 'cool' solution. In addition, programmers were under a form of social pressure from their external community to help fellow members solve their difficult problems, often attempting to 'show off' in front of the others. This was found to lead to conflicting goals for the programmers: best company versus best function. Creating a cool solution or trying to impress a global community through solving another member's difficult problem leads to longer hours worked, using unnecessary resources, as well as causing delays in product delivery to the customer.

The challenge for management is then to be able to balance the use of these external sources, ensuring creativity and access to the latest solutions while at the same time avoiding the overuse of these, leading to an inefficient use of resources. This is no new challenge, merely the exploration versus exploitation balance in a new setting. What perhaps has intensified this challenge is that as the internet technology develops so rapidly, management may have difficulty in keeping abreast of the developments, making it a challenge to know whether employees are working on necessary value-adding activities. One manager summed up this situation with reference to the programmers. 'Programmers take us [management] hostage. We never know whether they're working on extra bells and whistles to impress their buddies or whether it's really a value-adding activity for the customer.'

A second challenge for management is how to link the external knowledge networks with the internal networks in order to ensure that creative, new ideas are passed on throughout the firm from the entry-point. As I have shown, a high level of the use of external codified sources was related to a high level of creative performance. In order for new creative knowledge then to be applied in different settings and exploited throughout the rest of the firm, this knowledge needs to be spread through the internal knowledge networks of the organization.

Another point to raise, with both theoretical and practical implications, is that different patterns of knowledge acquisition are associated with different outcomes. Intuitively this is not surprising at all, but it is important because it allows us to take a more critical perspective on the field of knowledge management. The normative bias among many researchers in the knowledge management field is simply to assume that more knowledge flow is better. In this study I have shown clearly that too much codified external knowledge acquisition is detrimental to on-time performance. Again, there is not the space here to explore this finding in any detail, but it confirms that once one actually measures patterns of knowledge flow in detail, there are cases when 'more is not better'.

In terms of the limitations of this study, I acknowledge that there is a need to look at more than one firm, and preferably with a larger sample of respondents, before coming up with any definitive conclusions. The questionnaire suffers from common-method bias, so ideally I would also complement some of these measures with secondary data on, for example, meetings attended, e-mails sent, hours on the web. But such a data collection process would be extremely time-consuming and difficult to arrange.

Finally, it is important to acknowledge that my choice of communities of practice as my theoretical lens has its drawbacks. As noted several times, it is almost impossible to define communities of practice in an operational way, so one ends up falling back on measuring individual-level patterns of interaction. And having moved in that direction, there are a number of other theoretical angles that could and perhaps should be incorporated, such as the vast literature on groups, environmental scanning, and organizational cognition. These are issues that I will consider in future research.

PART III

Managing the Internal Network

8

Building an Internal Market System: Insights from Five R. & D. Organizations

JULIAN BIRKINSHAW AND CARL F. FEY

1. Introduction

The focus of this chapter is on the networks of relationships that exist between entities inside the boundaries of the firm. As argued in Chapter 1, there is a widespread shift away from what might be called the 'traditional' hierarchical organization model, and towards various 'network' models. One variety of network involves building stronger and more interdependent relationships between separate companies. These have been discussed at length in Chapters 2 to 4. Another variety involves freeing up the relationships within the firm, to foster entrepreneurship and responsibility in individual units, and to make the entire organization more adaptive to environmental changes. A number of different terms are used to refer to this model. In this chapter we will call it an 'internal market' as a means of highlighting several important features such as freedom of choice, entrepreneurship, competition, and the use of a price system.

The term 'internal market' is deliberately provocative. We know that the firm is not a market, so why confuse the terminology by mixing up the two concepts? Our answer is that a clear understanding of the advantages of the market, and the workings of the market process, shed light on a number of the shortcomings of traditional organizational design. The implication is that some form of hybrid organization can be construed that may—under certain circumstances—be superior to either a traditional market or a traditional hierarchy. This hybrid model can be justified on a theoretical basis, as this chapter will show. But more importantly, there is also evidence that it exists in practice as well. By way of introduction to the idea, then, it is worth while to highlight a few examples of what we mean by an internal market system.

1. Hewlett Packard operates with a highly decentralized divisional structure, whereby each division has more or less complete autonomy to decide

what technologies and products it will focus on. This often results in internal competition between divisions, or 'charter wars' in their terminology, as divisions vie with one another for the right to make, for example, HP's next-generation laser printer. This approach necessitates some duplication of resources, but it has also given HP great flexibility. Unlike most high-technology firms, HP has been very adept at 'catching the wave' every time a new technology or business emerges.

2. Ericsson's R. & D. organization operates on a fairly centralized basis when it comes to making large funding decisions, but the question of where a new investment will be made involves a considerable degree of choice. In most cases there are several design centres around the world that can take on a given piece of work (most work is software development), and Ericsson now encourages a process in which the two or three short-listed candidates are encouraged to 'bid' for the investment.

3. SEB, a large financial services firm in Sweden, deliberately uses competing channels to market. For example, SEB's customers can do their banking by walking into a branch, over the telephone, or by internet. Each of these channels is run by a separate business unit, with the clear understanding that they be allowed to 'steal' customers from one another. This creates some duplication, but at the same time it makes good business sense as a means of 'keeping options open'. No one knows how important telephone or internet banking services will be, so as long as SEB offers them alongside its traditional retail network, it will retain its strong position. Perhaps in the long run one channel will come to dominate, in which case the others can be closed down. Or perhaps each channel will end up specializing in a certain type of customer. But while there is a high degree of uncertainty in market evolution, a competing channel approach is appropriate.

4. ABB gives its operating companies great autonomy. Each company has its own financial statements, and is free to choose its own suppliers and customers from inside or outside the ABB system. By not requiring ABB companies to do business with one another, competition is introduced at every step in the value chain, and activities are made more efficient. At the same time, ABB's senior managers spend a lot of time building co-operative relationships between companies to ensure that the whole is greater than the sum of the parts.

As these brief examples suggest, the traditional logic of competition in the market-place and co-operation in the firm is too simplistic. Some firms, like HP and SEB, are happy to incur at least temporary competition between units while there is some uncertainty about what technology or product will prevail. Ericsson encourages competition for 'charters' as a means of ensuring that investment goes to the optimum location. And ABB pits internal suppliers and customers against external ones to ensure that every unit is competitive against the industry benchmark. The point, in short, is that market-like principles are often applied inside firms, and it is the purpose of this chapter to go some way towards understanding this phenomenon and to provide some systematic evidence for it.

The rest of the chapter is organized as follows. In Section 2 we provide a theoretical discussion of the concept of internal markets. In Sections 3 and 4 we describe the methodology and the findings from a recent empirical study, in which we examined the R. & D. organizations of five firms and considered the extent to which they were adopting an internal market model. Finally, in the discussion section we return to the broader issues—whether we really see internal market systems inside firms; how corporate management's role changes in such systems; and the sorts of capabilities that are needed to make them successful.

2. Theoretical Background

We define an internal market as a mode of governance in which market-like organizing mechanisms are used within the legal boundaries of the firm. In other words, an internal market is seen as a hybrid form of organizing between the polar forms of 'market' and 'hierarchy'. While the dichotomy between market and hierarchy has been widely understood since Coase (1937), it is increasingly recognized that most transactions end up taking place not within these polar forms but in the 'swollen middle' (Hennart 1993) between pure market and pure hierarchy—under such arrangements as strategic alliances, joint ventures, franchise arrangements, and internal markets.

Why is this? An important part of the answer is provided by Hennart (1993), who makes the distinction between organizing methods (hierarchy and price) and institutions (firms and markets). This suggests two different forms of hybrid: (1) market-based transactions that incorporate elements of hierarchy such as trust, forbearance, and identity; and (2) firm-based transactions that are organized through the price system. The former, as manifest in strategic alliances, joint ventures, outsourcing relationships, franchise arrangements, and so on, has received considerable research attention in recent years (e.g. Hennart 1988; Kogut 1988; Thorelli 1987). The latter has received far less research attention. There is a large literature on transfer pricing within the firm (Cook 1955; Eccles 1982; Hirschleifer 1956), but it has become more applied over the years and has therefore avoided the discrete structural analysis approach. And the broader idea of the internal market can be picked up sporadically in the literature (Arrow 1959; Buckley 1997; Halal 1994; March and Simon 1958; Williamson 1975) but without ever developing as a subject for research in its own right.[1]

---

[1] Note that this literature considers many different forms of internal markets: markets for capital, people, products, services, and so on. Our focus, as is discussed later, is explicitly on the internal market for intermediate technologies between R. & D. and business units.

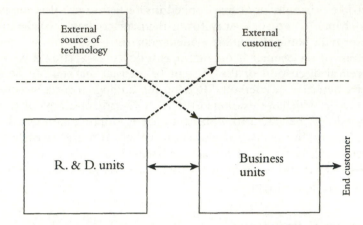

FIG. 8.1. Internal market relations between R. & D. unit and business unit

Under what conditions might the internal market be an efficient mode of governance? In large part we subscribe to Hennart's (1993) answer to this question. He argues that the price system encourages cheating and hierarchy encourages shirking. Thus, to minimize total organizing costs (costs of shirking plus cheating) most transactions embody elements of both market and hierarchy. However, we also concur with Simon's (1991: 28) argument that 'the economic system is nearly in neutral equilibrium between the use of market transactions and authority relations to handle any particular matter'. As he observes, we see a wide spectrum of governance modes coexisting, and we see firms shifting from one mode to another often without obvious efficiency gains or losses. If the system really is close to 'neutral equilibrium', the efficiency criterion becomes of lesser importance in determining which mode of governance will emerge.

2.1. Internal Markets in R. & D. Organizations

The empirical context of this study is the resource allocation process in the R. & D. organizations of large firms. This can be conceptualized as a market in which there are 'sellers' of R. & D. outputs, hereafter called R. & D. units, and there are 'buyers' of R. & D. outputs, hereafter called business units (see Figure 8.1). In some ways this may seem a strange context in which to study internal market systems. Both theory and casual observation suggest that the complexity and intangible nature of R. & D. outputs makes them unlikely candidates for market-like transactions. Our approach, then, is to see the R. & D. context as an extreme test of the internal market concept. If we can find evidence of firms using internal market systems in their R. & D. organizations, the chances are good that they are also being used in other contexts.

Historically, the R. & D. resource allocation process has been undertaken in large part within the boundaries of the firm using a hierarchical organizing system. There are two main theoretical arguments for explaining the dominance of this approach. One is the transaction cost logic, which suggests that internalizing the transaction between the R. & D. organization and the rest of the firm will be efficient. For example, Teece (1985) argued that the commercialization of an innovation typically requires co-specialized downstream assets which for transaction cost reasons are better kept within the firm. A second, but related, argument can be traced back to Schumpeter (1942). It suggests that breakthrough technologies cannot withstand the short-termism of the market-place because of the length of time they take to commercialize and the resistance they face from existing technologies. Schumpeter saw the firm as a vehicle for 'protecting' new ideas in their formative stages and thus as the principal enabler of breakthrough technological change.

While not denying these arguments, our supposition is that the internal market mode of governance can still provide most of the benefits of a pure firm, while also increasing the efficiency of internal resource allocation. It should be clear, then, that we are not assuming internal markets exist. Rather, we are starting with the base case scenario that resource allocation decisions in R. & D. organizations occur through a hierarchical organizing system, and we are looking for deviations from that base case.

Why do we believe that the internal market mode of governance may be emerging in large firms? The basic line of argument, as presented in Chapter 1, goes back to the assumptions underlying the concept of hierarchy. Hedlund (1994) offers a detailed critique of Simon's (1962) definitive work on hierarchy, and he suggests that the term refers to (1) pre-specification and stability, (2) instrumental parts and additive influence on the whole, and (3) universality and unidirectionality. Hedlund then goes on to argue that the contemporary business environment and the modern firm challenge all three of these assumptions. Technological change, globalization, and deregulation remove the stability that arguably existed in the post-war years. And instrumentality and universality are compromised when the subsidiary units of multinational corporations are the sources of new ideas and the home of strategic assets.

2.2. Characteristics of the Internal Market System

If we simply adopt Hennart's (1993) theory, the internal market system would be characterized by its use of prices as a means of organizing transactions in combination with administrative control of the sort seen in a traditional firm. Our belief, however, is that we can benefit from being much more explicit in defining the elements of the price system, and indeed in specifying what is meant by administrative control. In the empirical part of the chapter we will then consider each of the elements of this system in turn.

The value of the price system as an efficient means of organizing economic activity has been recognized for more than 100 years, but Hayek's (1945) seminal article provides the clearest elucidation of its benefits. Hayek argued that knowledge relevant to economic organization was dispersed among many people and could 'never be given to a single mind' (1945: 519), and furthermore that 'economic problems arise always and only in consequence of change'. On this basis, he showed that the price system was able to convey information more precisely and more rapidly than any other system. As he states (1945: 527):

the marvel is that in a case like that of a scarcity of one raw material, without an order being issued, without more than a handful of people knowing the cause, tens of thousands of people whose identity could not be ascertained by months of investigation are made to use the material or its products more sparingly, i.e. they move in the right direction.

While we subscribe to this argument, it seems that the underlying elements of the price system, as they affect the individual actor, can be more clearly explicated. The question, in other words, is what preconditions have to be in place for the individual actor or unit in the economic system to respond in the way Hayek described? The answer is provided in part by the thinking of Austrian economists on the 'market process' (Jacobson 1992; Kirzner 1973; von Mises 1949). Kirzner (1973), in particular, provided a detailed account of the entrepreneur whose 'alertness to opportunities' helps to reconcile the mismatches in supply and demand that exist at any moment in the market system and who thus keeps the market process moving forward towards equilibrium. If we examine this theory in terms of the market between R. & D. units and business units (Figure 8.2), we can identify two important sets of preconditions:

1. *Customer input into the resource allocation decision.* The decision by the R. & D. unit about what activities to undertake is based on the demands of the customer, which in this case is the firm's business units. Using Kirzner's (1973) logic, it is alertness to the needs of the customer that triggers a shift in the allocation of resources away from certain R. & D. projects and towards others. This is, of course, very different from the traditional approach in which resource allocation decisions are made centrally, and with a technology-driven focus.[2]

2. *Choice—for the business units, and for the R. & D. units.* It is a fundamental tenet of economic theory that competition between firms drives market efficiency. In Kirzner's (1973: 12) terms, actors systematically 'revise their bids and offers in the light of newly acquired knowledge of alternative

---

[2] Note, though, that by focusing on the immediate customer, i.e. the business unit, there is some risk that the long-term needs of the end consumer are not being addressed effectively. As discussed in Section 2.3, this is one of the biggest problems of the internal market system, in that it promotes efficiency ahead of effectiveness.

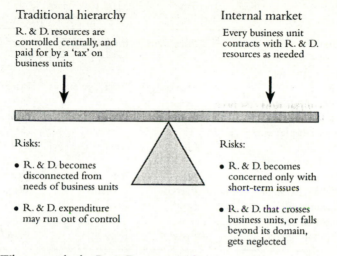

Traditional hierarchy	Internal market
R. & D. resources are controlled centrally, and paid for by a 'tax' on business units	Every business unit contracts with R. & D. resources as needed

Risks:

- R. & D. becomes disconnected from needs of business units

- R. & D. expenditure may run out of control

Risks:

- R. & D. becomes concerned only with short-term issues

- R. & D. that crosses business units, or falls beyond its domain, gets neglected

FIG. 8.2. Who controls the R. & D. resources?

opportunities. The alteration process renders each opportunity offered to the market more competitive than that offered in the preceding period.' This competitive process is what drives the system towards equilibrium[3] and which ultimately ensures that resources are allocated in the most efficient way. The alternative scenario is that the business unit is forced to buy from one R. & D. unit, either because that unit is in a monopoly position or because the relationship is mandated (e.g. in a centrally planned economy or in a hierarchical setting). The Kirznerian market process will not emerge in such a setting, resulting in a concomitant loss of efficiency in resource allocation. Using the same logic, R. & D. units should also be allowed a choice in an internal market, in terms of which business units they sell to, and whether they can sell to outside entities. Thus the R. & D. unit is Kirzner's entrepreneur, continuously on the lookout for new opportunities in the market-place.

It should be clear that these elements are intertwined with the price system, in that prices are what provide the buyers and sellers in Kirzner's market process with the information they need to revise their bids and offers. The importance of these three elements is that they represent an operational definition of the market process that can be examined in the setting of a large firm.

---

[3] Though it is important to realize that in Kirzner's world the system can never reach equilibrium. Under equilibrium there would be no need for suppliers to revise their offerings because all current plans can be carried out in the market without disappointment. Competition would therefore cease.

TABLE 8.1. *Characteristics of pure firm, internal market, and pure market*

Characteristic	Pure firm	Internal market	Pure market
Overarching system for co-ordination	Hierarchy	Price system	Price system
Customer input into resource allocation process	Indirect	Direct	Direct
Choice of suppliers for buying unit	No	Yes	Yes
Choice of customers for selling unit	No	Yes	Yes
Administrative control	Present	Present	Weak or absent
Incentive intensity	Low	Low	High
Identification with superordinate goals	Present	Present	Absent

So far we have focused on those elements of the internal market system that are also present in the pure market. But the internal market is by definition a hybrid, so we also need to consider what characteristics the internal market shares with the pure firm. Three such characteristics are frequently mentioned:

1. *Administrative control*. This refers to the systems used within firms to enforce desired behaviours. Central to administrative control is the authority relation, 'an agreement that the employee will accept as premises of his behaviour orders and instructions supplied to him by the organization' (March and Simon 1958: 90). Williamson (1991) also talks in terms of forbearance (as opposed to contract law) as the means by which contracting parties within the firm resolve their disputes.

2. *Low-incentive intensity*. Whereas markets rely on a tight coupling between outcome and reward for the individual actor, such a link is deliberately suppressed in the firm (Williamson 1991). The incomplete nature of the employment contract makes it hard to measure outcomes with accuracy, and as a result employees are rewarded at least in part through fixed salary (Simon 1991).

3. *Identity*. Kogut and Zander (1996: 506) argue that firms 'provide the normative territory to which members identify', which helps to define the rules of co-ordination between individuals and fosters learning. Simon (1991) uses a similar approach in arguing for organizational identification as a motivation for individuals to contribute to the firm beyond the level their monetary compensation would predict.

All these characteristics are present in the firm and therefore also in the internal market. Table 8.1 provides a summary of these and the earlier characteristics. We should be clear that this is not a definitive list. The question of what makes the firm a firm is a subject of ongoing debate, and to a large extent it is beyond the scope of this chapter because our empirical study is restricted to a comparison between the internal market and the pure market modes of governance. A comparison of the internal market and hybrid modes will have to be left for future research.

2.3. Performance

We should briefly consider the performance implications of the internal market compared to the pure firm and pure market modes of governance. The argument here is quite straightforward. Pure markets are very 'efficient' in terms of their ability to adapt autonomously to changes in supply or demand (Hayek 1945). Efficiency is defined as the extent to which production of required output at a perceived minimum cost is achieved (Schmidt and Finnigan 1992: 347). However, pure markets lack the ability to achieve a co-ordinated response between multiple actors. In the context of the current study, such a co-ordinated response might be the decision to continue investing in a new technology even though no immediate demand for that technology is forthcoming. This is usually referred to in the strategic management literature as 'effectiveness' (Drucker 1954). Effectiveness is defined as how closely an organization's output meets its goal and/or the customer requirements (Schmidt and Finnigan 1992: 347).

If pure markets are efficient and pure firms are effective, what sort of performance would be expected from internal markets? Given that the explicit comparison is with the pure firm, our expectation is that the internal market will achieve greater efficiency, but at the possible expense of effectiveness. Of course as a hybrid, the intention is to get the best of both worlds, and the role of management is essentially to 'step in' and overrule the market if it feels that effectiveness is being damaged. But ultimately trade-offs have to be made in choosing any mode of governance, and in the internal market our a priori expectation is that effectiveness will probably be compromised ahead of efficiency.

To summarize the discussion thus far, we have argued that changes in the business environment are leading to the emergence of new flexible organizational forms. One such organizational form we suggest is the internal market, which exhibits many of the characteristics of the pure market system but is undertaken within the boundaries of the firm. In comparison to the traditional hierarchical firm, the internal market is predicted to be more efficient, but at the possible expense of effectiveness.

3. Research Methodology

The research was undertaken in five firms: ABB, Ericsson, Hewlett Packard, Pharmacia & Upjohn, and Omega (disguised name). All of these firms are large and present in multiple countries, and provided us with very generous access, allowing the sort of detailed case-studies needed to undertake this form of exploratory research. It is perhaps an obvious point that Pharmacia & Upjohn (P&U) is the 'odd one out' in this study, being the sole pharmaceutical firm in a sample dominated by electrical and electronic engineering firms. Our logic is simply that the process of generalization involves taking ideas and testing them in both similar and different contexts. As will be shown, P&U ends up looking different from the other four firms on a number of dimensions, and this information provides some valuable insight into the internal market concept. Table 8.2 provides an overview of the five firms' R. & D. organizations, in terms of where their R. & D. activities are located and how they are structured.

3.1. Data Collection

Data were collected between August 1997 and October 1998. Interviews were the primary source of insight into the systems used by the firms. We conducted a total of seventy interviews, each lasting between one and two hours, with at least twelve interviews in each firm. Our initial point of contact was a director or vice-president in the R. & D. organization. He then provided us with access to other individuals. We selected individuals to interview in order to get a broad array of experiences, from managers and technical people in the R. & D. organization to employees working in the business units either as general managers or as technical managers. Table 8.2 provides a breakdown of whom we spoke to. The second source of data was a questionnaire survey that was designed as the interview stage neared completion. The questionnaire was mailed to all the seventy individuals met during the interview stage, and fifty-one of these were returned. Its purpose was to provide quantitative verification for our qualitative findings. Note, though, that the level of analysis in the questionnaire was the firm not the individual, and thus the only way to analyse the data was to aggregate answers from respondents in the same firm and look for differences in means.

Finally, data on firm performance were collected in two ways. Subjective items on the questionnaire asked respondents to assess their firm's performance relative to others on a number of dimensions. Annual reports of the firms provided data on R. & D. expenditure, sales growth, and profitability.

3.2. Construct Operationalization

As described above, the study focused on two aspects of the internal market system and two dimensions of performance. These were then split further into specific constructs which were measured using either questionnaire items or qualitative indicators. Details of these measures are provided in the Appendix to this chapter.

TABLE 8.2. *Characteristics of sample firms and data collected*

Dimension	ABB	Ericsson	HP	P&U	Omega[a]
Total sales revenues, 1997	$31.3 bn.	SEK 168 bn.	$43.2 bn.	$6.59 bn.	$23 bn.
R. & D. headquarters	Zurich	Stockholm	Palo Alto, Calif.	New Jersey	USA
R. & D. expenditure, 1997	$2.6 bn.	SEK 21 bn.	$3.1 bn.	$1.22 bn.	$1.1 bn.
Amount of total R. & D. done at corporate level	$300 m.	0[b]	$250 m.		$345 m.
Major R. & D. locations	Switzerland Sweden USA Germany Finland Italy Norway	Stockholm USA Germany UK Canada Smaller sites in 40 other countries	USA Japan UK France	USA Sweden Italy	USA Japan UK France
Interviews:					
Senior managers in R. & D. organization	5	7	3	6	7
Technical people and lab managers	3	11	3	5	6
Managers in business units	3	4	6	2	4
Locations for interviews	Sweden Germany Finland USA	Sweden USA Japan Canada UK	USA UK Canada	USA Sweden Italy UK	USA Japan Canada
Questionnaires returned	10	12	11	8	10

[a] Some figures for Omega have been altered to ensure anonymity.
[b] R. & D. in Ericsson is all conducted either at the business area or business unit level, rather than through corporate research labs.

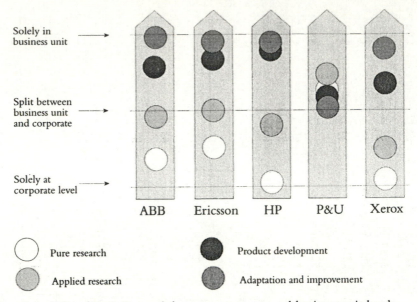

Solely in business unit →

Split between business unit and corporate →

Solely at corporate level →

ABB   Ericsson   HP   P&U   Xerox

○ Pure research   ● Product development

◐ Applied research   ◐ Adaptation and improvement

FIG. 8.3. Split of R. & D. work between corporate and business unit levels

TABLE 8.3. *Split of R. & D. work between corporate and business unit levels in the sample firms*

Where R. & D. work is done?	ABB	Ericsson	HP	P&U	Omega	Anova (sig.)
Pure research	1.25[a]	1.45[a]	1.00[a]	2.25[b]	1.00[a]	7.96 (0.047)
Applied research	1.90	2.05[b]	1.73	2.33[b]	1.40[a]	10.12 (0.018)
Product development	2.55	2.68	2.91[b]	2.17[a]	2.30	8.81 (0.03)
Adaptation, improvement	3.00[b]	2.95[b]	2.91[b]	2.00[a]	2.70	4.81 (0.18)

Note: 1 = corporate level; 2 = split; 3 = division level.

[a] Significantly low.
[b] Significantly high.

4. Findings

This section of the chapter reports on the qualitative and quantitative evidence collected during the research, broken down into the various elements of the internal market system and firm performance. The interpretation of the findings in terms of implications for the internal market model will be reserved for the discussion section.

4.1. *Influence of Customer on R. & D. Funding Decisions*

The first issue to consider is the extent to which the internal customer, i.e. the business unit, influences resource allocation decisions in R. & D. Figure 8.2 illustrates the spectrum of choices facing a company on this issue. At one extreme a company can provide all R. & D. resources centrally, and get the business units to pay for them through a 'tax' on revenues; at the other extreme the business units own their own dedicated R. & D. Obviously the more the business units control their own R. & D. resources, the more input the customer will have on R. & D. decisions, and the more 'market-like' the system. The results suggest a shift towards the right-hand side of this spectrum, though with a great deal of variation between firms. The first thing we looked at was the level in the firm (corporate or business unit) that the various activities of R. & D. were undertaken. Figure 8.3 illustrates this analysis. As one might expect, research is done predominantly at the corporate level, and development work predominantly at the business unit level. But there were significant differences between the five firms, revealing three different models.

1. HP and Omega have a clear split between research (pure and applied) and development (product, adaptation, and improvement). Research is done at a corporate level; development at the business unit level; and there is little overlap between the two.
2. ABB and Ericsson have a stronger business unit involvement in all parts of R. & D. Pure research is still done mostly, but not exclusively, at the corporate level, but applied research is split, and development work is done almost exclusively at the business unit level.
3. Pharmacia & Upjohn have all parts of R. & D. split, but most done at the business unit level. In part this is simply a function of the industry setting, because the whole innovation process, including research, is split by therapeutic area.

Table 8.4 provides some further data on how the five firms split up their R. & D., though it should be observed that the differences we see here are partly a function of definitions. Three major observations can be made. First, the money devoted to pure research is relatively small these days: 11 per cent in P&U and 12.6 per cent in Omega, but below 4 per cent in the other three firms. Secondly, there is a very clear focus on development work in

TABLE 8.4. *How R. & D. expenditure is split among research and development work in the sample firms*

How is total R. & D. expenditure split?	ABB (%)	Ericsson (%)	HP (%)	P&U (%)	Omega (%)	Anova (sig.)
Pure research	3.3	3.0	3.7	11.0	12.6	5.94 (0.11)
Applied research	16.1	23.3	69.0	30.2	28.6	9.18 (0.03)
Product development	52.2[b]	52.4[b]	17.8[a]	52.0[b]	45.0[b]	10.36 (0.02)
Adaptation, improvement	25.6	31.7	8.5	14.8	12.1	14.52 (0.002)
Spend on technology from external sources	5.75	8.7	6.4	16.4	6.4	3.09 (0.002)

[a] Significantly low.
[b] Significantly high.

ABB and Ericsson, to a much greater degree than the other three firms. Finally, we see P&U spending a much greater percentage of the total on external sources of technology than the other four firms. Again, this is an industry-specific finding because all major pharmaceutical firms today are actively in-licensing technologies to fill out their product pipelines.

A second question we addressed on the influence of the 'customer' was how corporate research projects get funded. Table 8.5 summarizes the data collected on this issue. Again, some interesting differences emerged, suggesting several different models.

1. In ABB most corporate R. & D. projects are contracted by the business units. Very little funding is given to corporate R. & D. through a centrally collected 'tax'. This is a clear example of an internal market system at work.
2. HP is the other extreme, with corporate R. & D. funding almost exclusively through a central 'tax' on business units. One respondent commented that HP labs actively resist funding from business units, because it would compromise their independence.
3. Ericsson and Omega both use hybrid funding models, with a mixture of the four systems indicated by us. Essentially they are seeking to achieve the benefits of both the ABB and HP approaches.
4. Pharmacia & Upjohn appears to use none of the systems we indicated to a very great extent. Perhaps this suggests that we did not accurately capture the full range of funding approaches used in the pharmaceutical industry.

TABLE 8.5. *Funding systems for R. & D. in the sample firms*

For R. & D. work done at a corporate level, which of the following systems are used for funding?	ABB	Ericsson	HP	P&U	Omega	Anova (sig.)
A fixed 'tax' paid by divisions	3.0[a]	4.9	6.7[b]	3.0[a]	5.6[b]	5.2 (0.01)
A negotiated 'tax' depending on what work is done	2.0	4.0[b]	1.0[a]	1.0[a]	2.7[b]	4.6 (0.01)
Jointly funded projects, part by corporate, part by divisions	6.2[b]	3.8[a]	1.7[a]	2.3[a]	3.2[a]	10.7 (0.001)
Projects 'contracted' by divisions	4.9[b]	3.7	1.3[a]	2.7	5.0[b]	6.0 (0.01)

Note: 1 = not used at all; 7 = used to a great extent.

[a] Significantly low.
[b] Significantly high.

The third question we addressed was the extent to which R. & D. decisions are made by commercial managers rather than technical managers. Obviously the more this happens, the more voice the customer has in the decision-making process. Table 8.6 summarizes the data we collected on this issue. The basic finding is that technical managers are in charge where it concerns long-term research trajectories and identifying new research opportunities, but commercial managers have a strong role to play in deciding overall funding and killing a project in difficulties. But again, there are some important differences between the five firms.

1. ABB and Pharmacia & Upjohn have significantly more commercial input in R. & D. decisions than the other three firms, especially those decisions that are traditionally the preserve of technical managers (e.g. long-term research trajectories).
2. In HP and Omega technical managers are in control of decisions around long-term research trajectories and identification of new research opportunities, and share other decisions with commercial managers.
3. Ericsson has a hybrid system, in which commercial managers have little input in many decisions but they do end up explicitly paying additional costs when projects are delayed.

4.1.1. Summary   In terms of our general observations, there seems to be a clear emphasis in most of these firms today towards linking development work more closely to the customer's needs. Examples of this are: meetings

TABLE 8.6. *Influence of commercial decision-makers over R. & D. decisions in the sample firms*

Extent to which decisions made by commercial managers, rather than technical	ABB	Ericsson	HP	P&U	Omega	Anova (sig.)
Overall funding levels	2.6	3.3	2.6	2.6	3.3	1.0[c]
Definition of long-term research trajectories	2.5[b]	1.8	1.2[a]	2.3[b]	1.3[a]	6.2 (0.001)
Identification of new research opportunities	2.2[b]	1.5	1.3[a]	2.1[b]	1.1[a]	5.2 (0.01)
'Killing' a project that is delayed or in difficulties	3.0	3.0	1.9	2.7	2.6	1.9[c]
Paying additional costs when projects are delayed	3.1[b]	3.2[b]	1.7[a]	2.4	2.7	2.8 (0.05)

Note: 1 = technical; 5 = commercial.

[a] Significantly low.
[b] Significantly high.
[c] No sig.

between R. & D. labs and the respective business units they are offering services to; reference group meetings held with lead customers; movement of engineers and scientists between research and development functions; and a shift towards greater use of contracts between business units and R. & D.

But despite these efforts, the overriding sense we got was that more needs to be done. Typical quotes we heard were 'Development groups sit too far from customers' and 'We need to do more of this [innovation support]'. Another interesting point that was mentioned in a couple of the electronics firms was the importance of having a 'window' on the final customer wherever you are in the R. & D. organization. For example, one R. & D. unit we talked to was responsible for developing the entire value chain through to customer delivery, and seemed to derive enormous satisfaction from that, whereas most other development groups were building modules of a system where the final customer was never seen.

To summarize the positions of the five firms on the spectrum, ABB has clearly moved the furthest towards the internal market model, while HP has the most 'traditional' model with a strong, central R. & D. group. The other three firms have intermediate positions. Of course, we cannot say at this stage which approach is better, because, as Figure 8.2 illustrates, there are costs and benefits with both models.

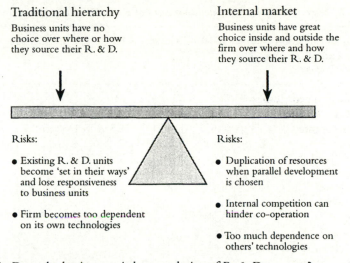

Traditional hierarchy

Business units have no
choice over where or how
they source their R. & D.

Internal market

Business units have great
choice inside and outside the
firm over where and how
they source their R. & D.

Risks:

- Existing R. & D. units
  become 'set in their ways'
  and lose responsiveness
  to business units

- Firm becomes too dependent
  on its own technologies

Risks:

- Duplication of resources
  when parallel development
  is chosen

- Internal competition can
  hinder co-operation

- Too much dependence on
  others' technologies

FIG. 8.4. Does the business unit have a choice of R. & D. sources?

4.2. Choice of R. & D. Sources for Business Units

The second issue is the extent to which internal business units have a choice about their sources of R. & D. In a traditional hierarchy the relationship between an R. & D. unit and the business unit is fixed, such that the business unit has no choice but to make use of whatever technologies are developed in the R. & D. unit. Under the internal market system that relationship gets decoupled, and the business unit only sources technology from the R. & D. unit if it wants to. If it believes better technology exists elsewhere in the corporation, or indeed outside, it is free to source from them. This element of choice puts pressure on the existing R. & D. unit to be more responsive to the demands of the business unit.

In global firms there is another important dimension to the sources of R. & D. Sometimes there will be several R. & D. centres with broadly similar capabilities, which means that—in theory—development work can be moved between locations relatively cheaply. This creates another element of choice for the business unit. Not only do they have options about what R. & D. they want to pay for, they also have options regarding where that R. & D. should be done. And again, those options put pressure on the development centres to perform.

Figure 8.4 reminds us, however, that there are also risks to having a great choice of internal and/or external sources of R. & D. The risk in having an internal choice of sources of R. & D. is primarily one of duplication. Most firms today realize that they cannot afford the 'parallel development' approach in which two or more R. & D. units explore alternative paths which business

TABLE 8.7. *Importance of various external sources of R. & D. in the sample firms*

How valuable are the following entities as sources of R. & D. expertise	ABB	Ericsson	HP	P&U	Omega	Anova (sig.)
Universities located close to your R. & D. sites	4.6	4.7	4.8	4.7	4.5	0.05[c]
Universities located elsewhere	4.6	3.4[a]	4.5	6.1[b]	3.8	3.9 (0.01)
Alliance or joint venture partners	3.6[a]	3.7[a]	3.9[a]	5.3[b]	5.1	2.4 (0.05)
Supplier firms	4.1[b]	4.0[b]	2.6[a]	4.0[b]	4.7[b]	2.9 (0.05)
Customers	5.2[b]	4.1[b]	3.4	3.2	2.8[a]	3.0 (0.05)
To what extent is technology bought or licensed from other firms?	3.0	3.4	4.1	3.9	4.2	1.5[c]
What percentage of technology embodied in your products is proprietary?	≃76	≃88[b]	≃70[a]	≃78	≃76	1.8 (0.10)

Note: 1 = not important; 7 = extremely important.

[a] Significantly low.
[b] Significantly high.
[c] No sig.

units are then free to choose from. The Ericsson approach of having multiple R. & D. centres with similar capabilities and thus an implicit competition over which one will undertake which projects is better, but still creates some significant co-ordination and administration costs. Internal competition also creates a risk that co-operation between units will be damaged, though in practice that is rarely an issue. One manager we spoke to commented that 'We encourage development centres to co-operate and compete at the same time.'

Making greater use of external sources of technology in explicit competition with internal ones has two risks. One is simply the cost of developing a technology in-house and then not using it, though that may be preferable to putting a sub-standard technology in the product. The second risk is that the firm ends up becoming very dependent on external technologies, which can have grave consequences if the technologies in question end up being core components of the new product.

Table 8.7 examines the use to which various external sources of technology are put in the five firms. We asked about the value of universities, suppliers, and customers as sources of R. & D., and about the extent to which the firms in-license technology. A number of observations can be made.

1. Pharmacia & Upjohn appears to be the least 'self-sufficient' when it comes to technology. Like most pharmaceutical firms, in-licensing of technology is an important strategy, and this is manifested in the value P&U puts on universities and joint venture and alliance partners.
2. HP and Omega rate low on self-sufficiency, but do not appear to value external sources of R. & D. like universities particularly highly. Our sense is that these two firms make a lot of use of *de facto* standards in operating systems and microprocessors—these do not require strong links to other firms, but they do reduce the level of proprietary technology in a product.
3. Ericsson is the most self-sufficient firm in the study, with the highest percentage of its product 'proprietary' and relatively low value put on external sources of R. & D. From the interviews we conducted, Ericsson appears to be moving away from this self-sufficient philosophy, and towards a greater acceptance of the open standards of the computer industry.

The second issue we looked at was the extent to which we see mobility of R. & D. activities between different locations. Here a very complicated picture emerges. All the companies in the study have many different development centres around the world, but the extent to which those centres' capabilities and physical assets overlap varies enormously. As suggested by Table 8.8, though, we can make a number of general observations.

1. Pharmacia & Upjohn has the least 'market-like' system for allocating projects between sites. In other words, decision-making is quite tightly controlled from the centre, which is what one would expect in the pharmaceutical industry.
2. ABB appears to have the most 'market-like' system for allocating resources. In part this is a reflection of their philosophy of giving operating units considerable autonomy, but it is also indicative of the number of overlapping locations in which any given R. & D. project can be undertaken.
3. Ericsson is a hybrid. There are a very large number of R. & D. centres around the world doing similar system development work, but respondents rated Ericsson's use of an internal market–bottom-up process quite low. From our interviews, it seems that while the system has the potential for fostering internal competition between locations, the reality is that most R. & D. sourcing decisions are made in a fairly top-down manner.
4. HP and Omega both scored very low on the extent to which there is a 'market-like' system, in part because both firms have relatively few R. & D. sites. HP, however, scored highest on the existence of

TABLE 8.8. *Choice of where R. & D. will be sourced inside the firm in the sample firms*

Please indicate the extent to which you agree with the following statements	ABB	Ericsson	HP	P&U	Omega	Anova (sig.)
There is an active 'bottom-up' process whereby managers of different sites bid for or request specific projects	4.1	3.7	4.7	3.1	3.8	0.7[c]
For any given R. & D. project there are several sites that could potentially undertake the work	4.7	4.8	4.6	3.4	3.3	1.7[c]
There is a 'market-like' system for allocating projects between different sites	4.1[b]	2.6	1.6[a]	1.3[a]	2.5	5.1 (0.01)
The location of 'physical' assets such as laboratories and test equipment dictates where R. & D. projects are located	4.7	3.4[a]	4.7	5.1[b]	5.1[b]	2.5 (0.05)
R. & D. work is sometimes moved between sites as a result of performance differences between sites	3.1	3.5[b]	2.3	3.0	1.9[a]	2.0 (0.10)

Note: 1 = disagree completely; 7 = agree completely.

[a] Significantly low.
[b] Significantly high.
[c] No sig.

a 'bottom-up' process, suggesting that R. & D. managers are still encouraged to take initiative and bring ideas forward.

4.2.1. Summary Taken together, these findings suggest a rather complex picture. The decision to use external sources of technology is made for many reasons, and, as the results suggest, such technology comes from many different places. Overall, though, the trend in both the electronics and pharmaceuticals industries is towards a greater openness to external sources—through acceptance of open standards in electronics, and through in-licensing in pharmaceuticals.

On the question of competition between R. & D. centres, we see little evidence for this actually happening. In Omega and P&U, it seems there is a clear demarcation of roles for individual R. & D. centres, which of course precludes the possibility of internal competition opening up. The other three firms all see some overlap in the roles of R. & D. centres, but the evidence for a market-like process for allocating roles is scanty. For example, in Ericsson and ABB the contracts between business units and development centres are in principle open to renegotiation but in reality they ossify over time. Partly because of the development of specialized expertise in a given centre, and partly because it is easy to maintain an existing relationship, it is very rare that development work is shifted between locations. And when this happens, it is often on the initiative of the development centre manager, who wants to rationalize his/her activities, and not because the business unit is dissatisfied. Put another way, there is a lot of inertia in the internal market for development work, with the result that it ends up functioning in a rather similar way to some of the other companies in which development centres are owned by the business units.

But one area in which Ericsson's internal market works well is in the allocation of new development projects. Increasingly it seems that two or more centres will be explicitly considered whenever a new piece of work is needed, and the contract is then given to the one that scores best on a list of factors including productivity, cost, capabilities, enthusiasm, and synergies. ABB, and to a lesser extent HP, also use this approach for allocating new development projects.

4.3. The Price System in the Internal Market

The use of a price system was argued by Hennart (1993) to be a key indicator of the existence of an internal market. Under a traditional hierarchical system price is irrelevant because each unit is simply passing its products or services on to the next unit in the chain. But under a true internal market system pricing is critical because it provides the strong signals from which the buyers and sellers in the market take their cues. Typically, for such a system to work, internal transfer prices have to be more or less harmonized with external market prices for the same products; otherwise the choice of buying from or selling to the independent companies cannot be made wisely.

The point, then, is that there has to be a fit between the structure and the pricing system. Market pricing in a traditional hierarchy does not make sense; and cost-plus pricing in an internal market system does not make sense either. And indeed, that is more or less what we found in the five firms. ABB's internal pricing was the closest to what we would call a 'market price' system. R. & D. units and business units are defined as profit centres and charge their transactions with outside firms, and with other ABB units, at approximately market prices. This approach makes it possible for business units explicitly to compare technology sourced from inside versus outside, and for research centres explicitly to compare sales to inside versus outside entities. Ericsson also has a price system for contracting between development centres and business units. However, prices within Ericsson are not market prices; they are internal estimates of the cost and productivity of the development centre in question. These estimates are held centrally and are used to calculate the internal transfer pricing between units.

HP labs do not charge business units for their work. As noted, since the labs are financed solely through a corporate tax, it is then up to the business units to get access to as much technology as they can, on the basis that they have already paid for it. Pharmacia & Upjohn, likewise, does not use a price system. Because major development decisions are centralized by therapeutic area, there is no need to create an internal market for evaluating R. & D. projects. Of course, all projects are subject to extensive review on a variety of criteria, but no attempt is made to convert this into prices. Finally, Omega uses a hybrid system, whereby some R. & D. is funded centrally (and therefore not 'priced' as such) while the rest is charged out on a cost basis. None of the work done by Omega's corporate R. & D. is sold at 'market' prices.

Overall, the evidence suggests that market-based pricing is relatively rare in R. & D. organizations. This is in large part because there are significant drawbacks to adopting market pricing inside the firm. Some products or services are very hard to value, so market pricing does not work for them. Market pricing can also encourage R. & D. centres to favour selling to outsiders, which is obviously inappropriate, and it can also favour short-term development projects ahead of long-term. All these risks have to be managed by corporate management, whose role is to step in, when necessary, and 'fix' the price system when it seems to be adversely affecting the performance of the firm. But having said that, there are still some important benefits to using market pricing inside the firm if the other elements of the internal market system are already in place.

4.4. Firm Performance

Finally, what are the implications for the internal market system on firm performance? We looked into this question by collecting data on various aspects of performance, but unfortunately it is impossible to come to any strong conclusions, just because all five companies had similar ratings on performance. These, as shown in Table 8.9, are self-rated performance measures, which are, of course, not a very accurate reflection of reality. They are presented anyway, as a way of showing how well the five companies feel they are doing in comparison to their competitors. The biggest differences are seen in the dimension of technological leadership, in which ABB and Ericsson rated themselves very high, and P&U rated themselves

TABLE 8.9. *Measures of performance in the sample firms*

Estimate performance of your division/business area over the last three years in comparison to a competitor in your industry	ABB	Ericsson	HP	P&U	Omega	Anova (sig.)
Getting new products to market rapidly	4.6	4.8	4.2	4.3	3.5	1.6
Bring breakthrough technologies to market	4.7	4.8	3.9	3.3	3.9	1.9
Making good use of outside sources of technology	4.1	4.0	4.3	3.9	3.2	1.2
Technological leadership in your industry	5.6[b]	5.6[b]	5.1	3.7[a]	4.9	3.7 (0.05)
Combining different technologies in your products	5.5	5.2	5.8[b]	4.1[a]	5.4	2.3 (0.10)
Speed, e.g. time to market	3.4	3.8	3.8	3.7	2.8	1.6[c]
End customer satisfaction	4.9	4.1[a]	5.3	5.2	4.6	2.2 (0.10)

Note: 1 = much worse; 7 = much better.
[a] Significantly low.
[b] Significantly high.
[c] No sig.

relatively low. We also see significant differences on the question of 'combining different technologies', which HP is rated highest on and P&U lowest, and on 'end customer satisfaction', where again HP is rated highest and Ericsson is rated the lowest. But on other dimensions the most notable thing about the data is the similarities between firms.

The interviews conducted during this research provided some qualitative insights into the performance question. Several managers mentioned concerns they had with their existing R. & D. systems, and it was also apparent that the systems were constantly in a state of change. Regardless of which system is being used, it appears, the awareness of the system's problems is often as great as awareness of its benefits, and as a result there are changes being made on a frequent basis. Most noticeably, there is a debate over the level of customer input into resource allocation decisions. As one manager noted, the corporate labs in his firm are always under critical review, but one year the concern is that they are 'working too closely with the business units' and two years later the concern is that they are doing too much 'ivory tower research'.

Thus, one insight that can be drawn from this discussion is that, regardless of the resource allocation system the firm uses, it is possible to create checks and balances to guard against the worst drawbacks of the chosen system. Thus, ABB uses the most internal-market-like system, but there are still systems to ensure that long-term projects can be protected. And Omega probably has the least internal-market-like system but it has built in systems to increase the responsiveness of its corporate labs to the demands of business units.

5. Discussion and Conclusions

The data presented here provide some rich insights into the systems used by five firms to manage their R. & D. resource allocation. To some extent we see evidence of the internal market at work, but in other ways the data suggest a fairly traditional and centralized approach. Let us briefly consider a number of general points that emerge from the research.

First, does the internal market system really exist? Going back to Hennart's (1993) theory, we certainly see some evidence of the price system in use within the firm, but it is not very much like the price system that is used in the 'pure' market. Most prices are internal transfer prices that do not reflect the true value-added of the product or service; and in parts of HP and Omega we see the deliberate withdrawal of price-based transactions as a means of keeping the research labs independent. Only ABB approximate to what we would recognize as a price system.

But while the price system is mostly absent, we do see many other systems in these four firms that are designed to create choice and competition internally. In particular, R. & D. units are increasingly being asked to compete with one another for the right to undertake a specific project, and business units are finding ways of making the chosen R. & D. unit more accountable for its performance. These approaches provide stronger incentives for R. & D. units to perform than would be the case in a traditional firm (because a non-competitive unit will not win contracts) but of course rather weaker incentives than would be the case if the R. & D. unit were a separate legal entity. On that basis, they clearly fall into the 'swollen middle' between firm and market.

Secondly, what is the new role of the corporate centre in the (hypothetical) internal market system? The idea is that resources are allocated through a give-and-take process rather than in a top-down fashion, but instead of eliminating the job of the corporate centre, it actually makes their job much harder. Their first important job is to define 'the rules of the game' such that every R. & D. and business unit in the firm understands its own responsibilities, who it can sell to and buy from, and what prices will be used. Their second important job is to monitor the internal market system, and to be prepared to step in if it appears to be resulting in a counter-productive solution. Markets are very good for achieving efficiency but sometimes that is achieved at the expense of effectiveness. The corporate centre, then, has to keep an eye out for the effectiveness of the whole firm, and be prepared to overrule the internal market if a serious conflict emerges. Finally, the corporate centre also has responsibility for building a corporate 'culture' to encourage individual units to co-operate and share best practices.

How does this work in the firms we studied? Moderately well, in our estimation. For ABB and Ericsson in particular (i.e. the firms where the internal market approach was most used), corporate managers clearly devote a lot of time to overseeing the activities of their various business units and development centres through their memberships in these entities' boards. These boards provide the vital function of ensuring that the unit in question is operating efficiently while also making sure the wider interests of the firm are taken care of.

Where there would seem to be room for improvement is in the definition of the 'rules of the game' around the allocation of projects to development centres. As observed several times, relationships ossify over time, so the internal market system that exists in theory ends up not working in practice. And the responsibility for this lies clearly with the 'rule-makers' and not with the business units and development centres that live by the rules. One way of enhancing the efficiency of this internal market, for example, would be to encourage bids for projects that were up for renewal, in which the incumbent development centre did not automatically get the next year of the contract. Such a mechanism might well not work, but it is steps like that that corporate management needs to consider.

Finally, what does all this tell us about the capabilities that a firm needs to develop to function effectively in an internal market system? The necessary capabilities can be considered at two levels. At the lower level of analysis—the business unit or the R. & D. unit—there is a need for managers to take greater responsibility for the destiny of their own unit. The internal market only works well when both 'supplier' and 'buyer' are actively seeking out opportunities to make it work more efficiently. This means R. & D. managers have to be prepared to hawk their ideas around multiple business units, and it means business unit managers have to actively consider different sources of technology rather than relying on an existing relationship. At the higher level of analysis—the corporate level—the challenge is to create a superstructure that encourages these sorts of behaviour. In part this is about 'letting go'—allowing individual business unit and R. & D. managers to make their own decisions. But it also involves creating incentives for entrepreneurship and defining new 'rules of the game' to facilitate choice.

To conclude, this chapter's objective was to describe how resource allocation decisions are made in five R. & D. organizations, with a view to understanding the extent to which an internal market system could be identified. As is often the case with case-study research, we ended up with an inconclusive and messy set of results. The internal market model can be seen quite clearly in ABB, and to some degree in the other firms, but for the most part the empirical evidence was more consistent with the traditional hierarchical system of resource allocation. The verdict is that the internal market model is 'not disproven'. Progress was made on a number of fronts, but this really just sets the stage for the next phase of research in which the internal market model is tested in other settings and with a larger sample of firms.

APPENDIX: CONSTRUCT OPERATIONALIZATION

Influence of Customer on Resource Allocation Decisions   This dimension can be seen as the balance between the short-term commercial needs of the business units (high customer influence) and the long-term technological objectives of the firm (low customer influence). This was split into the following three dimensions, all of which were measured through the questionnaire:

1. *Business unit control of R. & D. activities.* This was measured by asking respondents to state how R. & D. work is divided in their firm, where 1 = done at a corporate level, 2 = split between corporate and divisions, and 3 = done by the divisions. This question was asked for pure research, applied research, product and process development, and adaptation–improvement work.

2. *System for funding R. & D. activities.* Funding typically falls on a scale from a pure 'tax' system in which business units contribute funds to a central source, to a pure 'contract' system in which the business units specify exactly what they will get in return for their expenditure. This was measured using three questions about the firms' systems: (*a*) projects are contracted by divisions; (*b*) projects are jointly funded, part by corporate, part by divisions, and (*c*) a fixed tax is paid by divisions (reversed). The scale was 1 = not used at all to 7 = used to a great extent. Reliability for this three-item scale was good ($\alpha = 0.80$).

3. *Commercial input into R. & D. resource allocation decisions.* Respondents were asked to assess the relative input of commercial and technical managers into the following decisions: (*a*) overall funding levels, (*b*) definition of specific projects, (*c*) definition of long-term research trajectories, (*d*) identification of new research opportunities, (*e*) killing a project that is delayed or in difficulties, (*f*) paying additional costs when projects are delayed. 1 = decided by technical managers, 5 = decided by commercial managers. Reliability for this scale was good ($\alpha = 0.76$).

Choice of R. & D. Suppliers for Business Units   This dimension focuses on the various choices that the business unit has regarding its sources of R. & D. We created three quantitative measures from the questionnaire data, two concerning the opportunity to source R. & D. from outside, and the third concerning the opportunity to choose between various internal R. & D. units. We also used our interview material to complement these measures.

1. *External choice.* Respondents assessed the extent to which they used the following three systems in their firm: (*a*) business managers contract with R. & D. sources if they do not believe the necessary capabilities exist in-house, (*b*) business managers use both in-house R. & D. and external sources at the same time for their development work, and (*c*) technology is bought or licensed from other firms. 1 = not used at all, 7 = used to a great extent. Reliability was satisfactory ($\alpha = 0.63$).

2. *Value of external sources.* Respondents were asked the value of the following entities as sources of R. & D. expertise: (*a*) universities located close to the R. & D. sites, (*b*) universities located elsewhere, (*c*) alliance or joint venture partners, (*d*) supplier firms, (*e*) customers. 1 = not important, 7 = extremely important. Reliability was satisfactory ($\alpha = 0.68$).

3. *Internal choice.* Respondents were asked to assess the extent to which they agreed with the following statements regarding their level of internal choice: (*a*) for any given R. & D. project there are several sites that could potentially undertake the work, (*b*) there is a market-like system for allocating projects between different sites, (*c*) R. & D. work is sometimes moved between sites as a result of performance differences between sites. 1 = disagree completely, 7 = agree completely. Reliability was satisfactory ($\alpha = 0.64$).

9

Knowledge Management in the Multinational Enterprise

NIKLAS ARVIDSSON

> If only ABB knew what ABB knows, we'd be unbeatable
>
> (Allegedly said by Percy Barnevik, former chief executive of ABB)

1. Introduction

The multinational enterprise (MNE) is glorified as one of the most successful phenomena of the modern era. No matter how you measure its importance—number of employees, shares of global trade and currency flows, wealth, etc.—the end result is the same. The MNE—as an institution—is very powerful. One reason why the MNE is so successful is its unique abilities to transfer resources across geography but inside its own organizational boundaries (Buckley and Casson 1976). In fact, the *raison d'être* for the MNE is its ability to combine favourable location-specific advantages—such as inexpensive raw material or labour—with unique organization-specific advantages—such as brand names, technologies, or patents—by internalizing markets for input factors to the production processes (Dunning 1977, 1980). In this manner, the MNE takes the best parts from many different regions in the world at the same time, and combines them into powerful production processes and products. In short, the main advantage of the MNE when compared to national firms as well as over market transactions is its ability to internalize transfers of resources over geographical distances.

If the MNE has a competitive advantage built on, for instance, a marketing capability, it has the possibility to leverage this skill across several markets (Kogut and Zander 1992). It can also combine it with other, geographically determined advantages—e.g. inexpensive and/or skilled labour. In combination, this creates advantages that may be very difficult for other firms to match. A firm that is based in one country alone has to use the market if it wants to access input factors or output markets in other countries, and the market conditions usually reflect a realistic value of that which is sold. The MNE can quite flexibly access and use input or output factors in a multitude of countries at favourable conditions.

The traditional input factors to production processes include land, raw material, unskilled labour, and capital. These input factors are still important even if the advantages based on the traditional input factors have become necessary but not sufficient conditions for competitive advantage. Moreover, the traditional factors of production were characterized by the fact that ownership was closely associated with access to the profit that accrued. Even if competitive forces restrict the return, a landowner controls the revenues from farming and the capital owner controls the ones emanating from capital management.

In today's society, where knowledge is gaining importance as a factor for competitive advantage, the ability of the MNE to capitalize on capabilities *per se* has become important. In fact, during the last century knowledge has become the most important input factor for firms' competitive advantage. Consequently, one of the main concerns in the modern MNE is to leverage knowledge on a global scale. The MNE benefits greatly if capabilities in, for example, the Spanish subsidiary are imitated by subsidiaries in Italy, Sweden, Japan, Canada, and New Zealand. The basic question is whether a firm really controls the knowledge residing in its employees, and whether it can capitalize effectively on that knowledge. More specifically, can the MNE leverage capabilities across subsidiaries?

Initially, technologically based knowledge was the main issue in research on MNE knowledge (see e.g. Caves 1971; Hymer 1976; Dunning 1977). As a consequence, research studies focused on the articulability of knowledge, i.e. the degree to which it was possible to codify and document knowledge in such a way that others could understand and use the knowledge residing in the firm (Zander 1991). The firm could protect itself against competitors' imitation of its unique skills through patents. Today, knowledge focused on non-technological activities—such as logistics, quality control, or marketing—has become increasingly important (Kostova 1996). Still, the unique knowledge is often located in the hands and/or minds of individuals. Moreover, in many instances patents are no longer viable protective measures against competitors. Brand names or secret working methods have replaced patents as important protective measures.

As a result of these changes, studies of transfers of best practices have come into vogue. In line with this evolution, the current chapter is focused on marketing activities, which fundamentally deal with how to interact with and satisfy other human beings. Marketing, with its emphasis on providing a service, is therefore argued to involve skills that are difficult to observe, articulate, and codify (cf. Shostack 1977; Grönroos 1990). The implication of this is that we would expect transfers of marketing capabilities to be extraordinarily difficult. Thus, this study is devoted to the identification and transfer of marketing capabilities within the MNE.

2. Knowledge in the MNE organization

Knowledge that is put into action has been described as capabilities (Kogut and Zander 1992). There are several different types of knowledge and capabilities (see Machlup 1980), but I will only use and discuss the most common distinction. Knowledge can be separated in two broad groups (Polanyi 1969). One group—articulated knowledge—contains knowledge that is relatively easy to describe and codify. This group includes, for instance, knowledge that is stored in the blueprint of a television set. The other group—tacit knowledge—contains knowledge that is difficult to articulate and describe for other people. This group includes knowledge that mainly resides in our head, and concerns skills such as the solving of mathematical problems. It is these two types of knowledge that the MNE is interested in managing on a global scale. More specifically, tacit knowledge is often believed to be more valuable, and the MNE would therefore be more interested in achieving effective management of tacit knowledge. The overall question is how the MNE effectively leverages articulated and tacit knowledge from its subsidiaries.

The MNE has subsidiaries in many different parts of the world. These subsidiaries are shaped both by the internal organization of the MNE and by its local environment. Their local network is an important factor for their ability to develop unique skills. The secret behind leveraging such dispersed skills across the MNE lies in the internal organization and integration of dispersed subsidiaries. This includes the firm's ability to build information technology–information systems (IT–IS) systems that promote transfers of practices, or the organization's ability to create shared values that promote discussion and joint problem-solving across departments and subsidiaries. These two principles constitute the 'hard' and the 'soft' methods on how to leverage skills. The hard method—the IT–IS solution—tends to focus on articulated knowledge, while the soft method—building on shared values— tends to focus on tacit knowledge. Research also shows that transfers are dependent upon the receivers' learning ability (Szulanski 1996), the atmosphere of the relationship between parties in the transfer process (Kostova 1996), and characteristics of knowledge *per se* (Zander 1991).

One problem with tacit knowledge is that one cannot always articulate what one knows. The tennis player may have problems describing exactly how he/she hits the ball in order to drive home an ace, or the sales manager may have problems articulating exactly how he/she handles customers in certain situations. As a consequence, learning and transfer of knowledge becomes complicated. A poor learning ability implies a malfunctioning ability to absorb knowledge and/or a poor incentive system to learn a new behaviour. Detrimental personal relationships can, of course, create barriers to any type of transfer. Lastly, the institutional environment— including things like career paths, cultures, reporting systems, and general attitudes—influences the benefits of receiving skills from other institutional environments.

Another potential problem related to knowledge transfers is that of actually knowing which subsidiaries are particularly capable, and which should act as sources in the transfer of best-practice processes. The process of identifying which units are capable and which are not is seldom discussed in research. Consequently I am reducing the analysis of knowledge transfers to one of its fundamental questions: Are firms and managers able to identify how capable their subsidiaries are? Paradoxically, the most tacit knowledge is the most valuable knowledge, and—at the same time—it is the most difficult knowledge to leverage within the MNE. It is difficult to transfer capabilities since they are 'sticky', but there may also be another factor: capabilities may be 'invisible'.

Most previous studies focus on the process of transferring skills once the sender and the receiver have been identified. Thus, once sources and recipients are identified, the barriers to global leverage of capabilities relate to articulation of tacit knowledge (Zander 1991), the learning ability of recipients (Szulanski 1996), the relationship between sources and recipients (Szulanski 1996; Kostova 1996), and the proximity of actors' institutional environments (Kostova 1996). I argue that an overall effective transfer process must build on three prerequisites. First, one should acknowledge that all units in the MNE are potential contributors to the shared pool of skills of the MNE (Perlmutter 1969). Secondly, one should know how capable the units are so that the less skilled can learn from the skilled. Thirdly, one should make an effort to implement knowledge-sharing, and overcome transfer constraints—the 'stickiness' (von Hippel 1998) of knowledge (Zander 1991; Szulanski 1996; Kostova 1996). In sum, my main contribution is a discussion of the second of the three prerequisites.

Two paradoxes are found in knowledge management discussions. The transfer paradox, which is well known and elaborated upon, argues that the most valuable knowledge—tacit knowledge—also is the most sticky. It is expensive and difficult to materialize and codify so that others can easily absorb it. I also introduce a second—not so well known—knowledge management paradox. The evaluation paradox argues that the most valuable knowledge—tacit knowledge—is also the most difficult knowledge to evaluate and assess.[1] It is very difficult for a corporate manager to assess knowledge that resides in the hands and heads of subsidiaries. Consequently, it is difficult to decide which subsidiaries should act as sources in the knowledge transfer process.

There are two fundamental research questions. First, do corporate and subsidiary managers evaluate the marketing capabilities of a particular

---

[1] Two recent articles that acknowledge this idea are Earl and Scott (1999) and Manzoni and Barsoux (1998).

subsidiary in a consistent way? Secondly, do the evaluations as such explain the choice of sources and recipients in the capability transfer process? To answer these two questions I have collected empirical data in two different but complementary ways. Qualitative data have been collected in order, first, to make a preliminary test of the issues and questions that govern the study, and, secondly, to enable understanding of the phenomenon as such. Quantitative data were collected in order to test the questions in a significant number of firms, which allowed me to draw firmer conclusions. The following sections will analyse and discuss the qualitative as well as the quantitative data.

3. Qualitative Research Findings: The Managerial Issues

More than fifty interviews were conducted between fall 1997 and spring 1999, beginning at the corporate headquarters and subsequently involving managers in the subsidiary companies. In the rest of this section I present some of the interesting issues that emerged from these interviews. As a general observation, it became apparent that headquarters and subsidiary managers held very different perceptions about the locus and value of marketing knowledge. While corporate managers claimed that they wanted to be able to tap into the knowledge base of their subsidiaries, subsidiary managers often felt that their ideas were not given a fair hearing at headquarters. Moreover, new initiatives that were developed in the corporate head office often received the 'Oh no, it's another vision from the corporate space cadets' treatment by operative managers in the subsidiaries.

3.1. The Centre of Excellence Approach

An extensive set of interviews was conducted in one firm, Electra Services, because the degree to which it had actively sought to tap into the knowledge base in its foreign subsidiaries was unusual. Electra had created a European 'centres of excellence' programme with the aim of leveraging particularly important skills across Europe. A corporate manager had been made responsible for the process of selecting and appointing the centres of excellence. Seven departments or subsidiaries were appointed as a European centre of excellence in areas such as customer loyalty measurement, customer-focused marketing, and strategic management. They were located in Germany, the UK, Sweden, and France. As the centres of excellence were set up, they became independent entities with back-up from the European corporate head office in Brussels. They still remained within the budgetary domain of the country in which they were located, however.

But the system proved difficult to manage on an ongoing basis. The first problem that appeared related to the issue of whom should be held accountable for the costs and benefits the units created. The managers in the units often had dual responsibilities and worked simultaneously with subsidiary activities for the local managing director as well as with centre of excellence activities for the European operations. The main costs of the centre of excellence were the time, salary, and travel expenses of the manager. As it happened, the centre of excellence project never received a budget of its own. Instead, the country managing directors had to include these costs in their budgets. On the other hand, the revenues, i.e. the good that a centre of excellence brought with it, often benefited subsidiaries located in countries other than that of the centre of excellence. This was expected since the aim was to transfer know-how across geography. In fact, the sole aim of the venture was to create revenues in units other than the centre of excellence.

Nevertheless, this budgetary conflict harmed the project. One managing director simply told the centre of excellence manager to work exclusively with units within the particular country. Another centre had developed a concept that allowed it to work closely with customers in terms of actually trying to be a part of their problem-solving activities instead of just selling products to them. This proved to be very successful and subsidiaries in other countries were very keen to learn from this particular centre of excellence. Moreover, the local managing director was working very close to the managers behind the 'customer marketing' concept and gave his full support to the project.

A second problem related to the issue of how valuable the skills residing in the centres of excellence actually were for operative units in other countries. The decision of which units should serve as centres had been the work of one man. In practice, there were disputes over how valuable the capabilities of some centres actually were. First, were the skills valuable for other subsidiaries? Secondly, were the selected centre of excellence managers the best equipped managers to run the designated centres? The manager of the centre for strategic management had met a lot of opposition from operative subsidiaries since the issues he worked with sometimes threatened the ambitions and objectives of the subsidiary management. As a result, subsidiary managers sometimes ignored the centre of excellence and even called in external consultants who gave different advice. All in all, an internal study showed that about two years after the centres of excellence had been set up, less than 10 per cent of the European employees knew of their existence and less than 2 per cent knew what they actually were doing.

3.2. *The Information Systems Approach*

Another firm focused on the IT–IS-based solution, and was developing a global information system that aimed to serve primarily as an information provider but, it was hoped, also as a database for experience and knowledge. The system was set up as an internal information system based on Lotus Notes. Initially, the system focused on storing and making available product information, such as size dimensions, availability, applications, combination possibilities, etc. The idea was that a salesman in, for instance, Japan would be able to access this information immediately when needed by the use of a laptop computer and a mobile telephone. This made his customer service more effective. The ultimate goal was for salesmen also to store experiences and solutions to particular problems that they had encountered during the course of their work. If a salesman happened to face an unfamiliar situation, he would be able to search the database for possible solutions to his dilemma. The system was open to all, in terms of both input and usage. The firm's experience was that the system handled *information* transfer quite well. *Knowledge* transfers, on the other hand, were unseen.

3.3. Reconciling Different Perceptions

During the interviews one particularly interesting case was detected in which the corporate and the subsidiary managers had very different views of how things actually were. A marketing manager in the Swiss subsidiary of one of the firms ranked his unit much higher than the corporate managers had ranked the unit. It was a clear case of a perception gap.[2] During the interview the Swiss marketing manager—let's call him Günther—spontaneously touched upon the potential problem of determining how capable a specific unit is by stating that he could not definitely say how corporate managers had evaluated his unit. 'We can never be sure. Knowing and believing are two different things!' He explained this by the fact that the firm does not use formal recognition, e.g. through formally assigned centres of excellence, of how capable units actually are. When Günther was confronted with the data showing that corporate management did not rank his unit as very capable, he was silent for a long time. After some time he said that he always creates trouble for corporate management since he fights for his subsidiary's rights and needs. He explained that his subsidiary was given a low ranking by corporate management by the fact that he had unusually high objectives. Günther thought himself to be 'problematic for the corporate guys and probably rated lower because of that'. It was obvious that he was very troubled by the data he was shown. When the corporate marketing manager—a Swede —was confronted with the same data, he was not surprised. He explained the situation by saying: 'Günther is a proud gentleman who has very high self-esteem. He has poor self-judgement and poor judgement.'

What is interesting is the actual differences in opinion that existed between the two managers. It was very difficult to decide who was right and who was wrong. Still, the different opinions *per se* are interesting. How could the corporate manager work with knowledge management in the Swiss unit?

---

[2] A perception gap is defined as a difference between division and subsidiary managers' perceptions of how capable a subsidiary is to solve its operative problems effectively.

It is probably impossible to force the Swiss unit to adopt a practice from another subsidiary. If the Swiss manager thinks highly of his own subsidiary—rightly or not—it is very likely that he will be reluctant to receive practices from other units in the firm. Instead, it may even be likely that he would like to transfer practices from his own subsidiary to other subsidiaries. If he does transfer, and if his unit really is capable, everything is fine. But if he does transfer, and if his unit is incapable, we may see a case of transfer of a rather poor practice. The intended best-practice transfer could become a worst-practice transfer.

4. Research Methodology

In order to be able to answer the research questions in a more systematic manner, I conducted a quantitative study focusing on capabilities in marketing departments of subsidiaries in seven Swedish firms: Skandia, Sandvik Coromant, Sandvik Steel, Ericsson, Volvo, Pharmacia & Upjohn, and Alfa Laval Agri. The aim of the study was to understand how the MNE identifies the operative units that have 'best practices' in certain activities, and how the MNE leverages these practices between subsidiaries. The marketing practice used in the study is market orientation (Jaworski and Kohli 1993; Narver and Slater 1990), which includes a subsidiary's ability to collect, internally disseminate, analyse, and act upon market information on customers and competitors. This measure has been used in many studies in marketing and is regarded to be one of the best measures of marketing competence.

I structured the survey so as to receive evaluations of a particular subsidiary's capabilities from two different sources. I polled, first, the CEO and/or the marketing manager of each subsidiary, and, secondly, corporate managers responsible for global marketing activities. All subsidiaries in each firm were included in the study, and an overall response rate at the subsidiary level of 84 per cent meant that answers were received from almost all subsidiaries that were polled. Answers were also received from twenty-two corporate managers, which represents a response rate of 88 per cent at the corporate level. All in all, the data covered 176 subsidiaries in seven MNEs. Multiple responses were also collected—at both corporate and subsidiary levels—for as many subsidiaries as possible. In total there are multiple respondents covering thirty-six subsidiaries. The goal behind the idea of multiple respondents was to validate the results.

5. Findings from the Quantitative Study

The analysis of the quantitative data built on comparing the evaluations of, for instance, the French subsidiary made by corporate managers with the evaluations made by the French subsidiary managers themselves. This procedure was undertaken for all subsidiaries in all firms. If the evaluations were

found to be very similar, I concluded that the issue of evaluating competence was not a major problem in the MNE. As a result, the firms would
be expected to be able to identify sources and recipients in knowledge transfer processes without significant problems. If large differences between the
evaluations were found, the matter would appear in a very different light.
The transfer process would be expected to face problems such as the
'not-invented-here' syndrome[3] (Katz and Allen 1982), the 'don't listen to
me' problem,[4] or the more generic problem that transfers of best practices
actually become transfers of worst or mediocre practices.

The results broadly confirmed what was discovered during the interviews.
First, it was found that in only two of the seven firms did corporate and
subsidiary managers share the same beliefs of how competent the marketing departments in the subsidiaries were. In the other five firms there were
no shared beliefs regarding the competence of the subsidiaries. The results
indicated large perception gaps,[5] i.e. differences in how corporate and subsidiary managers evaluate competence, in a majority of the firms.

Questions were also asked regarding the financial performance of the
subsidiaries. The reason for these questions was to compare evaluations of
competence—market orientation—with evaluations of financial performance
—sales, operating results, and market share. When comparing corporate and
subsidiary evaluations of financial performance, the pattern was very different from the pattern regarding evaluations of competence. There was a much
higher level of agreement between evaluations of financial performance than
there was for evaluations of marketing capabilities. In other words, there
are more perception gaps for marketing capabilities than for financial performance (Table 9.1).

Thus, on average corporate and subsidiary managers shared opinions on
how capable the subsidiaries are in marketing activities in about 30 per cent
of cases. At the same time on average corporate and subsidiary managers
shared opinions on how well the subsidiaries perform in financial terms in
about 60 per cent of cases. Overall, opinions regarding how capable the
subsidiaries are show much greater differences as compared to opinions of
how well the subsidiaries perform in financial terms. There are substantial

---

[3] i.e. that the potential recipient of a practice believes that anything thought up elsewhere
must be inferior to that he/she has developed by him/herself. Thus, it is not worthy of becoming adopted and being implemented in the receiving unit. The result is a lack of willingness
to receive practices from other units.

[4] i.e. that the potential recipient of a practice believes that anything thought up elsewhere
must be superior to that he/she has developed by him/herself. Thus, his/her own ideas are
not worthy of becoming transferred to other units. The result is a lack of willingness to transfer practices to other units.

[5] The perception gap at the firm level is calculated by analysing the correlation between
corporate and subsidiary managers' evaluations of the same subsidiary. If the correlation is positive and significant, there is not a perception gap. In all other cases, there is a perception gap.
In practice, the correlation within a firm for a particular dimension ranged between +0.780,
which was highly significant ($\alpha = 0.000$), and –0.725, which was not significant ($\alpha = 0.165$).

TABLE 9.1. *Dimensions (capability v. financial) with hierarchical perception gaps (%)*

Firm	Capability performance dimensions with perception gaps	Financial performance dimensions with perception gaps
1	100 (4)	75 (4)
2	67 (6)	0 (4)
3	86 (7)	0 (4)
4	80 (5)	75 (4)
5	50 (6)	75 (4)
6	80 (5)	75 (4)
7	33 (6)	0 (4)
All (weighted average)	71	43

Note: Total number of dimensions in parentheses.

perception gaps regarding how capable subsidiaries are in performing the most important marketing activities.

5.1. How do we Explain the Perception Gaps?

From a theoretical perspective, the existence of perception gaps can be explained by three different factors. First, the managers have access to different pieces of information regarding the subsidiaries that are evaluated. Secondly, the managers have access to identical pieces of information regarding the subsidiaries, but asymmetrically choose to focus their attention on different pieces of information within the identical pool of information. Thirdly, the managers have access to identical pieces of information regarding the subsidiaries that are evaluated and symmetrically focus their attention on the same pieces of information, but interpret these identical pieces of information in different ways. In short, the three alternative explanations are:

Access to different pieces of information.
Selective attention to specific pieces of information.
Different—or selective—interpretation of identical pieces of information.

I should emphasize that the three different complementary explanations represent different stages of rationality. The first explanation—lack of access to important information—represents a mild degree of bounded rationality (Simon 1991). This is the most accepted restriction to the hypothetical perfect rationality. In practice, this restriction almost always holds. The third explanation—different interpretation of identical pieces of important information—represents a severe degree of bounded rationality. This restriction to perfect rationality is very seldom accepted—or even discussed—in research or practice. The possibility that a severe degree of boundedly

TABLE 9.2. *Results of regression analysis for perception gaps*

	Independent variable	Cronbach alpha	Beta-coefficient	Significance
Constant	—		—	0.313
Firm effects	Firm 4	—	−0.332	0.056
	Firm 6	—	−0.056	0.755
	Firm 7	—	+0.218	0.214
Control	Awareness of how much the corporate manager knows about the unit	—	+0.497	0.009
Access to information	Communication between subsidiary and corporate management	0.7639	+0.322	0.040
	Communication between subsidiary and other subsidiaries	0.7597	−0.197	0.196
	Use of IT as a communicative tool	0.9419	+0.289	0.098
Attention to the unit by corporate management	Strategic importance of market	0.6439	−0.210	0.198
	Financial performance of subsidiary	0.7922	+0.545	0.004
	Size of local market ($US)	—	+0.303	0.047
Symmetric interpretation of information	Dummy indicating if subsidiary manager is Swedish	—	−0.156	0.266
	Cultural distance to Sweden	—	+0.212	0.154
	Degree to which the subsidiary manager agrees with corporate management actions	0.7363	−0.224	0.178
F test			2.368	0.022
Adjusted R^2			0.275	

Note: The firm dummy items 1, 2, 3, and 5 are excluded in the final model.

rational behaviour could exist in knowledge management is most often disregarded.

To explain perception gaps, I used the three factors outlined in the previous paragraph and built a model that was tested in a multiple regression analysis (Table 9.2). The model had the perception gaps—calculated for each subsidiary as the difference between corporate and subsidiary managers' evaluations—as the dependent variable. The three main explanatory variables were the ones outlined above. I used different constructs to represent each of the main variables. In addition, I controlled for firm effects by using dummy variables for each firm, but also used a variable reflecting the degree to which corporate managers were aware of how much they actually knew about each subsidiary's capabilities. The multiple regression analysis tells us that perception gaps are explained by access to information by corporate managers and the attention corporate management assigns to a specific subsidiary. I conclude that there is no support for the most severe form of bounded rationality as an explanation behind perception gaps. The strongest support is found for the second form of bounded rationality: the hypothesis that selective attention explains perception gaps. The overall explanatory power of the model is high (adjusted $R^2 = 0.275$).

The control variable—the awareness of how much corporate managers actually know about the subsidiary—is also significant. This indicates that corporate management—at least to some extent—is aware of how much they know about each subsidiary. The result also validates the model as such. However, the relation between corporate managers' awareness and perception gaps is not intuitive. It was expected that the more corporate managers knew about a subsidiary's activities, the less the likelihood of perception gaps. My findings indicate that when corporate managers know a good deal about a subsidiary they tend to be slightly more critical[6] than when they know less. This means that more information about a subsidiary tends to make corporate managers more critical about the unit's capabilities, which is intuitively correct. In relative terms, corporate managers tend to underestimate subsidiaries' capabilities as compared to the subsidiaries' self-evaluation when the corporate managers know more about the subsidiary. Thus, as the corporate manager improves the degree to which he is informed about a subsidiary's activities, he decreases his evaluation of the subsidiary relative to the unit's self-evaluation.

As already stated, the strongest finding is that selective attention matters most. One of the indicators of corporate attention—the financial performance of the subsidiary—has a positive relation to the perception gaps. The better the subsidiary's financial performance, the more positive is the perception gap, i.e. the higher is the self-evaluation in relation to the corporate evaluation. As the financial performance of the subsidiary improves, the corporate manager decreases his/her evaluation of the subsidiary's capabilities. Meanwhile, the self-evaluations increase. This is surprising but interesting, given the way the financial performance measure is constructed. It is based on a combination of data from both subsidiary and corporate

---

[6] The correlation between corporate evaluations of marketing capabilities and degree of insight into the unit's activities is -0.106 ($\alpha = 0.185$).

managers,[7] and is reliable ($\alpha = 0.79$). The evaluators have similar views on how well the subsidiaries perform financially, but it affects their views on how capable the unit is in opposite directions. My preconception was that corporate managers would base their evaluations of marketing capabilities merely on the subsidiaries' financial performance, but the data show that this is not the case.

The size of the local market—measured by the subsidiary respondents' assessment of the total market expressed in US dollars—has the same relation to perception gaps as the financial performance construct. As the market size increases, the subsidiary manager increases his/her self-evaluation of the subsidiary's capabilities relative to the corporate managers' evaluations. It seems that the subsidiary managers tend to connect a large market—as an indicator of large overall sales by the subsidiary—with strong marketing capabilities.

The frequency of communication between subsidiary and corporate managers affects the perception gaps. Surprisingly, the communication frequency has a positive relation to perception gaps. The more frequent communication is, the more positive is the perception gap. In other words, more communication brings a higher self-evaluation in relation to the corporate evaluation. I conclude that more communication is associated with a relative overestimation by subsidiary managers of their own subsidiary's capabilities.

The main conclusion is that the attention that corporate managers assign —or do not assign—to a specific subsidiary explains the existence of perception gaps. More attention—as indicated by the unit's financial performance— does not automatically lead to lower perception gaps. Instead, it seems to increase perception gaps. One explanation of this result is that corporate managers do not assign much attention to units that perform the best (see above). Instead, their attention tends to be focused on units that they believe perform worse than average. As a consequence, the corporate managers may be poorly informed about the capabilities of the subsidiaries performing well both in terms of capabilities and in financial terms. This explanation has a positive and a negative side. The positive side is that if corporate managers focus their attention on units that perform poorly, they could help them to upgrade their capabilities. On the other hand, corporate managers face the risk of not understanding why the high performers are so successful.

To sum up, the perception gaps are mainly caused by lack of attention by corporate managers. This lack of attention, however, may very well be caused by low degrees of socialization, leading to a rather superficial knowledge of the subsidiaries and their operations by corporate management. We also argue that the inherent nature of valuable knowledge makes it 'invisible'. As an effect, hierarchical knowledge *management* seems doomed to fail.

---

[7] A factor analysis proved that corporate and subsidiary managers' evaluations of financial performance actually formed one construct, while their evaluations of marketing capabilities did not.

5.2. Transferring Best Practices within the Corporate Network

The discussion so far has dealt with whether managers are able to evaluate capabilities in a coherent way. The answer was that only in a minority of cases—around 30 per cent—were the managers able to do that. The result for evaluating financial performance was much better. The next question is whether the evaluations of competence matter in the transfer process. Do the units that are thought to be extraordinarily capable transfer their skills to other units in the firm? Moreover, since corporate and subsidiary managers' evaluations are often not identical, which of the evaluations is most influential when units are selected as sources?

When we relate the evaluations—corporate and subsidiary—of a subsidiary's capabilities to the unit's outward transfer frequency of best practices and products, we find that both corporate and subsidiary evaluations are positively related to the transfer frequency. The better the evaluations, the more frequent are practice transfers from these units. None of the relations is very strong, however.[8] In order to test how much of the selection of transfer sources the evaluations and other important variables explain, a multiple regression analysis was run.

In the analysis, variables were included that have been found to be important explanatory factors in previous research. These were:

1. Connectedness with rest of firm (see e.g. Kostova 1996). My indicators are communication with corporate management or other subsidiaries, use of IT, and degree of centralized decision-making.
2. Ability to share knowledge (Szulanski 1996). My indicators are effectiveness of the corporate knowledge management system, and the marketing experience of the unit manager.
3. Stickiness of capabilities (Zander 1991). My indicators are observability and codifiability of capabilities.
4. The local market. My indicator is the strategic importance of the local market.

In addition to the variables above, evaluation variables were added to test if they were important for the selection of source units in capability transfers. The test primarily showed that outward transfer frequency is explained by subsidiary managers' experience in marketing, as well as the codifiability and observability of the capabilities that are to be transferred. Moreover, the strategic importance of the local market and the financial performance of subsidiaries explain the frequency of outward transfers, i.e. the selection of sources in the knowledge management processes in the firm. The strongest indicator is the marketing experience of the subsidiary managers. The explanatory power of the model was high (see Table 9.3; adjusted $R^2 = 0.271$).

---

[8] The correlation is +0.240 ($\alpha < 0.01$) for corporate evaluations and transfer frequency, and +0.187 ($\alpha < 0.05$) for subsidiary evaluations and transfer frequency.

TABLE 9.3. *Results of regression analysis for outward transfer frequencies*

	Independent variable	Beta-coefficient	Significance
Constant		—	—	0.780
Firm effects	Firm 2	−0.164	0.176
	Firm 4	+0.091	0.523
	Firm 5	+0.011	0.932
	Firm 7	−0.039	0.755
Connectedness with rest of firm	Communication with other units	+0.119	0.253
	Use of IT	−0.013	0.908
	Degree of centralized decision-making	−0.085	0.422
Ability to share knowledge	Effectiveness of the corporate knowledge management system	−0.033	0.782
	Marketing experience by unit's CEO–marketing manager	+0.310	0.003
Stickiness of capabilities	Observability of capabilities	+0.180	0.070
	Codifiability of capabilities	+0.207	0.053
Local market	Strategic importance of market	+0.222	0.047
Capabilities, performance	Evaluation by corporate managers	+0.034	0.788
	Self-evaluation	+0.158	0.111
	Financial performance	+0.212	0.053
F test		3.254	0.000
Adjusted R^2		0.271	

Note: The firm dummies for firms 1, 3, and 6 are excluded in the model.

Thus, when studying how evaluations of capabilities relate to transfer patterns, the principal measure is that the selection of sources in transfer processes—as indicated by outward transfer frequency—is based on the financial performance of the unit. Financial performance is the most important measure when (explicit or implicit) selection of transfer sources is made. There is a weak indication that self-evaluations, i.e. that the source is confident that they are capable, also relate to the sourcing decision. The corporate evaluations have no bearing on the outward transfer frequency.

Overall, the transfer frequency is not determined by an intentional milking strategy in which particularly fat (capable) cows (subsidiaries) are milked to the benefit of particularly skinny (incapable) cows (subsidiaries). Instead, it seems that the process is much more *ad hoc* than that. A slightly exaggerated description would be that knowledge just happens to flow from whoever, and is received by whoever happens to be around.

6. Discussion and Conclusions

The study found that in some firms corporate managers' evaluations of subsidiaries' marketing capabilities differed significantly from subsidiary managers' evaluations of their own capabilities. There were perception gaps. Furthermore, the analysis of the selection of source units in transfers of marketing capabilities showed that it was primarily financial performance that was used as a capability indicator. If anything, self-evaluations had a weak explanatory power over the selection of source units. This shows that, first, perceptions of capabilities differ significantly between corporate and subsidiary managers. In addition, evaluations of capabilities do not explain the selection of source units in transfer processes. Instead, the source units are selected upon criteria such as the characteristics of capabilities or the personal experience of the subsidiary's marketing manager. The evaluation and transfer patterns indicate that the firms are *not* succeeding in transferring practices from undisputed top achievers to less capable subsidiaries. Moreover, corporate managers do not seem to be well informed about the capabilities of the subsidiaries.

6.1 Corporate Knowledge Management—an Oxymoron?

A key conclusion from this study is that corporate knowledge management, i.e. hierarchically controlled action in the capability transfer process, may be an oxymoron. Corporate managers cannot intentionally manage knowledge. The flows of knowledge are mainly explained by characteristics of the knowledge itself and the abilities to receive knowledge by recipients in the transfer process. Intentional leveraging of the absolutely most capable units' skills does not happen. Instead, it is the natural characteristics of the knowledge and the recipients that determine whether transfer happens. If anything, the subsidiary managers' opinions of how capable they and other subsidiaries are influence the selection of sources in the transfer processes. The corporate managers' opinions of how capable subsidiaries are often do not coincide with the subsidiaries' own views of their own skills, and do not seem to influence the selection of sources. Knowledge resides in the hands and heads of the operative managers and is best evaluated by these managers. In effect, hierarchical corporate knowledge *management* systems aimed at centralizing decisions regarding sources and recipients in the transfer processes are not likely to be effective. The heterarchical ideal (Hedlund 1986, 1993)—perhaps restricted to operative managers—seems to be a much better solution. The tacit characteristic of important knowledge suggests that it is difficult to know how capable a specific subsidiary is. This study proved this to be true. The implication is that corporate knowledge management is not likely to be effective. One cannot manage what one cannot understand.

One practical implication from these findings is that corporate managers should not centralize the capability management process. The selection of source units, for instance, is likely to be better managed by operative managers who have hands-on experience with the actual practices that are in question. One of the firms—firm 5—had intentionally built a system in which corporate managers were expected to have significant operational expertise. Their internal management system meant that corporate positions were only temporary and corporate managers were expected to take assignments in subsidiaries after the corporate position ended. This created high rotation of managers between subsidiary and corporate positions, which stimulated shared experience and values in the firm. This, in turn, brought harmonized views on the capability levels in different subsidiaries (see Table 9.1).

The results also show another risk. The selection of source units is likely to be heavily influenced by financial performance. All managers in a firm are very familiar with measures of financial performance, and are likely to base most decisions on this type of information since it is globally standardized and readily available. When it comes to decisions regarding capability management, however, there is a risk that financial performance does not harmonize with the actual level of capabilities in the subsidiary. In this study financial performance and marketing capabilities were not altogether positively related.[9] Still, the interviews did not show that managers were aware of this discrepancy. It is evident that financial performance is governed by many factors, such as local competition and cost structures, in addition to actual capabilities. All in all, financial performance is a poor indicator of capabilities.

Effective capability management clearly needs a balance between decentralized action and centralized support systems. This study indicates that one of the most important decisions in capability management—the selection of source units in the transfer process—is likely to benefit from being left in the hands of subsidiary managers. Centralizing *action* in capability management does not seem to be successful. This does not exclude the possibility that corporate management has an important function to fulfil in the capability management process. There has to be a budget for intra-firm action, there must be forums for intra-firm interaction, there must be corporate recognition schemes for top achievers, and there must be a supportive corporate function that can resolve potential disputes between subsidiaries and set the objectives. More importantly, when an undisputed best practice exists, corporate management may be able to achieve economies of scale via global co-ordination of decentralized action. Thus, corporate capability management is important since it provides the institutional framework in which subsidiaries may pursue capability management.

[9] The correlation between self-evaluations and financial performance—the combined construct—was +0.152 ($\alpha = 0.065$) and the correlation between corporate evaluations and financial performance—the combined construct—was −0.366 ($\alpha = 0.000$).

To sum up, this study showed that corporate and subsidiary marketing managers often did not have the same opinions regarding how capable a marketing unit in the firm actually is. There are sometimes considerable perception gaps, i.e. differences between corporate evaluations and subsidiaries' self-evaluations, regarding how skilled subsidiaries are. In the chapter I show that perception gaps exist, and relate the evaluations of skills to the patterns of knowledge transfers in the MNE. In doing this, I have found that practices, in fact, do not always flow from the units believed to be the most capable to those believed to be the least capable. Using this unique finding, I have drawn conclusions for the MNE knowledge management process.

10

New Wine in Old Bottles: Information Technology Evolution in Firm Strategy and Structure

PETER HAGSTRÖM

1. Introduction

Are firms inexorably moving into the brave new world of the information society or does information technology merely provide advances—albeit dramatic advances—in firm efficiency? Arguably, if we were to see these views as extremes on a continuum and confine our population to academics, the centre of gravity would be closer to the 'hype' side. In firms the situation appears to be more complicated. Painting the picture with broad brush strokes, operational management is likely to lean towards the efficiency side, professionals (in particular within the IT function) are more prone to see the sky as the only limit, while corporate management often finds itself in the role of innocent and incredulous bystander. Stark simplification as this undoubtedly is, it may still be a helpful point of departure when trying to make some sense of the impact on firm strategy and structure of the dizzying development of information technology.

This chapter will revisit some of the simple but salient features of IT that have emerged with the by now fairly protracted use of computer-related tools in organizations. Some more recent developments such as the internet, mobility, and enterprise-wide systems will also be examined. In the course of the chapter there will be an attempt to clarify the varying approaches to IT usage among and within firms. The basic line of argument is straightforward:

1. IT enables new strategies and structures;
2. IT and its usage change rapidly (cf. 'new wine'), but less so than is commonly held;
3. there are simple, stable, and useful ways to think about IT and its impact (cf. 'old bottles'), but although they are easy to understand, they appear to be hard to internalize; and
4. there is no single, superior answer to the question of the best way to run a firm in the age of IT.

The fundamental issue is that of IT as cast in the role of enabler; of being a necessary, but not sufficient, condition for much contemporary strategic and structural change. In this way, IT displays infrastructural properties, which, in turn, have a direct bearing on how networks inside and outside the firm are established and configured, and how capabilities can be honed at different levels within and between firms. As in Chapter 1, the claim is not that networks or capabilities are totally new phenomena *per se*; only that they have come to receive more attention by both scholars and practitioners fairly recently as the concepts have been explored and developed further. This chapter continues along this path. Empirically, IT does seem to broaden the scope for networks to arise as space and time constraints are relaxed, and as new possibilities for control and co-ordination of activities emerge. Apart from previous research, the narrative will seek very practical support in illustrative case facts drawn from a string of recent firm interviews and from written depositions by middle-level managers. Initially, however, a context for the terminology used here needs to be identified.

2. More than Four Decades of Debate

The first shot across the bow was fired by Leavitt and Whisler (1958). This original statement had computers prompting greater centralization in firms and, by implication, undermining impediments to firm growth. Authoritative literature reviews of the organizational impact (e.g. Markus and Robey 1988; Swanson 1987) have since convincingly shown that the use of IT can be associated with centralization and/or decentralization in firms. A parallel controversy coming out of research in economics during the 1980s is concerned with whether markets or hierarchies are stimulated by the use of IT; parallel, since proponents of markets over hierarchies tend to favour decentralization over centralization, and vice versa (Hagström 1991). In the strategy field academics (and companies) around the same time primarily seized on the possibilities of IT to undermine the market by introducing dedicated vertical electronic relationships and service innovations, thereby excluding competitors (e.g. Parson 1983; McFarlan 1984; Porter 1985). These courses of action are natural, since the essence of strategy arguably is to create temporary monopolies in order to make profits.

The above discussions raise the underlying issue of causality. Has the use of IT, broadly defined, been associated with specific outcomes? Much of the earlier strategy literature would say yes, stressing the instrumental nature of IT. Interpretations grounded in organization theory tended to have IT play the part of an intervening (rather than an independent) variable (e.g. Robey 1977) or stressed the strong malleability of the technology (e.g. Kling 1980). More dramatic is perhaps the conclusion that we simply have not understood what is going on and that 'constructive theoretical progress has been minimal' (Swanson 1987: 196).

The bottom line appears to be a strong correlation between configurations of strategy and structure, on the one hand, and IT usage, on the other. Clearly, there is little consensus on what the relationship looks like, so that predictability can be argued to be quite poor. However, this rather dismal lowest common denominator is all that is required in order to draw some other conclusions. First, the centralization–decentralization debate in the context of IT implies usage associated with firm activities being concentrated or dispersed in new ways within the organization. Secondly, the market versus hierarchy debate suggests that activities may move across firm borders in connection with the IT deployed, i.e. IT usage is associated with the changing scope of a firm.

Whether these changes would tend to be marginal or substantial is an empirical question, and as such a contentious one. Actually, the issue is one not only of magnitude, but of kind as well. An early proponent of this latter approach is Zuboff (1988), who argued that IT either automated an existing way of doing things or 'informated' employees to be able to do things radically differently. The latter term carries the connotations of empowerment and teamwork as information is made available for discretionary use by employees. Automation can suggestively be seen as IT allowing for something like 'electronic scientific management' (cf. Taylor 1947). A very practical example of the choice involved is the way insurance companies have chosen to use IT for claims-processing. An automating approach would have productivity increases by running highly specialized, functional processing of claims on a large scale. An 'informating' approach would instead have claims-processing by customer, letting the employee deal with the customer across activities (claims, billing, etc.) and claims (e.g. a tree falling over the garage, also damaging the car inside). Hence, rather than technological determinism, outcomes follow voluntaristic choices. This translates into the essence of the enabling characteristics of IT.

With movement of activities hierarchically in the organization and across organizational boundaries in place, and with a terminology allowing us to discuss magnitude and type of change introduced, we are well equipped. However, a third dimension of activity movement can readily be deduced: a spatial dimension.[1] A seminal piece by Nanus (1969) introduced the international application of computers by multinational corporations (MNCs). This early vision saw simple MNC activities, e.g. payroll, being automated and thus 'disappearing', whereas more complicated information flows would be centrally managed, thus allowing local decision-making to become more informed. The international aspects of computing were not really addressed again in the fields of strategy and organizational behaviour until the mid-1980s.[2] The next step came with Keen (1986), who is widely credited with

---

[1] For a more complete argument of the underlying logic, see Hagström (1991, 1996).

[2] Actually, some pioneering work by economists, starting with Antonelli (1981), and by individual geographers (e.g. Bakis 1980) came earlier but was in practice ignored by the various disciplines close to business administration.

explicitly bringing telecommunications into what hitherto had been the realm of computing only.

One final element of establishing a vocabulary and a context for a discussion of different types of usage of IT in firms is temporal change in emphasis. Largely driven by technological development as translated into changing costs, there is a basic story of moving from mainframes, via mini computers, to personal computers, which lately have been complemented by significant network capabilities through the rise of the internet and a widespread expectation that 'non-wired' IT will take off.[3] Of course, firms differ in when they got onto the bandwagon and in how far the technical possibilities have been exploited. The accelerated development of IT makes these considerations progressively more important. It is a humbling fact that the first commercial computer generally is regarded to be the Univac of 1951 and that even ten years later there were only a total of about 6,000 computers world-wide (McKenney *et al.* 1995).

The main reason for worrying about these historical debates and concepts is that they still have validity and are shaping the way firms tend to think about IT usage today. First, both people and systems from those days are still around, and, secondly and more importantly, some effects of IT usage are generic. In sum, we have a mobility of activities induced by IT usage and the technical possibilities as they have changed over time. The mobility can be seen to take place along three dimensions: hierarchically, across firm boundaries, and spatially. The upshot of mobility of activities is that performing activities is tantamount to deploying firm resources. Hence, we have a concept —activities—that is neatly sandwiched in between the resources controlled by the focal firm and the capacity for the firm to deploy those resources (capabilities).[4] If the location where the activities take place—organizationally, geographically, and in relation to the firm boundary—changes, then the firm capabilities underlying the activities may also be affected. For expository purposes, capabilities can here be thought of as recipes for the deployment of resources, i.e. recipes for the performance of activities.

The gathering of qualitative data for this exploratory inquiry is of two types: interviews have been carried out in firms partaking in the CaMiNO (*Ca*pability *M*anagement *in* *N*etwork *O*rganizations) research programme, and questions have been posed to middle-level executives through the executive education programmes at the Stockholm School of Economics.[5]

---

[3] The stories vary somewhat and have done so over time since Gibson and Nolan (1974) proposed an evolutionary model of IT growth by passing through various stages. For more recent and complete evaluations, see McKenney *et al.* (1995), and Castells (1996).

[4] On resources and the deployment of the same, see Ch. 1, and cf. Amit and Schoemaker (1993).

[5] In the latter case, participants in the executive MBA programme as a part of their mandatory evaluation had to answer questions about their IT applications structure and about how work has been affected over time as a function of IT usage. All in all, in excess of forty firms have supplied data. There are both Swedish and non-Swedish firms in the sample. However, the sample is neither random nor carefully selected, and data should be interpreted in that light. Firms' experiences are consequently used to illustrate and make credible—rather than 'prove' —our propositions.

The population of firms providing data and illustrations for the present chapter are firms active on the Swedish market.[6] This is no disadvantage since, by most measures, Sweden is among the most advanced countries in IT penetration and usage.[7] Far from giving accolades to Sweden (accolades that are, by the way, quite transient) the point is only to establish that Sweden is a reasonable area from which to choose a sample of firms, or, at least, was so in 1998.

3. Fixed or Flexible Infrastructure?

The standard approach towards first 'automating the mess' basically means going for the simplest, local, control-orientated applications. It is reasonably well established that firms started computerizing the transaction-heavy, simple applications like payroll and general ledger. Of course, these types of systems can also be found at the very heart of a firm's business. Good examples of this are the reservation systems at the airline SAS and the card transactions at the bank SEB. Another example is a logistics system for retailers, such as the one in place for ICA, Sweden's biggest food retailer, allowing it to reduce the number of major stocking locations from twenty-two to seven at the rate of about one a year. These are examples of automating given operations, reaping often dramatic productivity gains. Typically, both concentration of activities and an improved scope for control result from the process; in the latter case since the electronic transactions leave a trace. Not surprisingly, this general experience tallies well with early findings of IT usage being associated with centralization in firms (e.g. Whisler 1970).

In effect, what we see is how automation and scale effects typically coincide to move what often were dispersed activities to one particular location in terms of both geography and organization. This kind of IT application can perhaps best be likened to that of a utility, where the focus is on reducing costs for performing a set of often rather simple activities (see also Weill and Broadbent 1998). Simplicity notwithstanding, these types of systems are typically well entrenched in the organizations, in part because they are often idiosyncratic to the individual firm and in part because they tend to be fairly old. The characterization describes well the situation at both SEB and SAS. But the constraints of legacy systems in place can be worse still. Telia, the main Swedish telecommunications services operator, ran a major administrative system[8] that identified customers by telephone number,

---

[6] This should not be taken to mean only Swedish companies, as large firms like Coca-Cola, Lucent Technologies, and Baxter are included in the sample.

[7] For some figures, see Teldok (1997). Regarding fixed and mobile telephones, as well as personal computer and internet usage, available statistical data tend to put Sweden and other Nordic countries at or near the top internationally.

[8] Televerkets Administrativa Datasystem (TAD).

meaning that when customers started acquiring several lines, they also got several bills, service calls, etc. The system was so large and dominant that it was almost impossible to change. Adaptation being prohibitively expensive, the system far outlived its useful life at the hard-to-measure expense of deteriorating customer service as competition heated up before actually being replaced. Legacy systems are typically not only an irritating sunk cost; they also frequently inhibit thinking about how to best utilize a versatile tool like IT. Cross-selling of services, including customer support etc., are not on the agenda if the system in place does not have that option.

In terms of capabilities, a well-defined set tied to the system is often in evidence. Legacy constraints do tend to freeze those capabilities in time. One could expect these well-defined systems to be outsourced, but when the systems are close to the key activities performed by the firm, there is a definite reluctance to lose control over the (typically outdated) capabilities. SEB and SAS share this experience. When such systems are deemed less critical, outsourcing is a real option. Ericsson Sweden thus outsourced logistics for many of the components used in manufacturing to Caterpillar, safe in the conviction that Caterpillar would maintain its expertise given its own need to work with fast and efficient parts replacement. In this case, we see how an activity is concentrated geographically and organizationally, but also how it has moved outside the focal organization; a very unlikely move prior to the advent of the IT applications of the last decade or so. In fact the argument could be made that outsourcing activities in a way that, at times, makes the firm look like Swiss cheese is greatly stimulated by developments in IT usage. Using Thompson's (1967) terminology, IT may help in outsourcing not only the traditionally pooled and sequentially dependent activities, but also the reciprocally dependent activities, as systems have become more versatile.

In general, systems have become more complex over time, while growing more flexible. Dealing with complexity and incorporating flexibility can, however, play out quite differently for different firms. When ABB was created out of the merger between ASEA of Sweden and Brown Boveri of Switzerland in 1988, a common reporting system—ABACUS[9]—was put in place from day one. Only slightly modified since, the system is still the key common IT application in ABB. ABACUS is a very cheap and simple application developed in-house (for the history, see Simons 1992). The fundamental logic of ABACUS is to break down ABB into the smallest possible parts that could have a meaningful balance sheet,[10] hence going one step further than the more common assignment of only a profit and loss statement to a unit. The aim is to achieve consistency and to accommodate small units, e.g. manufacturing light switches, with large ones, e.g. manufacturing gas

[9] *Asea Brown Boveri Accounting and Communication System.*
[10] The main performance measure is return on capital employed.

turbines. In this fashion, data can readily be aggregated along the product and geography dimensions of ABB's matrix organization. With authority over data access strictly following the aggregation hierarchy, management can selectively choose to release information internally in order to induce competition among units. Competition is thus indirectly brought into the organization. Although different units do find themselves in customer–supplier relationships internally, competition fostered through ABACUS is more one of competition for inputs (e.g. investment funds) and for sheer survival.[11]

The upshot of the ABB control system is the ambition to push responsibility for a balance sheet as far out in the organization as possible, constituting a dispersal of business management in both geographical and organizational terms. Flexibility within the organization is achieved through a mix of internal competition and strong corporate control. ABB has also found a way to make a complex organization work. It hinges on the availability of accurate and timely monthly reporting. For all practical purposes, such reporting did not exist until the 1980s, which goes a long way to explain the failed matrix organizations of the 1970s. The different dimensions simply yielded different data, the reconciliation of which just took too much time. Also, complete electronic reporting is perhaps not as pervasive as is often assumed. Even Microsoft relied primarily on a paper-based reporting system until 1997.[12]

Skandia AFS, the hitherto successful long-term savings arm of the insurance and financial services firm Skandia (see Chapter 6), presents quite a different situation, although again the firm-wide application has infrastructural characteristics. The division was set up separately from the parent's insurance activities. The essential business idea is embedded in the communications network and specific applications that Skandia AFS has developed. The backbone is an IT platform that provides for an accommodating framework for applications, thus being widely different from the transactions-based legacy systems discussed above. Indeed, Skandia AFS is positioned as an arbitrator between the market for long-term savings and for fund management. In what traditionally is a vertically integrated business, Skandia AFS provides the communications infrastructure and a very limited range of support services, which are codified in its IT applications. The 'externalized' activities still need to be managed on a relationship (rather than a market) basis. The application of IT is arguably the network, and apart from managing that and the ancillary service activities, the main effort of Skandia AFS goes into managing the stable, dispersed relationships providing final customer access and customer fund management. In this sense, Skandia AFS is a good example of an IT-enabled 'external network'.

---

[11] The reasoning is similar to that of Cappelli (1999) in his recent book on how the market is indirectly brought into the employment relationship.

[12] Panel discussion by Robert Herbold, chief operating officer, Microsoft, and the author, 20 Oct. 1998 at the Grand Hotel, Stockholm.

More limited (in terms of firm coverage) applications also exhibit dramatic effects regarding location of activities and shifting locus of capability development. ABB Power Systems can supervise electrical grids jointly with the local customer without visiting the site. Trouble-shooting and proposed preventive maintenance is conveniently carried out by ABB from a remote location, so that they are able to concentrate the activity and subsequently develop it further than previously possible when it was dispersed in the field. In Ericsson a malfunction in a mobile system in Tokyo can instantly be re-created and corrected in a testbed in Stockholm. Although such more recently available systems allow ABB and Ericsson to improve on specific capabilities, the situation is far from clear-cut. The transport of field activities to a supplier location across the world is conceivably a two-way issue. In so far as knowledge can be articulated so as to be incorporated in software, activities will tend to shift to customers. Both ABB Power Systems and Ericsson Mobile can see how customers will begin to take over in particular the activity of analysing new electrical grids and mobile networks. Powerful simulation applications will to an increasing extent be available off the shelf, allowing the operator to make its own system pre-studies without necessarily possessing all the skills required to do the same thing from scratch. With activities shifting across firm boundaries, the vast majority of the firms in the sample showed an acute awareness of the need to learn how to manage these fluid external firm relationships. In terms of technology available, this has become easier. Still, external relations were seen by the firms as primarily a people issue, not least as a function of the evolution of the technology.

Unfortunately, the rather neat story of how IT applications have evolved over time is a bit more complicated than acknowledged above. In parallel to the simple transactions-based systems, different varieties of electronic mail systems have evolved. The early systems of the 1980s are perhaps best not remembered, being very cumbersome and restrictive in their format. Electronic mail and groupware of the 1990s have, by virtue of their ease of use, really taken off during the latter half of the 1990s. The sample firms were unanimous in their appreciation of the 'free-form' communication now possible. Without exception, the firms reported heavy usage of electronic mail. Given the lack of user-friendly early applications, electronic mail systems were rarely regarded as particularly important. The situation in Pharmacia & Upjohn was not extreme when they found that in 1996 there were twenty-two different electronic mail systems in use in the company. ABB never counted, but now report more than 100,000 users on a single system. The most enthusiastic firms were, however, the distant (sales) subsidiaries. Interviewees from Baxter, Lucent, and Coca-Cola in particular stressed the upgrading of local service offerings, and stronger integration with the rest of the company. Interpreting the practioners' reactions, the message that came across was very much one of free-form communication being a demand-driven opportunity, with benefits accruing according to local and individual initiative. In fact, such usage has been found to support spontaneously emerging communities of users within, but also across, firms (see Hagström 1990; and Chapter 7).

What come across as applications with profound impact on how work is organized and carried out tend to be 'simple' things such as electronic mail and rather straightforward, free-form groupware. Respondents in firms were in agreement to a remarkable extent on this score.

4. After Distributed IT, an Era of Mobility?

Increased demand for flexible applications has gone hand in hand with demand for what often is referred to as 'mobility'. Mobility is not only the characteristic of the majority of Ericsson products by sales, it is also a basic tenet for IT development at Ericsson. However, the company is keenly aware that 'mobile' is a less than unambiguous concept. To Ericsson it means moving from cell to cell within a radio network. That type of mobility for data communication (as opposed to voice communication) is still rare in firms. What most people tend to have in mind when saying 'mobility' is ubiquitous access. In principle, that has been available at Ericsson for years. At Hewlett-Packard the PC common operator environment platform provides the same service. Wherever in the world an employee finds himself or herself, it is possible to log on to his or her domain. Originally, these applications relied on proprietary standards. The wider, now totally dominating, standard of the internet protocol (TCP–IP[13]) is also widely used for intra- and extranet solutions.

However, it is easily forgotten how recent this wider standard really is. Peter Keen's widely acclaimed book *Every Manager's Guide to Information Technology* (Keen 1991) selected the 140 most important IT terms for careful explanation. Internet was not one of those terms. It is by no means uncommon that influential books published in the last few years barely afford the internet a mention.[14] The same story comes across from managers in firms. Everybody knows about the internet and even smallish firms frequently have a home page. However, they typically contain information for external use and applied internet usage is in effect less common than typically assumed.

---

[13] Transmission control protocol–internet protocol.

[14] By no means wanting to single any books out, since this state of affairs is the norm rather than the exception, one could anyway, for instance, note that an insightful and important book such as *Strategic Planning for Information Systems* (Ward and Griffiths 1996) mentions the internet once, but then as a synonym for the information super highway. Similarly, the edited volume *Global Information Technology and Systems Management* (Palvia *et al.* 1996) brings up the internet three times on its more than 600 pages, but more *en passant* than anything else. Moreover, it is often forgotten that the world-wide web came into existence as late as 1993.

Internet protocol (IP) based solutions are different, particularly in the respect that the standard can be used externally as well as internally. Two main effects seem to follow: first, that information very much goes from being 'sent' to being 'searched', and, secondly, that spatial reach becomes less dependent on scale.

ABB Power Systems and Baxter report that it is expected that employees should keep themselves informed, rather than it being the responsibility of management to inform employees. At Swedish Match there is a policy of making information more widely available by making it less dependent on individual employees. A side-effect of improved availability and demand-driven acquisition of information is the alleviation of tendencies towards 'information overload'. Several respondents pointed to the advantages of not having information broadcast in the firm, but rather simply that information is available as it is in a traditional library. As with free-form applications, practitioners seem to stress the importance of local initiative when it comes to honing capabilities. The feeling of access to support from the whole firm appears to underpin this notion.

The impression is reinforced when turning to spatial reach. One obvious difference, however, is that whereas information search primarily was identified as being active in an internal information market, the reach observation tended to refer to external parties. One recurring point relates to the internet replacing the traditional dedicated customer and supplier links of yesteryear (so called inter-organizational systems). Firms like Baxter achieved almost folkloric status back in the early 1980s in studies of how they managed to tie in their customers with dedicated communication lines and applications (e.g. Wiseman 1985). A more topical illustration is Astra's US marketing subsidiary (formerly the Astra Merck Inc. joint venture), which has created a site called www.acidcontrol.com. The site offers advice particularly on how to deal with heartburn, and about the uses of its ulcer drug Losec. The main target audience is heartburn sufferers, but also physicians. The regulations surrounding this type of direct marketing are more liberal in the United States than elsewhere. Through the internet's global reach, the channel is available also to non-US consumers, although a prominently displayed notice proclaims the site to be directed to US consumers only. The bottom line here for Astra is that locally developed capabilities in marketing and customer interface are immediately available for inspection by other parts of the organization and by external parties world-wide.

Lastly, there is a note of caution regarding the flexibility of IP solutions. Cisco Systems is arguably one of the major companies that uses the internet most actively, recording more than half of their sales over the net. However, the spatial reach here makes for a global approach that to a large extent rules out local adaptation. There is consequently no contradiction between IP applications and tight control that curtails the independence of foreign sales subsidiaries.

5. Comprehensive Approaches to IT Support for the Business

'In effect, it is easier to organise the company around the system rather than to adapt the system to the organisation' is an authentic comment from Ericsson when a manager was discussing the travails of implementing an enterprise resource planning (ERP) system.

During the period 1998–9 Ericsson was in the process of 'rewiring' the whole company. The existing IT infrastructure had become hopelessly outdated as the company was saddled with a plethora of legacy systems. They had been established successively and had not come through any major acquisitions. As one middle manager in Ericsson Radio Systems expressed it: 'All the different company functions, and on top of that, often even the geographic units, had their own systems, so we had to do something.' In fact, Ericsson has a history of being an early adopter of IT, not least as a function of being in the business. Indeed, the Ericsson story is confirmed by very similar experiences by other firms. And legacy systems are not only of the simple transactions-based category as discussed earlier. Firms have tended to keep adding to the stock of such systems. When preparing to deal with the year 2000 problem (Y2K), Telia found that they had more than 1,300 applications running in the company. The situation was similar in ABB Sweden, when the need to know exactly how important a particular customer was became a competitive necessity (see also Chapter 3). These illustrations are all powerful arguments for an ERP-type application. ABB Sweden has spent in excess of $US 250 million on such an implementation, as has Ericsson. Attractive as consolidation may seem, ERP systems raise some issues in addition to the obvious one of price.

Earlier received—and also often quite expensive—'wisdom' has instructed firms to 'align IT and business strategy', or, worse, has recommended that 'IT should drive business strategy'; that they should somehow 'fit' (e.g. Rockart and Scott Morton 1984). This is, indeed, a tall order, and clearly so when tackled in a complex company like Ericsson, where more than 80,000 employees in more than 100 countries work in one of the fastest-moving business environments. The old idea of 'fit', which is an intuitively appealing concept (who would want to wear size 9 or 11 shoes when having size 10 feet?), is also quite misleading. Technology, the environment, and strategy change, so fit becomes a problem over time. Such a static view inspired by notions of fit could easily be a recipe for introducing tomorrow's legacy systems.[15]

In the ERP world fit can be seen to be taken to an extreme, as the initial quotation in this section demonstrated. Furthermore, one effect of this

---

[15] More flexible approaches to the idea of fit have, however, started to surface. An empirically grounded approach that has gained some currency is one of tying business maxims to IT maxims (Weill and Broadbent 1998), thus implicitly avoiding the requirement of the snug fit.

situation is that of the IT department commonly being responsible for implementing what amount to fundamental business processes and often a new structure for the firm. Given the average age of corporate managers,[16] they typically have great difficulty in getting the required overview and fully understanding what is going on. Earl (1996) describes the chief information officer 'mark 2', which can be interpreted to amount to the IT function *de facto* taking the lead in business development (although it was never intended to be this way).

Another perhaps somewhat troubling observation is that ERP systems return in spirit to the days of the mainframe, when the prevailing concept was to build giant, single, integrated systems (e.g. Kanter 1977): in effect complete computer models of the firm. Most of those endeavours failed, as did, for instance, the attempt in the 1970s by the world's leading roller bearing manufacturer, SKF, to build STICS, the SKF totally integrated computer system. If IT is an enabler by virtue of its infrastructural properties, then flexibility becomes all the more important. If IT affects where activities are carried out, there is an obvious danger that firms will support and develop 'legacy capabilities' when making constraining technology choices. A middle manager in SAS made the comment that 'Today, SAS's organization is more flexible than many of the company's [computer] systems.' The empirical data demonstrated that there is quite some apprehension among managers over the implementation of some of these modern large-scale applications.

6. Designing IT Usage or being Designed by IT Usage?

Firms have considerable leeway over how IT is employed in the firm. The enabling characteristics present the firm with some fundamental choices. The firm can choose to operate as usual, employing IT primarily to automate given activities. Choosing instead to change, there appear to be two fundamental dimensions to consider. First, IT allows for vastly improved control of even the smallest units in a complex organization; a control that the firm can decide to exercise to its fullest or not. In the extreme, one can think of each individual, or even each activity of an individual, being a profit centre. Improving control makes it easier to live with a 'messier' organization, as a particular, consistent structure is not needed for control functions the way it used to be.[17] Differently put, firms can let organizations become more idiosyncratic in response to particular needs without losing control. Of course, idiosyncrasy is not confined to the focal firm; it is also relevant for the firm's external relationships.

---

[16] The chairman of ABB, Percy Barnevik, introduced the notion of BC and AC (Before Computers and After Computers) into ABB. The idea was that the employees could be divided into these two groups and that if you were 'born BC', you had a bit of catching up to do.

[17] For a historical context to this argument, see Beniger (1986).

The second dimension of change is the degree to which a detailed organizational blueprint is implemented. With IT allowing information to be easily accessed far from corporate centres, firms can opt to keep the organization on a tight leash or to allow more local initiative as individuals or local units make use of the IT infrastructure. The former is like planning a new housing development and putting in the walkways from the beginning. The latter situation is more akin to letting people move in and then pave where they walk. Choice along this dimension is contingent on one's view of how capabilities and organizations evolve. IT can support a directive design procedure as well as a looser approach where the aim is to create favourable conditions for organic change. In some ways, these are extreme versions of what Burns and Stalker (1961) called mechanistic and organic organizations.

The picture that emerges is one of IT enabling more choice in how firms are structured. In so far as firms exercise their possibilities for choice, the result is likely to be greater variation in the way different firms operate—something that also showed up repeatedly in the empirical material. Contemporary IT usage can then possibly add some weight to the thought that the variance in the structure of surviving organizations may actually be increasing (Hagström and Chandler 1998).

Again, structural choice is not confined to the focal firm. Internal as well as external networks fit well into this story. Opting for more organic self-organizing makes internal relations more market-like in character. Conversely, using the ability to accommodate more complex structures may well make external relationships more likely as more—and more varied—links can be managed.

In the end, the enabling characteristics of IT also imply that the better and more malleable the technology becomes, the less technical management and the more people management is required when thinking about the firm structure. Restrictions on what can be done may then rest more in the minds of people than in the technology.

11

Relaxing the Boundaries of the Firm

PETER HAGSTRÖM

1. Introduction

An underlying theme of the contributions in this book is that firms find themselves embedded in internal and external networks of relationships within which there are neither 'pure' arm's-length nor formal hierarchical transactions. It follows that it is these relationships—rather than the nodes *per se*—that are of primary interest. It has also been posited that capabilities are nourished and grow in such networks.

Essentially we are then left with 'the firm' defined as a legal entity and with a claim to be the natural and only unit of analysis. This is problematic as we then lack unambiguous terminology for identifying the 'correct' unit(s) of analysis. Many of the contributions point to capabilities residing at different organizational levels. They come at the group, individual, or sub-unit level as well as in the organization as a whole. In addition, they can arise between firms, hence also raising the problem of rent appropriation. The firm is then not always the relevant unit of analysis for strategy and structure, but different networks may be. Admittedly the question is largely left unresolved in the book and will remain so in this postscript, although a discussion of the problems is offered.

2. The Firm

When markets do not work, firms or organizations arise. The dominant theory of the firm views the firm as a nexus of contracts (for a review, see Holmström and Tirole 1989). Consequently, the firm must be able to enter into contracts, and hence the firm is defined by its legal boundaries, which, in practice, are its balance sheet. In line with Coase's (1937) original hypothesis, firms are then the most efficient response to contractual constraints. In this world the structure of the firm is invariably a hierarchy.[1] The market versus hierarchy framework is at odds with the more empirically grounded contributions in the present volume by virtue of being too parsimonious to be particularly helpful when trying to understand observed phenomena.

---

[1] For a fuller argument on this point, see Hagström and Hedlund (1998).

The reductionism need not be taken to its extreme, however. Relational and implicit contracts are offered as remedies in situations when explicit contracts are inconvenient or impossible to write (Williamson 1985; Milgrom and Roberts 1992). In short, some blurring of organizational boundaries is accepted. Whether a vague relational contract or an unarticulated implicit contract is in place, it is expected that the parties nurture their relationship and act in good faith. On the other hand, as transactions become more complex and uncertain, the assumption is that they will be brought into the non-market governance mode, i.e. the hierarchy. The dividing line between when hierarchy is the more efficient outcome and when incomplete contracts are is not obvious. The theoretical proposition is that the arrangement that minimizes transaction costs will survive (Williamson 1975), and that consequently less efficient arrangements will not be observed in the economy.

Still, these alternatives seem to be less than the whole story when considering the way that Skandia AFS puts so much effort into making the relationships with its partner firms 'thicker' (Chapter 6), or when considering the intricate and diverse exchanges between Volvo and its suppliers (Chapter 2). Given that these situations also are characterized by an extremely limited set of alternative partners (if any at all), and with considerable relation-specific investments, they should be good candidates for being vertically integrated (cf. Milgrom 1992), yet that is clearly not the case.

3. Fuzzy Networks

The term 'network organization' has been used throughout this book to denote these 'thick' relationships, be they internal or external to the legal boundary of the firm (cf. Baker 1992; Chapter 1). This view of networks is both flexible and imprecise: flexible as these notions of patterns of roles and relationships are employed in a highly exploratory fashion, and imprecise for the same reason.

A related problem is that 'network' has been used in many different contexts already. Physical networks such as communications networks imply a measure of standardization and permanence of links between nodes, and are at times used to describe organizational relationships (cf. Hagström 1991). Such a rigid interpretation is not relevant here as flexibility, dispersal of control and co-ordination, and preponderance of lateral relations are not captured. On the other hand, information and communications networks can be used to promote the evolution of such organizational networks (Chapter 11). The enabling characteristics of modern information technology has also been a recurring theme in the preceding chapters.

Other uses of 'networks' in the realm of organizations have tended to be more precise, and hence restrictive, compared to the empirical approach taken throughout the book. For instance, like most authors Nohria and

Eccles (1992) take the existing relationships as given, which is difficult here, since capabilities not only exist, but are being created in the networks.[2]

We have been left with a notion of networks that encompasses complex roles and relationships, and that change over time, in terms of both participants and the quality of the links. These 'fuzzy networks' are, of course, no match for Occam's razor, but work reasonably well for exploratory and descriptive purposes. Within the legal boundary of the firm any directional centre of gravity in the fuzzy network is anyway far less dominant and commanding than an apex of a hierarchy. Although more market-type relationships may enter the traditionally defined firm,[3] they are typically not arm's-length relationships. However, centralized control is forgone, which, in turn, raises the issue of appropriation of profits and distribution of costs also within the traditional firm.

4. Strategic Investments

One, more formal, way to deal with investments in network relationships is to view these investments as options on future states of nature. Standard treatments of corporate finance (e.g. Brealey and Myers 1991) look at uncertain investments in this way, and a similar logic can be applied to internal investments (cf. Kogut and Zander 1992). These types of investments are typically prerequisites for profitable follow-up investments. These strategic investments have to be treated as options, since they fail standard calculations of the net present value kind. Investment in new capabilities falls into this category. Typically firms under-invest in such platforms—in opportunities to act in possibly new markets (Kogut and Kulatilaka 1994). In addition, they may be established in unexpected places—in peripheral or external parts of the network (cf. Chapter 5).

Appropriation of rents can be seen in the light of strategic investments or options pricing. The problem does not seem to be too dissimilar from that of public goods, the provision of which always seems to be a practical problem. Still, firms seem to be able to handle it (as governments do in the case of public goods) although no claim should be made that this is always done efficiently. A reasonably acceptable example of how such a situation can be handled formally can be taken from the aircraft engine industry and the experience of Volvo Aero. Broadly, a major manufacturer like General Electric or Pratt & Whitney takes the lead in a consortium that develops a new engine. Volvo Aero then typically takes a 5–10 per cent share in such a consortium. That translates into Volvo Aero assuming 5–10 per cent of the costs and being entitled to the same share of all future revenues from

---

[2] See also the extensive argument in Ch. 5 on different views of networks.

[3] Market-like mechanisms can be used even for quite complex activities such as R. & D., as can be seen from Ch. 8.

that engine, including spare parts. In particular, Volvo Aero has to do its share of the work before any revenues materialize. Without going into detail, problems can arise if, for instance, the lead manufacturer puts less effort into selling the engine in favour of another one from another development consortium in its portfolio. Similarly, the engine could be the one to suffer heavy discounts when a whole range of engines are sold to a large customer etc. The only defence in such situations is the reputation built up over a long time in the relationship and the prospect of maintaining this relationship, since there is no formal recourse.

One way of interpreting the described situation would be to see it as an implicit contract, but that is a catch-all for a rather rich context. Another way would be simply to put it down to the parties' relative bargaining strength (cf. Dyer and Nobeoka 1998). However, in practice, rents may not be exactly appropriated, but be approximately so. The value of reputation, common norms, and expectations of future collaboration tend to yield a reasonable outcome. What we have called 'fuzzy networks' are set in a rich context, and mutual adjustment mostly seems to be able to handle the division of profits and costs satisfactorily. If it did not work reasonably well, the courts would be swamped by disputes, given the large number of intensive customer–supplier relationships we know are in existence.

The appropriation issue can also arise within the legal entity, particularly if more market-like mechanisms are introduced. In large, and/or 'decentralized' organizations, sub-units operate on different budgets or belong to different profit centres or the like. The potential for conflict is there, but the ability for the internal network to handle the situation should be no worse than that of an external network. In fact, here we come across classical issues such as charging out of corporate overhead, payment for research and development, etc.

Conceivably, it becomes really complicated if different levels of analysis (e.g. supra-firm, firm, and sub-unit) are involved at the same time for development of a 'platform' or of a set of new capabilities. At least that would be the case with the view of the firm as a nexus of contracts. A critical assumption that guides the establishment of contracts is similarity of bounded rationality. Multiple levels of analysis would, however, imply the existence of different rationalities, since one of the main reasons for having an organization at all is that it supplies the framework for how decisions should be taken by sub-units (cf. March and Simon 1958). This is the hierarchical principle at work. It is clearly unsuited for multiple-level capability development, again pointing to the need for a different conceptualization.

5. Increased Complexity

Thompson (1967: 70) noted more than three decades ago that crossing international boundaries probably is the most dramatic complexity for organizations to deal with. This increased complexity shows up in the contributions to this volume. In practice all of the firms involved in the empirical studies were active internationally. Limiting our foray into yet another area of inquiry, a few brief observations may nevertheless be in order in light of the previous discussion.

First, there has been a forceful debate about new organizational forms in an international context as the dissatisfaction with traditional models grew. Lateral, complex organizations with well-developed internal and external links were discussed more than a decade ago under terms such as the heterarchy (Hedlund 1986), the transnational (Bartlett and Ghoshal 1989), or the horizontal organization (White and Poynter 1990) to name a few influential contributions. Secondly, the *raison-d'être* of multinational corporations is often put down to the need to internalize exchange relationships that cannot be adequately enforced through explicit contracts, and/or the multinational possessing network advantages by virtue of its international presence. The internalization approach interestingly allows explicitly for internal markets through shadow pricing and for labour contracts (e.g. Hennart 1982; Buckley 1988). Network advantages are framed in terms of holding options not too dissimilarly to the situation with strategic investments. However, advantages are exploited, for example by shifting production between different locations in the multinational network of facilities in response to changes in the real exchange rate (Kogut 1983; Kogut and Kulatilaka 1994).

The three research traditions are all well established. The point of raising them here is not to explore them in detail, or because of any empirical overlap, but merely to draw attention to the fact that complex organizations, internal markets, and strategic investments are very much an ongoing concern in the research on multinational corporations and have been so for quite some time. The issues and the theoretical approaches used to deal with them parallel the earlier discussion in this chapter. Obviously, similar relationships have been able to develop and thrive across borders in spite of the increased complexity; or perhaps it is the very increased complexity of fuzzy networks that we find when studying multinational corporations. If even greater internationalization is inevitable, then multinational corporations may be trailblazers especially worthy of study. One sobering thought is that these networks—or whatever they are—are found where the legal structure varies considerably and with nodes in different cultural environments. In so far as approaches to organizations hinge on a uniform legal and culture-free environment, it seems unlikely that they can capture what we actually observe out there.

6. Concluding Remarks

The research programme reported in this volume has been about developing capabilities in fuzzy networks over relaxed firm boundaries. Although this is put forward with tongue in cheek, there is a long research agenda coming out of this largely explorative research. We know little about where and how capabilities are developed. It seems likely that capabilities materialize not only at the firm level, as is all too often assumed. Then there is the issue of direction; can capability development be managed, or is it the conditions for it that are to be managed? What is the relevant unit of analysis, and how do we deal with multi-level issues? How do we define and delimit networks? If we downplay traditional firm boundaries, what do we use instead?

The use of terminology such as 'external', 'internal', 'firm', 'market', etc. shows to what extent we are prisoners of the existing language. Disturbingly, arguing against the dichotomy of 'external' and 'internal' still means we need to use the very same dichotomy in order to make the point. Maybe some solace can be gained from practitioners. With activities shifting across firm boundaries, the vast majority of the firms[4] showed an acute awareness of the need to learn how to manage fluid external firm relationships. Interestingly, several of the interviewees also spontaneously indicated that the issue was extremely difficult to pin down. Subsequent probing revealed what appeared to be a lack of a common language or of a vocabulary to talk about these issues. Perhaps this volume can stimulate academics and practitioners to help fill that void.

---

[4] In the sample of firms from Ch. 10.

References

ABERNATHY, W. J. (1978), *The Productivity Dilemma* (Baltimore: Johns Hopkins University Press).

ALEXANDER, C. (1964), *Notes on the Synthesis of Form* (Cambridge, Mass.: Harvard University Press).

ALLEN, T. J. (1977), *Managing the Flow of Technology: Technology Transfer and the Dissemination of Technological Information within the R&D Organization* (Cambridge, Mass.: MIT Press).

—— (1986), 'Organizational Structure, Information Technology, and R&D Productivity', *IEEE Transactions on Engineering Management*, 33: 212–17.

AMIT, R., and SCHOEMAKER, P. J. (1993), 'Strategic Assets and Organizational Rent', *Strategic Management Journal*, 14: 33–46.

ANCONA, D. G., and CALDWELL, D. F. (1992), 'Bridging the Boundary: External Activity and Performance in Organizational Teams', *Administrative Science Quarterly*, 37: 634–65.

—— —— (1997), 'Rethinking Team Composition from the Outside In', in D. H. GRUENFELD (ed.), *Research on Managing Groups and Teams* (Stamford, Conn.: JAI Press).

ANDERSON, E., and WEITZ, B. (1989), 'Determinants of Continuity in Conventional Industrial Performance', *Marketing Science*, 8: 310–23.

ANDREWS, K. (1971), *The Concept of Corporate Strategy* (Homewood, Ill.: Dow-Jones-Irwin).

ANSOFF, I. (1965), *Corporate Strategy* (New York: McGraw-Hill).

ANTONELLI, C. (1981), *Transborder Data Flows and International Business: A Pilot Study*, DSTI/ICCP/81.16, Working Party on Information, C.a.C.P.E.G.o.T.D.F. (Paris: OECD).

ARGYRIS, C., and SCHÖN, D. (1978), *Organizational Learning: A Theory of Action Perspective* (Reading, Mass.: Addison-Wesley).

ARROW, K. J. (1959), 'Control in Large Organizations', *Management Science*, 10: 397–408.

ARVIDSSON, N. (1999), *The Ignorant MNE: The Role of Perception Gaps in Knowledge Management* (Stockholm: Institute of International Business, Stockholm School of Economics).

ASHBY, W. R. (1956), *Introduction to Cybernetics* (London: Chapman & Hall).

BAKER, W. E. (1992), 'The Network Organization in Theory and Practice', in N. NOHRIA and B. ECCLES (eds.), *Networks and Organizations* (Cambridge, Mass.: Harvard Business School Press).

BAKIS, H. (1980), *The Communications of Larger Firms and their Implications on the Emergence of a New World Industrial Order: A Case Study of IBM's Global Data Network.* (Tokyo: Commission on Industrial Systems, International Geographical Union, Chou University).

BARNEY, J. B. (1986), 'Strategic Factor Markets: Expectations, Luck and Business Strategy', *Management Science*, 32: 1231–41.

—— (1991), 'Firm Resources and Sustained Competitive Advantage', *Journal of Management*, 17/1: 99–120.

BARRAS, R. (1986), 'Towards a Theory of Innovation in Services', *Research Policy*, 15: 161–73.

BARTLETT, C. A. (1996), *Skandia AFS*, Harvard Business School Teaching Case N9–396–412 (Cambridge, Mass.: Harvard Business School).

—— and GHOSHAL, S. (1989), *Managing across Borders: The Transnational Solution* (Cambridge, Mass.: Harvard Business School Press).

BASTIEN, D. T. (1987), 'Common Patterns of Behavior and Communication in Corporate Mergers and Acquisitions', *Human Resource Management*, 26: 17–33.

BENIGER, J. (1986), *The Control Revolution: Technological and Economic Origins of the Information Society* (Cambridge, Mass.: Harvard University Press).

BEST, M. (1990), *The New Competition* (Cambridge, Mass.: Harvard University Press).

BIRKINSHAW, J. M. (1995), 'Entrepreneurship in Multinational Corporations: The Initiative Process in Canadian Subsidiaries', Western Business School PhD thesis.

—— and HOOD, N. (1998), 'Multinational Subsidiary Evolution: Capability and Charger Change in Foreign-Owned Subsidiary Companies', *Academy of Management Review*, 23: 773–95.

BOLAND, R. J., and TENKASI, R. V. (1995), 'Perspective Making and Perspective Taking in Communities of Knowing', *Organization Science*, 6: 350–72.

BOWER, J. L. (1974), 'Planning and Control: Bottom-Up or Top-Down', *Journal of General Management*, 1: 20–31.

BREALEY, R., and MYERS, S. (1991), *Principles of Corporate Finance* (New York: McGraw-Hill).

BROWN, J. S., and DUGUID, P. (1991), 'Organizational Learning and Communities of Practice', *Organization Science*, 2: 40–57.

—— and GRAY, E. S. (1997), *The People are the Company* (Boston: Fast Company).

BUCKLEY, P. J. (1988), 'Organizational Forms and Multinational Companies', in S. THOMPSON and M. WRIGHT (eds.), *Internal Organization, Efficiency and Profit* (Oxford: Philip Allan).

—— (1997), 'The Economics of Business Process Design in Multinational Firms', in M. RICKETTS and R. MUDAMBI (eds.), *The Organization of the Firm: International Business Perspectives* (London: Routledge).

—— and CASSON, M. (1976), 'Alternative Theories of the Multinational Enterprise', in *The Future of the Multinational Enterprise* (London: Macmillan).

BURGELMAN, R. A. (1983*a*), 'A Model of the Interaction of Strategic Behavior, Corporate Context, and the Concept of Strategy', *Academy of Management Review*, 8/1: 61–70.

—— (1983*b*), 'A Process Model of Internal Corporate Venturing in the Diversified Major Firm', *Administrative Science Quarterly*, 28: 223–44.

—— (1991), 'Intraorganizational Ecology of Strategy Making and Organizational Adaptation: Theory and Field Research', *Organization Science*, 2/3: 239–62.

BURNS, T., and STALKER, G. M. (1961), *The Management of Innovation* (London: Tavistock).

CAPPELLI, P. (1999), *The New Deal at Work: Managing the Market-Driven Workforce* (Boston: Harvard Business School Press).

CARTER, J. R., and MILLER, J. G. (1989), 'The Impact of Alternative Vendor–Buyer Communication Structures on the Quality of Purchased Materials', *Decision Science*, 20: 759–75.

CASTELLS, M. (1996), *The Rise of the Network Society* (Oxford: Blackwell).

CAVES, R. (1971), 'International Corporations: The Industrial Economics of Foreign Investment', *Economica*, 41: 176–93.

CHANDLER, A. D. (1962), *Strategy and Structure: Chapters in the History of the American Industrial Enterprise* (Cambridge, Mass.: MIT Press).

CHESBROUGH, H. W., and TEECE, D. J. (1996), 'When is Virtual Virtuous', *Harvard Business Review*, 74/1: 65–73.

CHRISTENSEN, C. M. (1993), 'The Rigid Diskdrive Industry: A History of Commercial and Technological Turbulence', *Business History Review*, 67: 531.

—— (1997), *The Innovator's Dilemma* (Boston: Harvard Business School Press).

CLARK, K. B. (1985), 'The Interaction of Design Hierarchies and Market Concepts in Technological Evolution', *Research Policy*, 14: 235–51.

—— (1989), 'Project Scope and Project Performance: The Effect of Parts Strategy and Supplier Involvement on Product Development', *Management Science*, 35: 1247–63.

—— and FUJIMOTO, T. (1991), *Product Development Performance* (Boston: Harvard Business School Press).

COASE, R. A. (1937), 'The Nature of the Firm', *Economica*, 4: 386–405.

COHEN, M. D., MARCH, J. G., and OLSEN, J. P. (1972), 'A Garbage Can Model of Organizational Choice', *Administrative Science Quarterly*, 17: 1–25.

COHEN, W. M., and LEVINTHAL, D. A. (1990), 'Absorptive Capacity: A New Perspective on Learning and Innovation', *Administrative Science Quarterly*, 35/1: 128–52.

CONFERENCE BOARD OF EUROPE (1995), *The Changing Global Role of the Marketing Function: A Research Report*, 1105-95-RR (Brussels: Conference Board of Europe).

CONNER, K. R. (1991), 'An Historical Comparison of Resource-Based Theory and Five Schools of Thought within Industrial Organization Economics: Do we have a New Theory of the Firm?', *Journal of Management*, 17: 121–54.

COOK, P. W. J. (1955), 'Decentralization and the Transfer-Price Problem', *Journal of Business*, 18: 87–94.

CYERT, R. M., and MARCH, J. G. (1963), *A Behavioral Theory of the Firm*, 2nd edn. (Cambridge, Mass.: Blackwell).

D'AVENI, R. (1994), *Hypercompetition* (New York: Free Press).

DAY, G. (1994), 'The Capabilities of Market-Driven Organizations', *Journal of Marketing*, 58: 37–52.

DEEPHOUSE, D. L. (1999), 'To be Different, or to be the Same? It's a Question (and Theory) of Strategic Balance', *Strategic Management Journal*, 20: 147–66.

DIERICKX, I., and COOL, K. (1989), 'Asset Stock Accumulation and Sustainability of Competitive Advantage', *Management Science*, 35: 1504–11.

DONALDSON, L. (1985), *In Defense of Organization Theory: A Reply to the Critics* (Cambridge: Cambridge University Press).

DOSI, G., FREEMAN, C., NELSON, R. R., SILVERBERG, G., and SOETE, L. (1988), *Technical Change and Economic Theory* (London: Printer Publishers).

DOZ, Y., and HAMEL, G. (1997), *Alliance Advantage* (Cambridge, Mass.: Harvard Business School Press).

DRUCKER, P. (1954), *Concept of the Corporation* (New York: Mentor).

—— (1990), 'The Emerging Theory of Manufacturing', *Harvard Business Review*, 68/3: 94–102.

DUNNING, J. H. (1977), 'Trade, Location of Economic Activity and the Multi-national Enterprise: A Search for an Eclectic Approach', in B. OHLIN, P. O. HESSELBOM, and P. J. WISKMAN (eds.), *The International Allocation of Economic Activity* (London: Macmillan).

—— (1980), 'Towards an Eclectic Theory of International Theory of Production: Some Empirical Tests', *Journal of International Business Studies*, 11: 9–31.

DYER, J. H. (1996), 'Specialized Supplier Networks as a Source of Competitive Advantage: Evidence from the Auto Industry', *Strategic Management Journal*, 17: 271–92.

—— (1997), 'Effective Interfirm Collaboration: How Firms Minimize Transaction Costs and Maximize Transaction Value', *Strategic Management Journal*, 18: 535–56.

—— and NOBEOKA, K. (1998), 'Creating and Managing a High Performance Knowledge-Sharing Network: The Toyota Case', Paper presented at the Academy of International Business Conference, Vienna, Austria, Oct.

—— and SINGH, H. (1998), 'The Relational View: Co-operative Strategy and Sources of Interorganizational Competitive Advantage', *Academy of Management Review*, 23/4: 660–79.

EARL, M. J. (1996), 'The Chief Information Officer: Past, Present, and Future', in EARL (ed.), *Information Management: The Organizational Dimension* (Oxford: Oxford University Press).

—— and SCOTT, I. (1999), 'What is a Chief Knowledge Officer?', *Sloan Management Review*, 40: 29–39.

ECCLES, R. G. (1982), *Transfer Pricing: A Theory for Practice* (Lexington, Mass.: Lexington Books).

EDVINSSON, L., and MALONE, M. S. (1997), *Intellectual Capital: Realizing your Company's True Value by Finding its Hidden Brainpower* (New York: HarperCollins).

EGELHOFF, W. G. (1991), 'Information Processing Theory and the Multinational Enterprise', *Journal of International Business Studies*, 27: 467–95.

EISENHARDT, K. M. (1989), 'Building Theories from Case Study Research', *Academy of Management Review*, 14: 532–50.

—— and TABRIZI, B. (1995), 'Accelerating Adaptive Processes: Product Innovation in the Global Computer Industry', *Administrative Science Quarterly*, 40: 84–110.

FIOL, C. M., and LYLES, M. A. (1985), 'Organizational Learning', *Academy of Management Review*, 10: 803–13.

FLAPP, H. B., and BULDER, B. B. and VOLKER, B. (1998), 'Intra-Organizational Networks and Performance: A Review', *Computational and Mathematical Organization Theory*, 4: 109–47.

FORBES (1998), 'The 300 Best Small Global Companies, 1998', *Forbes Global* (Oct.).

FROST, T. S. (1998), 'The Geographic Sources of Foreign Subsidiaries' Innovations', Richard Ivey School of Business, Working Paper (London, Ont.).

FRUIN, M. (1992), *The Japanese Enterprise System: Competitive Strategies and Cooperative Structures* (New York: Oxford University Press).

GALBRAITH, J. R. (1973), *Designing Complex Organizations* (Reading, Mass.: Addison Wesley).

—— (1997), *Managing the New Complexity*, IMD Working Paper 97–5 (Lausanne: IMD).

GALLOUJ, F., and WEINSTEIN, O. (1997), 'Innovation in Services', *Research Policy*, 26/4 and 5: 537–56.

GALUNIC, D. C., and EISENHARDT, K. M. (1996), 'The Evolution of Intracorporate Domains: Divisional Charter Loss in High-Technology, Multidivisional Corporations', *Organization Science*, 7: 255–83.

GHEMAWAT, P. (1991), *Commitment* (New York: Free Press).

GHOSHAL, S., and BARTLETT, C. A. (1990), 'The Multinational Corporation as an Interorganizational Network', *Academy of Management Review*, 15: 603–25.

—— —— (1997), *The Individualized Corporation* (New York: HarperCollins).

—— and NOHRIA, N. (1989), 'Internal Differentiation within Multinational Corporations', *Strategic Management Journal*, 10: 323–37.

GIBSON, C. F., and NOLAN, R. L. (1974), 'Managing the Four Stages of EDP Growth', *Harvard Business Review*, 52: 76–88.

GLASER, B., and STRAUSS, A. (1967), *The Discovery of Grounded Theory: Strategies for Qualitative Research* (Chicago: Aldine).

GOMEZ-CASSERES, B. (1994), 'Group versus Group: How Alliance Networks Compete', *Harvard Business Review*, 4: 4–11.

GRANSTRAND, O. E., BOHLIN, E., OSKARSSON, C., and SJÖBERG, N. (1992), 'External Technology Acquisition in Large Multi-Technology Companies', *R & D Management*, 22: 111–33.

GRANT, R. M. (1996), 'Prospering in Dynamically-Competitive Environments: Organizational Capability as Knowledge Integration', *Organization Science*, 7: 375–87.

GREVE, H. R. (1994), 'Patterns of Competition: The Diffusion of Strategy Adoption and Abandonment', Stanford University, Graduate School of Business, PhD thesis.

GRÖNROOS, C. (1990), *Service Management and Marketing: Managing the Moment of Truth in Service Competition* (Lexington, Mass.: Lexington Books).

HAGSTRÖM, P. (1990), 'New Information Systems and the Changing Structure of MNCs', in C. A. BARTLETT, Y. DOZ, and G. HEDLUND (eds.), *Managing the Global Firm* (London: Routledge).

—— (1991), 'The "Wired" MNC', Institute of International Business, Stockholm School of Economics, PhD thesis.

—— (1996), 'Information Systems in MNCs as an Infrastructure for Service Delivery', in P. PALVIA, S. PALVIA, and E. ROCHE (eds.), *Global Information Technology and Systems Management: Key Issues and Trends* (Nashua, NH: Ivy League Publishing).

—— and CHANDLER, A. D. (1998), 'Perspectives on Firm Dynamics', in A. D. CHANDLER, P. HAGSTRÖM, and Ö. SÖLVELL (eds.), *The Dynamic Firm: The Role of Technology, Strategy, Organization, and Regions* (Oxford: Oxford University Press).

—— and HEDLUND, G. (1998), 'A Three-Dimensional Model of Changing Internal Structure in the Firm', in A. D. CHANDLER JR., P. HAGSTRÖM, and Ö. SÖLVELL (eds.), *The Dynamic Firm: The Role of Technology, Strategy, Organization, and Regions* (Oxford: Oxford University Press).

HALAL, W. (1994), 'From Hierarchy to Enterprise: Internal Markets are the New Foundation of Management', *Academy of Management Executive*, 8: 69–83.

HAMEL, G. (1991), 'Competition for Competence and Inter-Partner Learning within International Strategic Alliances', *Strategic Management Journal*, 12: 83–104.

HAMILTON, C. (1994), *Absolut: Historien om flaskan* (Stockholm: Nordstedts).

HANSEN, M. (1996), 'Knowledge Integration in Organization', Stanford University PhD thesis.

HARRIGAN, K. R. (1986), 'Matching Vertical Integration Strategies to Competitive Conditions', *Strategic Management Journal*, 7: 535–55.

HARTLEY, J. H., MEREDITH, J. R., and McCUTCHEON, D. (1997), 'Supplier's Contributions to Product Development: An Exploratory Study', *IEEE Transactions on Engineering Management*, 44: 258–66.

HAUKNES, J. (1996), *Innovation in the Service Economy*, 7 (Oslo: STEP).

HAUPTMAN, O. (1986), 'The Influence of Task Type on the Relation Between Communication and Performance: The Case of Software Development', *R & D Management*, 6: 218–44.

HAYEK, F. A. (1945), 'The Use of Knowledge in Society', *American Economic Review*, 35: 519–30.

HAYES, R. H., and WHEELWRIGHT, S. C. (1984), 'The Experience Curve: A Framework for Manufacturing Performance Improvement', in HAYES and WHEELWRIGHT (eds.), *Restoring our Competitive Edge: Competing through Manufacturing* (New York: John Wiley & Sons).

HÅKANSSON, H. (1987), *Industrial Technological Development: A Network Approach* (London: Croom Helm).

—— (1989), *Corporate Technological Behaviour: Co-operation and Networks* (London: Routledge).

—— and JOHANSON, J. (1992), 'A Model of Industrial Networks', in HÅKANSSON and JOHANSON (eds.), *Industrial Networks: A New View of Reality* (London: Routledge).

HEDBERG, B., DAHLGREN, G., HANSSON, J., and OLVE, N.-G. (1994), *Imaginära organisationer* (Malmö: Liber).

HEDBERG, J., and RANDEL, M. (1997), 'A Study of the Swedish Market for Long-Term Savings: Will Vertical Integration among the Current Players Decrease?', Institute of International Business, Stockholm School of Economics, Master of Business thesis.

HEDLUND, G. (1986), 'The Modern MNC: A Heterarchy?', *Human Resource Management*, 25: 9–36.

—— (1993), 'Assumptions of Hierarchy and Heterarchy: An Application to Multinational Corporations', in S. GHOSHAL and E. WESTNEY (eds.), *Organization Theory and the Multinational Corporation* (London: Macmillan).

—— (1994), 'A Model of Knowledge Management and the N-Form Corporation', *Strategic Management Journal*, 15: 73–91.

—— and NONAKA, I. (1993), 'Models of Knowledge Management in the West and Japan', in P. LORANGE, B. CHAKRAVARTHY, J. ROOS, and A. VAN DE VEN (eds.), *Implementing Strategic Process* (Oxford: Blackwell Business).

HEIDE, J. B., and GEORGE, J. (1990), 'Alliances in Industrial Purchasing: The Determinants of Joint Action in Buyer–Supplier Relationships', *Journal of Marketing Research*, 27: 24–36.

—— and MINER, A. S. (1992), 'The Shadow of the Future: Effects of Anticipated Interaction and Frequency of Contacts on Buyer–Seller Cooperation', *Academy of Management Journal*, 35: 265–91.

HENDERSON, R. M. (1994), 'The Evolution of Integrative Capability: Innovation in Cardiovascular Drug Discovery', *Industrial and Corporate Change*, 3: 607–30.

—— and CLARK, K. B. (1990), 'Architectural Innovation: the Reconfiguration of Existing Product Technologies and the Failure of Established Firms', *Administrative Science Quarterly*, 35: 9–30.

—— and COCKBURN, I. (1994), 'Measuring Competence? Exploring Firm Effects in Pharmaceutical Research', *Strategic Management Journal*, 15: 63–84.

HENEMAN, H. G. (1974), 'Comparisons of Self and Superior Rating of Managerial Performance', *Journal of Applied Psychology*, 59: 638–42.

HENNART, J. F. (1982), *A Theory of Multinational Enterprise* (2nd edn., 1988; Ann Arbor: University of Michigan Press).

—— (1993), 'Explaining the "Swollen Middle": Why Most Transactions are a Mix of "Market" and "Hierarchy"', *Organization Science*, 4: 529–47.

HIRSCHLEIFER, J. (1956), 'On the Economics of Transfer Pricing', *Journal of Business*, 29: 72–84.

HOLLAND, J. H. (1975), *Adaptation in Natural and Artificial Systems* (Ann Arbor: University of Michigan Press).

HOLMSTRÖM, B. R., and TIROLE, J. (1989), 'The Theory of the Firm', in R. SCHMALENSEE and R. D. WILLIG (eds.), *Handbook of Industrial Organization* (Amsterdam: Elsevier Science).

HUBER, G. P. (1991), 'Organizational Learning: The Contributing Processes and the Literatures', *Organization Science*, 2: 88–115.

HYMER, S. H. (1976), *The International Operations of National Firms: A Study of Direct Foreign Investment* (Cambridge, Mass.: MIT Press).

IANSITI, M. (1998), *Technology Integration* (Boston: Harvard Business School Press).

ILLINITCH, A. Y., D'AVENI, R., and LEWIN, A. Y. (1996), 'New Organizational Forms and Strategies for Managing in Hypercompetitive Environments', *Organization Science*, 7: 211–20.

IMAI, K., NONAKA, I., and TAKEUCHI, H. (1985), 'Managing the New Product Development Process: How Japanese Learn and Unlearn', in K. B. CLARK, R. H. HAYES and C. LORENZ (eds.), *The Uneasy Alliance: Managing the Productivity–Technology Dilemma* (Boston: Harvard Business School Press).

JACOBSON, R. (1992), 'The "Austrian" School of Strategy', *Academy of Management Review*, 17: 782–807.

JARILLO, J.-C. (1988), 'On Strategic Networks', *Strategic Management Journal*, 9: 33–41.

JAWORSKI, B. J., and KOHLI, A. K. (1993), 'Market Orientation: Antecedents and Consequences', *Journal of Marketing*, 57: 53–70.

JOHANSON, J., and MATTSON, L. G. (1988), 'Internationalization in Industrial Systems: A Network Approach', in N. HOOD and J. E. VAHLNE (eds.), *Strategies in Global Competition* (London: Croom Helm).

—— and VAHLNE, J. E. (1992), *Management of Internationalization* (Stockholm: Institute of International Business).

JOHNSON, G. (1987), *Strategic Change and the Management Process* (Oxford: Basil Blackwell).

JOSKOW, P. L. (1987), 'Contract Duration and Relationship-Specific Investments: Empirical Evidence from Coal Markets', *American Economic Review*, 77: 168–85.

KANTER, J. (1977), *Management Oriented Management Information Systems*, 2nd edn. (Englewood Cliffs, NJ: Prentice-Hall).

KATZ, R., and ALLEN, T. J. (1982), 'Investigating the Not Invented Here (NIH) Syndrome: A Look at the Performance, Tenure, and Communication Patterns of 50 R&D Project Groups', *R & D Management*, 12: 7–19.

KEEN, P. G. W. (1986), *Competing in Time: Using Telecommunications for Competitive Advantage* (Cambridge, Mass.: Ballinger).

—— (1991), *Every Manager's Guide to Information Technology: A Glossary of Key Terms and Concepts for Today's Business Leader* (Boston: Harvard Business School Press).

KELLY, K. (1998), *New Rules for the New Economy* (Harmondsworth: Penguin).

KING, G., KEOHANE, R. O., and VERBA, S. (1994), *Designing Organizational Inquiry: Scientific Inference in Qualitative Research* (Princeton: Princeton University Press).

KIRZNER, J. (1973), *Competition and Entrepreneurship* (Chicago: University of Chicago Press).

KLING, R. (1980), 'Social Analyses of Computing: Theoretical Perspectives in Recent Empirical Research', *(ACM) Computing Survey*, 12: 61–110.

KNICKERBOCKER, F. T. (1973), *Oligopolistic Reaction and Multinational Enterprise* (Boston: Harvard University, Graduate School of Business Administration).

KNIGHT, F. H. (1921), *Risk, Uncertainty and Profit* (Boston: Houghton & Mifflin).

KOGUT, B. (1983), 'Foreign Direct Investment as a Sequential Process', in C. P. KINDLEBERGER and D. AUDRETSCH (eds.), *The Multinational Corporation in the 1980s* (Cambridge, Mass.: MIT Press).

—— (1988), 'Joint Ventures: Theoretical and Empirical Perspectives', *Strategic Management Journal*, 9: 319–32.

—— and KULATILAKA, N. (1994), 'Operating Flexibility, Global Manufacturing, and the Option Value of a Multinational Network', *Management Science*, 40: 123–39.

—— and ZANDER, U. (1992), 'Knowledge of the Firm, Combinative Capabilities and the Replication of Technology', *Organization Science*, 3: 383–97.

—— —— (1996), 'What Firms Do: Coordination, Identity and Learning', *Organization Science*, 7: 502–18.

KOSTOVA, T. (1996), 'Success of the Transnational Transfer of Organizational Practices within Multinational Companies', University of Minnesota PhD thesis.

KOZA, M. P., and LEWIN, A. Y. (1998), 'The Co-evolution of Strategic Alliances', *Organization Science*, 9: 255–65.

LAVE, J., and WENGER, E. (1991), *Situated Learning: Legitimate Peripheral Participation* (Cambridge: Cambridge University Press).

LAWRENCE, P. R. (1993), 'The Contingency Approach to Organizational Design', in J. GOLEMBIEWSKI (ed.), *Handbook of Organizational Behaviour* (New York: Dekker).

—— and LORSCH, J. W. (1967), *Organization and Environment* (Cambridge, Mass.: Harvard University, Graduate School of Business Administration).

LEAVITT, H. J., and WHISLER, T. L. (1958), 'Management in the 1980s', *Harvard Business Review*, 36: 41–8.

LEONARD-BARTON, D. (1990), 'A Dual Methodology for Case Studies: Synergistic Use of a Longitudinal Single Site with Replicated Multiple Sites', *Organization Science*, 1: 248–66.

—— (1992), 'Core Capabilities and Core Rigidities: A Paradox in Managing New Product Development', *Strategic Management Journal*, 13: 111–25.

—— (1995), *Wellsprings of Knowledge* (Boston: Harvard Business School Press).

LEVINTHAL, D. A., and MARCH, J. G. (1993), 'The Myopia of Learning', *Strategic Management Journal*, 14: 95–112.

—— and MYATT, J. (1994), 'Co-evolution of Capabilities and Industry: The Evolution of Mutual Fund Processing', *Strategic Management Journal*, 15: 45–62.

LEVITT, B., and MARCH, J. G. (1988), 'Organizational Learning', *Annual Review of Sociology*, 14: 319–40.

LEVITT, T. (1975), 'Marketing Myopia', *Harvard Business Review*, 53/4: 24–47.

LIEBENSTEIN, H. (1966), 'Allocative Efficiency vs. X-Efficiency', *American Economic Review*, 56: 392–415.

LIKER, J. K., KAMATH, R. R., and NAZLI WASTI, S. (1995), 'Supplier Involvement in Automotive Component Design: Are there really Large US Japan Differences?', *Research Policy*, 25: 59–89.

LIPPARINI, A., and SOBRERO, M. (1994), 'The Glue and the Pieces: Entrepreneurship and Innovation in Small Firm Networks', *Journal of Business Venturing*, 9: 125–40.

MACCORMACK, A. (1998), 'Drivers of Architectural Innovation', Harvard Business School PhD thesis.

MCFARLAN, F. W. (1984), 'Information Technology Changes the Way you Compete', *Harvard Business Review*, 64: 98–103.

MACHLUP, F. (1980), *Knowledge: Its Creation, Distribution and Economic Significance* (Princeton: Princeton University Press).

MCKENNEY, J. L., COPELAND, D. C., and MASON, R. O. (1995), *Waves of Change: Business Evolution through Information Technology* (Boston: Harvard Business School Press).

MANZONI, J. F., and BARSOUX, J. L. (1998), 'The Set-up-to-Fail Syndrome', *Harvard Business Review* (Mar.–Apr.), 101–13.

MARCH, J. G. (1991), 'Exploration and Exploitation in Organizational Learning', *Organization Science*, 2: 71–87.

—— and SIMON, H. A. (1958), *Organizations* (New York: Wiley).

MARKUS, M. L., and ROBEY, D. (1988), 'Information Technology and Organizational Change: Causal Structure in Theory and Research', *Management Science*, 34: 583–98.

MARPLE, D. L. (1961), 'The Decisions of Engineering Design', *IEEE Transactions on Engineering Management* (Mar.), 55–71.

MILES, M. B., and HUBERMAN, A. M. (1994), *Qualitative Data Analysis* (London: Sage).

MILGROM, P. and ROBERTS, J. (1992), *Economics, Organization and Management* (Englewood Cliffs: Prentice-Hall International).

MINTZBERG, H. (1978), 'Patterns in Strategy Formulation', *Management Science*, 24: 934–48.

—— (1990), 'The Design School: Reconsidering the Basic Premises of Strategic Management', *Strategic Management Journal*, 11: 171–95.

—— (1994), *The Rise and Fall of Strategic Planning* (New York: Free Press).

—— and WATERS, J. A. (1985), 'Of Strategies, Deliberate and Emergent', *Strategic Management Journal*, 6: 257–72.

MONTGOMERY, D., YIP, G., and VILLALONGA, B. (1998), 'The Use and Performance Effect of Global Account Management: An Empirical Analysis Using Structural Equation Modeling', Paper presented at the Academy of International Business Annual Meeting, Vienna.

MORGAN, R. M., and HUNT, S. D. (1994), 'The Commitment-Trust Theory of Relationship Marketing', *Journal of Marketing*, 58: 20–38.

NAHAPIET, J. (1994), 'Servicing the global client: Towards global account management?', Paper presented at the 14th Annual Strategic Management Society Conference, Groupe HEC, Jouy-en-Josas.

NANUS, B. (1969), 'The Multinational Computer', *Columbia Journal of World Business*, 4: 7–14.

NARVER, J. C., and SLATER, S. F. (1990), 'The Effect of Market Orientation on Business Profitability', *Journal of Marketing* (Oct.), 20–35.

NELSON, R. R. (1991), 'Why do Firms Differ and how does it Matter?', *Strategic Management Journal*, 12: 61–74.

—— and WINTER, S. G. (1982), 'Organizational Capabilities and Behaviour', in R. R. NELSON and S. G. WINTER (eds.), *An Evolutionary Theory of Economic Change* (Cambridge, Mass.: Belknap Press).

NISHIGUCHI, T. (1995), *Strategic Industrial Sourcing: The Japanese Advantage* (New York: Oxford University Press).

NODA, T., and BOWER, J. L. (1996), 'Strategy Making as Iterated Processes of Resource Allocation', *Strategic Management Journal*, 17: 159–92.

NOHRIA, N., and ECCLES, R. G. (1992), *Networks and Organizations: Structure, Form and Action* (Cambridge, Mass.: Harvard Business School Press).

NONAKA, I., and TAKEUCHI, H. (1995), *The Knowledge Creating Company* (New York: Oxford University Press).

NORMANN, R. (1993), *Service Management: ledning och strategi i tjänsteproduktion*, 3rd edn. (Malmö: Liber Ekonomi).

OLIVER, D. (1996), *Skandia: Managing Intellectual Capital*, IMD Teaching Case, GM 624-27-09-96 (Lausanne: IMD).

ORLIKOWSKY, W. (1993), *From Memo to Dialogue: Enacting Genres of Communication in Electronic Media* (Cambridge, Mass.: MIT, Alfred P. Sloan School of Management).

PALVIA, P., PALVIA, S., and ROCHE, E. (1996), *Global Information Technology and Systems Management: Key Issues and Trends* (Nashua, NH: Ivy League Publishing).

PARSON, G. L. (1983), 'Information Technology: A New Competitive Weapon', *Sloan Management Review*, 25: 3–14.

PAVA, C. (1983), *Managing New Office Technology* (New York: Free Press).

PENROSE, E. T. (1959), *The Theory of the Growth of the Firm*, 2nd edn. (Oxford: Basil Blackwell).

PERLMUTTER, H. V. (1969), 'The Tortuous Evolution of the Multinational Corporation', *Columbia Journal of World Business* (Jan.–Feb.), 9–11.

PETERAF, M. A. (1993), 'The Cornerstones of Competitive Advantage: A Resource Based View', *Strategic Management Journal*, 14: 179–91.

—— (1994), 'Commentary: The Two Schools of Thought in Resource-Based Theory: Definitions and Implications for Research', in P. SHRIVASTAVA, A. HUFF, and J. DUTTON (eds.), *Advances in Strategic Management*, vol. 10B (Greenwich, Conn.: JAI Press).

PETTIGREW, A. M. (1985a), *The Awakening Giant: Continuity and Change in Imperial Chemical Industries* (Oxford: Basil Blackwell).

—— (1985b), 'Contextualist Research and the Study of Organisational Change Processes', in E. MUNFORD et al. (eds.), *Research Methods in Information Systems* (Amsterdam: North-Holland).

—— (1987a), *The Management of Strategic Change* (Oxford: Basil Blackwell).

—— (1987*b*), 'Context and Action in the Transformation of the Firm', *Journal of Management Studies*, 24/6: 649–70.

PFEFFER, J., and NOWAK, P. (1976), 'Joint Ventures and Interorganisational Interdependence', *Administrative Science Quarterly*, 21: 398–418.

POLANYI, K. (1962), *Personal Knowledge: Towards a Post-Critical Philosophy* (Chicago: Chicago University Press).

—— (1969), *Knowing and Being* (London: Routledge & Kegan Paul).

PORTER, M. (1980), *Competitive Strategy: Techniques for Analyzing Industries and Competitors* (New York: Free Press).

—— (1981), 'The Contributions of Industrial Organization to Strategic Management', *Academy of Management Review*, 6: 609–21.

—— (1985), *Competitive Advantage, Creating and Sustaining Superior Performance* (New York: Free Press).

—— (1990), *The Competitive Advantage of Nations* (New York: Free Press).

POWELL, W. W. (1990), 'Neither Market nor Hierarchy: Network Forms of Organization', *Research in Organizational Behaviour*, 12: 295–336.

PRAHALAD, C. K., and DOZ, Y. (1987), *The Multinational Mission* (New York: Free Press).

PURSER, R. E., PASMORE, W. A., and TENKASI, R. V. (1992), 'The Influence of Deliberations on Learning in New Product Development Teams', *Journal of Engineering and Technology Management*, 9: 1–28.

QUINN, J. B. (1980), *Strategies for Change: Logical Incrementalism* (Homewood, Ill.: Richard D. Irwin).

—— ANDERSON, P., and FINKELSTEIN, S. (1996), 'Managing Professional Intellect: Making the Most of the Best', *Harvard Business Review*, 74/2: 19–28.

REBER, A. S. (1993), *Implicit Learning and Tacit Knowledge* (New York: Oxford University Press).

REGNÉR, P. (1999), *Strategy Creation in Complexity: Creative vs. Adaptive Learning Dynamics in the Firm*, doctoral thesis, Institute of International Business, Stockholm School of Economics.

RING, P. S. (1996), 'Fragile and Resilient Trust and their Roles in Economic Exchange', *Business and Society*, 35: 148–75.

—— and VAN DE VEN, A. (1992), 'Structuring Cooperative Relationships between Organizations', *Strategic Management Journal*, 13: 483–98.

ROBERTS, E. B., and BERRY, C. A. (1985), 'Entering New Business: Selecting Strategies for Success', *Sloan Management Review*, 26: 3–17.

ROBEY, D. (1977), 'Computers and Management Structure: Some Empirical Findings Re-examined', *Human Relations*, 30: 963–76.

ROCKART, J. F., and SCOTT MORTON, M. F. (1984), 'Implications of Changes in Information Technology for Corporate Strategy', *Interfaces*, 14: 84–95.

ROGERS, E. (1983), *The Diffusion of Innovations*, 3rd edn. (New York: Free Press).

RUMELT, R. P. (1984), 'Towards a Strategic Theory of the Firm', in R. B. LAMB (ed.), *Competitive Strategic Management* (Englewood Cliffs, NJ: Prentice-Hall).

—— (1987), 'Theory, Strategy and Entrepreneurship', in D. J. TEECE (ed.), *The Competitive Challenge* (Cambridge, Mass.: Ballinger).

—— (1995), 'Inertia and Transformation', in C. A. MONTGOMERY (ed.), *Resource-Based and Evolutionary Theories of the Firm: Towards a Synthesis*, 2nd edn. (Dordrecht: Kluwer Academic).

RUMELT, R. P., SCHENDEL, D., and TEECE, D. J. (1991), 'Strategic Management and Economics', *Strategic Management Journal*, 12: 5–29.

SCB (1998), *Företagens innovativa verksamhet* (Stockholm: SCB).

SCHMIDT, W. H., and FINNIGAN, J. P. (1992), *The Race without a Finish Line* (San Francisco: Jossey-Bass).

SCHOEMAKER, P. J. H. (1990), 'Strategy, Complexity and Economic Rent', *Management Science*, 36: 1178–92.

SCHON, D. A. (1983), *The Reflective Practitioner: How Professionals Think in Action* (New York: Basic Books).

SCHOONHOVEN, C. B. (1981), 'Problems with Contingency Theory: Testing Assumptions Hidden within the Language of Contingency "Theory"', *Administrative Science Quarterly*, 26: 349–77.

SCHUMPETER, J. A. (1942), *Capitalism, Socialism and Democracy* (New York: Harper & Brothers).

—— (1947), 'The Creative Response in Economic History', *Journal of Economic History*, 7: 149–59.

SCOTT, W. R. (1990), 'Technology and Structure: An Organisational-Level Perspective', in P. GOODMAN and L. S. SPROULL (eds.), *Technology and Organizations* (San Francisco: Jossey-Bass).

—— (1998), *Organizations: Rational, Natural and Open Systems*, 4th edn. (Englewood Cliffs, NJ: Prentice-Hall).

SHOSTACK, G. L. (1977), 'Breaking Free from Product Marketing', *Journal of Marketing* (Apr.), 73–80.

SIMON, H. A. (1962), 'The Architecture of Complexity', *Proceedings of the American Philosophical Society*, 106: 467–82.

—— (1991), 'Organizations and Markets', *Journal of Economic Perspectives*, 5: 25–44.

SIMONS, R. (1992), *Asea Brown Boveri: The ABACUS System*, 9-192-140 (Boston, Mass.: Publishing Division, Harvard Business School).

SINGH, H., and ZOLLO, M. (1998), *The Impact of Knowledge Codification, Experience Trajectories, and Integration Strategies on the Performance of Corporate Acquisitions*, Proceedings of the Academy of Management Conference, San Diego (CD Rom).

SJÖBERG, L., and LIND, F. (1994), *Work Motivation in Financial Crisis: A Study of Prognosis Factors* (Stockholm: Stockholm School of Economics).

SNOW, C. C., MILES, R. E., and COLEMAN, H. J. J. (1992), 'Managing 21st Century Network Organizations', *Organizational Dynamics*, 20/3: 5–21.

SNYDER, W. (1996), 'Organizational Learning and Performance: An Exploration of Linkages between Organizational Learning, Knowledge, and Performance', University of Southern California PhD thesis.

—— (1997), 'Communities of Practice: Combining Organizational Learning and Strategy Insights to Create a Bridge to the 21st Century', Paper presented at the Academy of Management Conference, Boston, Mass.

SOBRERO, M. (1996), *Inter-Organizational Architecture and Innovative Process* (Cambridge, Mass.: MIT, Alfred P. Sloan School of Management).

—— and ROBERTS, E. B. (1998), *The Trade-Off between Efficiency and Learning in Interorganizational Relationships*, Alfred P. Sloan School of Management, Massachusetts Institute of Technology Working Paper 3896 (Cambridge, Mass.: MIT).

SPENDER, J.-C. (1996), 'Making Knowledge the Basis of a Dynamic Theory of the Firm', *Strategic Management Journal*, 17: 45–62.

STEBBINS, M. W., and SHANI, A. B. R. (1995), 'Organization Design and the Knowledge Worker', *Leadership and Organization Development Journal*, 16: 23–30.

STEWART, T. A. (1997), *Intellectual Capital: The New Wealth of Organizations* (New York: Doubleday).

STRAUSS, A., and CORBIN, J. (1990), *Basics of Qualitative Research* (London: Sage).

SWANSON, E. B. (1987), *Information Systems in Organization Theory: A Review* (Chichester: John Wiley & Sons).

SZULANSKI, G. (1996), 'Exploring Internal Stickiness: Impediments to the Transfer of Best Practice within the Firm', *Strategic Management Journal*, 17: 27–43.

TAYLOR, F. W. (1947), *Scientific Management* (New York: Harper & Brothers).

TEECE, D. J. (1985), *Efficient Boundaries, Technological Innovation, and Strategic Management: An Application of the Transactions Cost Paradigm*, Working Paper BPP-8 (Berkeley: University of California Press).

—— (1987), 'Profiting from Technological Innovation', in TEECE (ed.), *The Competitive Challenge: Strategies for Industrial Innovation and Renewal* (Cambridge, Mass.: Ballinger).

—— PISANO, G., and SHUEN, A. (1997), 'Dynamic Capabilities and Strategic Management', in N. J. FOSS (ed.), *Resources Firms and Strategies* (Oxford: Oxford University Press).

TELDOK (1997), *Teldok Yearbook* (Stockholm: Teldok).

THOMPSON, J. D. (1967), *Organizations in Action* (New York: McGraw-Hill).

THORELLI, H. B. (1987), 'Networks: Between Markets and Hierarchies', *Strategic Management Journal*, 7: 37–51.

TRIPSAS, M. (1997), 'Surviving Radical Technological Change through Dynamic Capability: Evidence from the Typesetter Industry', *Industrial and Corporate Change*, 3: 341–77.

TSAI, W., and GHOSHAL, S. (1998), 'Social Capital and Value Creation: The Role of Intrafirm Networks', *Academy of Management Journal*, 41: 464–78.

TUSHMAN, M. L. (1977), 'Communication across Organizational Boundaries: Special Boundary Roles in the Innovation Process', *Administrative Science Quarterly*, 22: 587–605.

VAN DE VEN, A., and DRAZIN, R. (1985), 'The Concept of Fit in Contingency Theory', in L. L. CUMMINGS and B. M. STAW (eds.), *Research in Organizational Behavior* (Greenwich, Conn.: JAI Press).

—— and WALKER, G. (1984), 'The Dynamics of Interorganizational Coordination', *Administrative Science Quarterly*, 29: 598–621.

VON HIPPEL, E. (1987), 'Co-operation between Rivals: Informal Know-How Trading', *Research Policy*, 16: 291–302.

—— (1988), *The Sources of Innovation* (Oxford: Oxford University Press).

—— (1990), 'Task Partitioning: An Innovation Process Variable', *Research Policy*, 19: 407–18.

—— (1998), '"Sticky Information" and the Locus of Problem-Solving: Implications for Innovation', in A. D. CHANDLER, P. HAGSTRÖM, and Ö. SÖLVELL (eds.), *The Dynamic Firm: The Role of Technology, Strategy, Organization and Regions* (Oxford: Oxford University Press).

VON MISES, L. (1949), *Human Action: A Treatise on Economics* (New Haven, Conn.: Yale University Press).

WARD, J., and GRIFFITHS, P. (1996), *Strategic Planning for Information Systems*, 2nd edn. (Chichester: John Wiley).

WEILL, P., and BROADBENT, M. (1998), *Leveraging the New Infrastructure: How Market Leaders Capitalize on IT* (Boston: Harvard Business School Press).

WENGER, E. (1998), *Communities of Practice: Learning, Meaning, and Identity* (Cambridge: Cambridge University Press).

WERNERFELT, B. (1984), 'A Resource Based View of the Firm', *Strategic Management Journal*, 5: 171–80.

WESTNEY, D. E. (1993), 'Cross-Pacific Internationalization of R&D by US and Japanese Firms', *Research Policy*, 23: 171–81.

WEXLEY, K. N., ALEXANDER, J. P., GREENAWALT, J. P., and COUCH, M. A. (1980), 'Attitudinal Congruence and Similarity as Related to Interpersonal Evaluation in Manager–Subordinate Dyads', *Academy of Management Journal*, 23: 320–30.

WHISLER, T. L. (1970), *The Impact of Computers on Organizations* (New York: Praeger).

WHITE, R. E., and POYNTER, T. A. (1990), 'Organize for World-Wide Advantage', in C. A. BARTLETT, Y. DOZ, and G. HEDLUND (eds.), *Managing the Global Firm* (London: Routledge).

WIKSTRÖM, S., NORMANN, R., ANELL, B., EKVALL, G., FORSLIN, J., and SKÄRVAD, P.-H. (1994), *Knowledge and Value: A New Perspective on Corporate Transformation* (New York: Routledge).

WILLIAMSON, O. E. (1975), *Markets and Hierarchies: Analysis and Antitrust Implications* (New York: Free Press).

—— (1985), *The Economic Institutions of Capitalism* (New York: Free Press).

—— (1991), 'Comparative Economic Organization: The Analysis of Discrete Structural Alternatives', *Administrative Science Quarterly*, 36: 269–96.

WISEMAN, C. (1985), *Strategy and Computers: Information Systems as Competitive Weapons* (Homewood, Ill.: Dow Jones-Irwin).

WOODWARD, J. (1965), *Industrial Organization: Theory and Practice* (London: Oxford University Press).

YIN, R. K. (1989), *Case Study Research-Design and Methods* (London: Sage).

—— (1993), *Applications of Case Study Research* (London: Sage).

YIP, G. (1992), *Managing for Worldwide Competitive Advantage* (Englewood Cliffs, NJ: Prentice-Hall).

—— and JOHANSSON, J. (1993), *Global Market Strategies of US and Japanese Business* (Boston, Mass.: Marketing Science Institute).

—— and MADSEN, T. (1996), 'Global Account Management: The New Frontier in Relationship Marketing', *International Marketing Review*, 13: 24–42.

ZANDER, I., and ZANDER, U. (1998), *The Inside Track: On the Neglected Role of Customers in Strategy and Firm Growth*, Institute of International Business Working Paper (Stockholm: Institute of International Business).

ZANDER, U. (1991), 'Exploiting a Technological Edge: Voluntary and Involuntary Dissemination of Technology', Institute of International Business, Stockholm School of Economics, PhD thesis.

—— and KOGUT, B. (1995), 'Knowledge and Speed of Imitation: An Empirical Test', *Organization Science*, 6: 76–92.

ZUBOFF, S. (1988), *In the Age of the Smart Machine* (Oxford: Heinemann Professional Publishing).

Index